INVISIBLE PEOPLE

Edited and with an introduction by

SAM HOWE VERHOVEK

Foreword by

JOSE ANTONIO VARGAS,

Pulitzer Prize–winning journalist and author of
Dear America: Notes of an Undocumented Citizen

INVISIBLE PEOPLE

Stories of Lives at the Margins

ALEX TIZON

TEMPLE UNIVERSITY PRESS
Philadelphia • Rome • Tokyo

TEMPLE UNIVERSITY PRESS
Philadelphia, Pennsylvania 19122
tupress.temple.edu

Text design by Kate Nichols

Photograph on page v: Courtesy of Melissa Tizon

Library of Congress Cataloging-in-Publication Data

Names: Tizon, Alex, author. | Verhovek, Sam Howe, editor, author of
   introduction. | Vargas, Jose Antonio, writer of foreword
Title: Invisible people : stories of lives at the margins / Alex Tizon ; edited
   and with an introduction by Sam Howe Verhovek ; with a foreword by
   Jose Antonio Vargas.
Description: Philadelphia : Temple University Press, 2019. |
Identifiers: LCCN 2019009196 (print) | LCCN 2019009470 (ebook) |
   ISBN 9781439918326 (E-book) | ISBN 9781439918302 (cloth : alk. paper)
Classification: LCC PN4874.T465 (ebook) | LCC PN4874.T465 A25 2019 (print)
   | DDC 070.4493055/69—dc23
LC record available at https://lccn.loc.gov/2019009196

Printed in the United States of America

9 8 7 6 5 4 3 2 1

For Eudocia Tomas "Lola" Pulido

—MELISSA TIZON

All editor and author (Tizon estate) proceeds
from the sale of this book will benefit the scholarship fund
of the Asian American Journalists Association.

So I guess you could say I've written a lot about one thing as a journalist. But I hardly ever saw it as exclusively about race. To my mind, it was more about telling stories of people who existed outside the mainstream's field of vision. Invisible people. Barely discernible beings who lived among us, sometimes right next door . . . who moved through life largely unseen because their stories were largely untold.

—ALEX TIZON, BIG LITTLE MAN

. . .

Here's what I'm getting at. My own lifelong sense of feeling invisible, and living with others like my father who experienced the same, somehow became useful. I developed the sensory apparatus to apprehend fellow invisibles. In making them seen, even for just a few column inches on a Sunday morning, I had found a purpose.

—ALEX TIZON, BIG LITTLE MAN

CONTENTS

FOREWORD

by JOSE ANTONIO VARGAS

In our oversaturated, exceedingly ephemeral media era, it's all too easy to forget what journalism stands for.

Yes, journalism must provide facts: the what, where, and when. But journalism must also strive to explore the why and the how, to locate the mysterious gray area in a world often painted in black-and-white terms. Discovering that gray area while giving voice and dignity to invisible people is the legacy of Alex Tizon.

I first heard of Tizon when I was a student at San Francisco State University. I was working as a copy boy (answering phones, delivering faxes) at the *San Francisco Chronicle*, then home to a handful of Filipino American journalists who told me about Tizon—the first Filipino American journalist I had heard of to win a Pulitzer Prize. When I landed a reporting job at the *Washington Post*, I followed Tizon's work at the *Seattle Times* and the *Los Angeles Times*, always marveling at his ability to find people and subjects off the beaten path. Often, he went zig when most went zag.

No one was invisible to Tizon. No subject—however eccentric, however marginalized—escaped his microscopic lens. His was the kind of patient, penetrating journalism that has become all too rare in a news media consumed with hot takes and easy conclusions. He refused to paint people as archetypes, as mere "minorities" lost in the mainstream. He didn't simply investigate systems and structures and their impact on individual lives. He investigated, with inimitable skill and profound empathy, the human spirit, including his own.

Some of his most memorable work is autobiographical. *Big Little Man* stands as one of the most discerning memoirs about the struggles of being Asian in a country defined by its black-and-white binary. As long as writers need to examine themselves—and the role they play in how stories are told—"My Family's Slave," his cover story for *The Atlantic*, will be debated and dissected.

Collected in this volume is more than a life's work. It is a vision of humanity itself from a writer who was, and will continue to be, a big little man in American journalism.

INTRODUCTION

by SAM HOWE VERHOVEK

When my friend and former colleague Tomas Alex Tizon passed away in 2017 at the age of fifty-seven, he missed by hours hearing news that would have thrilled him and ratified the central thrust of his remarkable career as a reporter, author, and consummate storyteller. *The Atlantic* magazine called to tell Alex that the story his wife, Melissa, says he was "born to write," about the woman who raised and nurtured and loved him under conditions that amounted to indentured servitude, would be on the cover of an upcoming issue.

The story of Lola, starkly and provocatively headlined "My Family's Slave," is complicated, nuanced, at points horrifying, and at others touching—here it can make you weep; here it can make you laugh out loud. It is raw but minutely observed and beautifully written. It is a love sonnet folded within the layers of a crime story—or, maybe you find yourself asking whether it is the other way around. It has the ring not just of truth but of a certain type of painful honesty that was characteristic of Alex and his work. Deeply self-critical, as he often was—he authored an earlier book that *The Atlantic* described as a "self-lacerating examination of the complexities, humiliations and small victories" inherent in his quest for an identity as an Asian American male—in this story, Alex struggles to come to terms with how he and his siblings could ever atone for what he casts as a sin that began with his grandfather in a faraway country, in a different culture, in an earlier era. It is one that can never be put right, although largely because of the conundrum at the heart of the tale: he loved Lola, and she loved him.

The piece engendered enormous discussion and no small controversy, although much of the latter was chatter on the Internet so instantaneous and so vituperative that I found myself skeptical that the purveyors of it had fully read and truly thought through the complexity of the 8,500-word piece. In any event, it soon became the most read, the most commented on, and the most forwarded piece in the magazine's Internet-era history. Remarkably, according to Chartbeat's annual ranking of the one hundred most popular digital articles, it also became the most read English-language article on the Internet for all of 2017, consuming fifty-eight million minutes of readers' time—more than *triple* the combined reading time for the next most read piece. *New York Times* columnist David Brooks picked it for his annual Sidney Awards of must-read magazine articles, and a year after Alex's death, he won the National Magazine Award, the most prestigious honor in the industry.

To my mind, Lola's story is a vintage Tizon piece, reflective and worthy of his talents as a Pulitzer Prize–winning newspaper reporter, a rising star in long-form magazine journalism, and a widely admired professor at the University of Oregon, who stressed to his students that great writing is built only on a foundation of keen observation, having a patient eye and ear for the smallest of details. One can be a great reporter without being a great writer, but it is nigh impossible to be a great writer without being a great reporter. Alex, obviously, was both.

The idea for this book took root in my mind at Alex's funeral, a sad but also—as was very characteristic of Alex and his large extended Filipino American family—boisterous celebration of his life. It occurred to me then that all his many young nieces and nephews and cousins, the ones who talked about how much they would miss their goofy Uncle Alex, deserved to know much more about him in time. Of course, I hoped they would always remember Alex in all his goofy gloriousness, but they should also know the depth of his soul, the strains of sweetness and sadness and struggle that made him a very complex human being—and an exquisite writer. The more I thought about it, though, I realized that what Alex had to say, and how he viewed the world, should touch a much wider circle of people. Alex's work deserves to live on long past his tragic death at too young an age, and thus the best of it is collected in this book. It is one from which teachers, students, and general readers alike will benefit if they seek an answer to this basic question: *How do you tell a great story?*

Beyond that, I suppose, the book may be helpful to aspiring writers in another regard, to those who are perhaps struggling with this question: *How do you recognize a great story?* This was perhaps Alex's greatest journalistic gift of all. His interest—his mission, really—was to bring visibility to people at the margins of society, to explore the lives of those "who existed outside the mainstream's field of vision," as he puts it in his book, *Big Little Man*: "Invisible people. Barely discernible beings who lived among us, sometimes right next door . . . who moved through life largely unseen because their stories were largely untold." Hence, the title of this book as well as the epigraphs on page vii.

As his wife, Melissa, describes it, Alex believed very strongly that every person had an "epic story" within and that his job was to help coax it out.

"Somewhere in the tangle of the subject's burden and the subject's desire is your story," he told her.

The more inconsequential society at large considered the person, the more Alex was interested in the challenge of piecing together his or her life story. In our "look at me!" world, where getting yourself to "go viral" on the Internet is considered a thing to be celebrated, and in a nation with the loudest, most attention-desperate president in our history, Alex sought out the sounds—and sights—of human silence. What a gift. What a soul.

As suggested in *Big Little Man*, Alex was drawn to invisible people in large measure because he had contended with his own sense of invisibility for so much of his pre-adult life. As a Filipino American male in an immigrant family living an itinerant life, he struggled to find his place in the American narrative. Popular culture and professional sports in the United States were devoid of Asian male heroes; the West was always won by John Wayne–type cowboys on the screen, not by the Chinese immigrant workers who laid track for the transcontinental railroad in real life. He was generically derided by classmates as a "Chink" in elementary school in the Bronx or as "Oriental" by somewhat kinder-hearted teachers. Still, "Oriental" seemed soft, yellow, and feminine in the American interpretation, qualities that didn't align with the young man Alex wanted to be. This label, he said, was an even more insidious form of the invisibility he felt.

Once Alex became a reporter, his interests were far wider than those that could be seen through a racial lens. He was drawn to life's outsiders and misfits, to eccentrics, to loners and losers. He was interested in the people and places left behind by rapid changes in technology, in labor demands, and even in cultural mores. If a person was mocked or misunderstood or just ignored, Alex wanted to know more about him or her. He was interested in criminals, not because he liked them but because he wanted to understand how they reached their detours in life. In selecting the stories for this book, which I did in consultation with several of his editors, I decided it was best not to group them chronologically, even though that might have helped show Alex's evolution as a writer. Instead, I have compiled them loosely by the sort of "invisible person" he is profiling. Notice, please, that I do not use the term "archetype" in the previous sentence, if only because I can hear Alex in my mind: "'Archetype,' man? What the hell kind of word is that?"

Alex writes of lonely immigrants struggling to forge a new American identity; he takes seriously a group of people who call themselves "Surfers for Jesus," alienated from mainland life and preaching the gospel on Hawaiian beaches amid the eternal quest for the perfect wave. In "Thom Jones and the Cosmic Joke," a

2000 *Seattle Times* story included here, Tizon writes of a former high-school night custodian who became a celebrated writer, with a short story published in the *New Yorker,* followed by an O. Henry Award and a two-book contract with Little, Brown and Company. The cosmic joke? Writing was pure torture, a terrible amalgam of writer's block and self-doubt, a concept that Alex spins brilliantly into a complicated musing on career choices, the notion of a calling, the role of suffering, and the difference between satisfaction and happiness.

"Now, my life is hell," the author and former janitor tells him. On the other hand, he confesses, "I'm not happy if I don't suffer at least five hours a day."

Journalism is, in a way, a form of pointillism. Each story is a dot or a dash on the canvas—and, for the best reporters, across a long career, these small points and plots come together to form a larger narrative, a coherent sense of what makes his or her stories unique and what messages they convey. Alex's life and career were cut short, but what stands out nonetheless in the body of his work is his belief that every person has an epic story to tell, even—and perhaps especially—the invisible people.

Somewhere in the tangle of

the subject's burden and the subject's desire

is your story.

—ALEX TIZON

INVISIBLE PEOPLE

PART I

ALEX'S STORY

BIG LITTLE MAN: IN SEARCH
OF MY ASIAN SELF

Introduced by **DEANNE URMY,**
editor at Houghton Mifflin Harcourt

*E**arly on, Alex Tizon described to me his memoir,* Big Little Man,
*in a few sentences that now seem far more incisive and unflinch-
ing than the eventual marketing-approved jacket copy that appeared
on the book:* "Big Little Man *is about climbing out of shame," he
wrote. "The universal theme is shame. The first half investigates
the origins of that shame. The second half is about the intellectual
climb out of that hole."*

*Others have described Alex's gift for asking original, searching
questions. In* Big Little Man, *he asks these questions of himself.
What was this nearly disabling dose of racial shame, where did
it come from, and what did it do to him as a boy who immigrated
to the United States from the Philippines? How and why did the
shame cast a deep shadow well into manhood, and what was it
that finally allowed him to "climb out of that hole"? It wasn't an
easy set of questions to live with; an e-mail Alex wrote close to his
manuscript deadline reads, "Am struggling with this last chapter.
Personal stuff mostly. I need just a little more time. Have the material, just need to write."*

*Alex knew how to accept editing—most often, he transformed
halfway-decent suggestions into startling, powerful detail and insight—and how to counter less-than-helpful notes. He once commented on a descriptive phrase I'd suggested—"a landscape still
complex but life-saving for the Asian American man"—saying,*

"Can we change 'life-saving' to 'life-affirming'? I mean, nobody is really saved here." Editing Alex's writing was a deep pleasure, and I felt lucky on several occasions in Seattle and New York City to spend time with him and to meet his wife, Melissa, and two daughters; he was so proud of them.

While Big Little Man, as it was written, is a searing critique of American culture and an astonishingly honest personal exploration, the book detonates with further sense when read alongside Alex's final essay, "My Family's Slave," which appears in this book just after the excerpt from Big Little Man. (It is also now included as a coda to the paperback edition of Big Little Man.) Alex's struggles with the last chapter of his book take on poignant new meaning now; he must have understood that this wasn't truly his last chapter. And the phrase from that resurrected e-mail, "I need just a little more time," takes on new sense, too.

We needed so much more time from Alex Tizon. Surely, he would have given us further fiercely informed, gorgeously written pieces on what it's like to be shamed as an immigrant and a minority, especially as a child, and the damage the shaming and the shame bring to all of us. And so much more, including the unexpected, from this fine writer and big man.

. . .

IT WAS ALL new to my Americanized senses. I was awash in newness, as if I had landed on a never-discovered continent. And yet it was not my first time here. I was born on one of these islands. My blood, with its tinctures of Malay and Spanish and Chinese, came from the same pool as those of the masses we passed on the road. At age four I was brought by my parents to America, a land where people did not look too kindly on a groveler, for instance, anybody who said "sir" three times in a single sentence. . . . It was hard work, becoming an American, and I felt I'd succeeded for the most part.

Yet I was not "all-American." I could never be that. Most of us, when imagining an all-American, wouldn't picture a man who looked like me. Not even I would. You would have to take my word for it that more than a few times in my life I looked in a mirror and was startled by the person looking back. I could go a long time feeling blithely at home, until a single glance at my reflection would be like a slap on the back of the head. *Hey! You are not of this land.* Certainly during my growing up years in America, many people, friends and strangers, intentionally and not, helped to embed in me like a hidden razor blade the awareness of being an outsider.

I remember an encounter with a fellow student at JHS 79 in the Bronx, where my family lived in the 1970s. I was about thirteen. My school was just off the Grand Concourse on 181st, a five-story brick building with bars over all the windows and dark clanging stairwells that might as well have been back alleys. Some stairwells you did not dare travel alone, but I was new and didn't know better. One afternoon in one of these stairwells, an open hand with five impossibly long fingers fell hard against my chest and stopped me in my tracks.

"What you supposed to be, motherfukka?" the owner of the hand said. . . . "Are you a *Chink*, a *Mehikan*. What?" . . .

Joe's original query was a question I've been asked in various, usually more tactful ways ever since I could remember. *What you supposed to be?* From where on this planet did you come? What *are* you?

IN THE AMERICA that I grew up in, men of Asia placed last in the hierarchy of manhood. They were invisible in the high-testosterone arenas of politics and big business and sports. On television and in the movies, they were worse than invisible: they were embarrassing. *We* were embarrassing. The Asian male in cinema was synonymous with nebbish. They made great extras. In crowd scenes that required running away, Asian men excelled. They certainly did not play strong lead roles, because apparently there were no strong Asian men with sex appeal. . . . I could not point the finger of blame at anyone. Mine was an education that came from the air itself. At school, it was as much what was *not* taught. Asians simply did not come up in history class, except as victims who needed saving (Filipinos, South Koreans, South Vietnamese) or as wily enemies who inevitably lost (Chinese, Filipinos, Japanese) or as enemies who managed not to lose by withstanding mind-boggling casualties (North Koreans, North Vietnamese). Asia was a stage on which dynamic Westerners played out their own dramas and fantasies, with Asians as incidentals. I graduated from high school unable to name a single preeminent East Asian figure in history who was a force for good.

MY FATHER, who was a funny, dynamic conversationalist in his own language, a man about Manila, would never be quite so funny or dynamic or quick-witted or agile or confident again. He would always be a small man in America. My mother was small, too, but it was acceptable, even desirable, for women to be small. American men found my mother attractive. She never lacked attention or employment. My father was the one most demoted in the great new land. He was supposed to be the man of the family, and he did not know which levers to pull or push, and he didn't have the luxury of a lifetime, like his children, to learn them.

YET I ALSO KNEW it wasn't true. Somewhere in the middle of myself, like a corpuscle hidden under layers, I knew the mythology was a sham. I had lived too many secret moments in which I felt iron within me. . . . I began keeping files. Figurative files in my head, but also actual file folders with headings such as "Great Orientals" and "Asians in the News" and "Oriental vs. Asian?" scribbled in big Sharpie letters. Whenever I ran across anything fileable related to Asians, in particular pertaining to race and manhood and power and sex, I would make a note and tuck it away in one of the folders. . . .

"What's in those?" one of my little sisters asked.

"Files," I said cryptically.

"Of . . . ?"

"Top secret information," I said.

SOMETIME AFTER LISA AND ROSEMARY, I started a file— one of my first—labeled simply "Orientals." Inside went notes and newspaper or magazine clips, anything that made reference to the word. After a while I had to create sub-files, so large was the universe of things called Oriental: roots, rugs, religions, noodles, hairstyles, hordes, healing arts, herbs and spices, fabrics, medicines, modes of war, types of astronomy, spheres of the globe, schools of philosophical thought, and salads. It applied to men, women, gum, dances, eyes, body types, chicken dishes, societies, civilizations, styles of diplomacy, codes of behavior, fighting arts, sexual proclivities, and a particular kind of mind. Apparently, the Orient produced people with a singular way of thinking. There was no way, wrote Jack London, for a Westerner to plumb the Oriental mind—it was cut from different cloth, functioned in an alien way. . . .

A travel agency near where my mother worked in Harlem put up posters of the Orient on its walls and windows. My mother and I wandered in there a few times. The posters and pamphlets showed images of geishas and monks and fog-shrouded temples. Of elephants in gold jewelry. Of strange-looking boats in dark waters, open markets teeming with ant-like hordes in strange dress, women with baskets on their heads, children in paddy hats sitting on the backs of hulking black water buffaloes. Of farmers in pointy hats turned down toward the earth like rows of bent nails, and rice terraces wrapped around the foothills of green volcanoes still steaming from their last eruption.

What a mysterious place, the Orient. Menacing but also immensely alluring. So otherworldly. So alien, as London said. No wonder it spawned people with such unfathomable minds. I had read *White Fang* and *Call of the Wild*; Jack London was one of my favorite writers.

TO KNOW WHY the word "Oriental" chafes so many of us today, it helps to know its history. The word came from the Latin word *oriens*, meaning east or "the direction of the rising sun." . . . Europeans used the word to describe the vast stretch of the planet east of themselves all the way to the Pacific Ocean. The Orient came to encompass a quarter of the globe, including Egypt, Nepal, and Korea; Turkey, Mongolia, and Indonesia; Lebanon, India, and Japan.

Europeans popularized the concept of the Orient at a time when they were usurping much of it. Colonizers used scholarly studies on the Oriental mind, Oriental character, and Oriental society as guides to subduing and managing their subjects. Concept and conquest went hand in hand.

The underlying assumption of Orientalism was that the Orient represented the inferior opposite of Europe: the East was feminine and passive, the West masculine and dominating. The East was spiritual and inward-looking, the West rational and outward-seeing. The East was bound in tradition, the West impelled by progress. The East was primitive, vulgar and defenseless; the West was the beacon of civilization, the standard of refinement, and the wielder of unstoppable military power. The Orient needed to be civilized for its own good.

Aside from being backward, we Orientals were also cravenly submissive, incurably exotic (from the Greek *exotikos*, meaning "from the outside"), inscrutable, cunning, silently treacherous and highly penetrable. In fact, begging to be penetrated. We Orientals lived to be acted upon by virile, dynamic, rational Westerners. . . .

Yellow was the perfect color for Orientals. It was only superficially descriptive of skin tone. The cultural associations with the color resonated with the Western view of the Orient. *Caucasoids*, or Europeans, were white, the color of purity and power. *Negroids*, or Africans, were black, for their dark and animalistic character. *Mongoloids*, or Orientals, were yellow, the color of infirmity and cowardice. . . .

The vision of "the menace from the East was always more racial than national," writes historian John Dower in *War Without Mercy*. "It derived not from concern with any one country or people in particular, but from a vague and ominous sense of the vast, faceless, nameless yellow horde."

The "Yellow Peril" became a persistent theme in American politics and culture through World War II, when the term was applied to the Japanese, those treacherous simians who snuck up

'+ necessary to round up and lock

became the
us former
ere In-
g, and
ame

ly

assacre in Vietnam became news.
Life magazine pictorial of the kill-
women and children and old men, as
ot up and contorted in bloody piles along
s like giant sores on legs and arms and necks.
ome apart. And the faces: open-mouthed, some-
s still frozen in terror, brains spilled into black hair.
ooked like those of my family. My aunts and uncles,
rs. Oriental faces. I looked at the photographs a long time,
d not stop thinking about them.

The only American soldier convicted in the killings, Lieutenant William Calley, served three months under house arrest. What
the massacre drove home to me was that Oriental life was not
terribly valuable. You could extinguish hundreds of Orientals—un-
armed villages, farmers, women, toddlers, infants—and the penalty would be napping and watching television in your apartment
for twelve weeks. I still have that *Life* pictorial in my files and run
across it once in a while. The same emotions well up each time.

HAVING MET OTHER IMMIGRANTS like myself in America,
I can say that a great number of us came to our same "Oriental"
identity in a similar fashion. We arrived in the United States as
Japanese or Korean or Filipino, but over time we became Orientals. It wouldn't be until the 1970s, after Edward Said's book
Orientalism shook up the academy and garnered an influential
following, that "Oriental" began its descent into scholarly oppro-
brium, along the same path as "Negro" and "Indian."

Nevertheless, many older Americans still use the word, often
innocently. In the Midwest and South, I'm frequently referred to
as Oriental by kind and well-meaning people. I can walk a few
blocks from my house in the Pacific Northwest and order an Oriental salad and an Oriental chicken sandwich. (I've been tempted
to order an Occidental beverage to go with them.) . . .

But in academic and government circles, "Asian"[...] correct designation, and I became one in college. All o[...] Orientals were now officially and properly Asians. . . .

The second-wavers were more diverse. Among them [...] dians, Koreans, Vietnamese, Cambodians, Laotians, Hmon[...] Mien. Many came from war-ravaged countries. Very many [...] with nothing.

As a journalist in my twenties and thirties, I wrote extensive[...] about these communities. No surprise, I found each group exuber[...] antly complex and distinct, and perceiving themselves to be sepa- rate from—and often antipathetic to—other Asian ethnicities. . . .

It was the children and grandchildren, the ones growing up in America, who would find—or be coerced onto—common ground. Years of checking "Asian" on countless forms, of being subjected to the same epithets and compliments, of living in the same neighborhoods and housing projects, and sharing simi- lar challenges and aspirations—the most important to become Americanized—all of these would compel young Vietnamese, Cambodians, and Filipinos to accept their belongings to the cat- egory known as Asians. . . .

Young people who would have no natural ties in Asia found themselves bound together in America, and more so with suc- ceeding generations. The farther out in time from the point of arrival, the more Asian they became. [In one sense at least] it mirrored what happened to Africans brought to America as slaves. "We may have come on different ships," Martin Luther King Jr. said, "but we're in the same boat now." We Asians were now in the same boat. . . . Like Lisa said on the Grand Concourse [in the Bronx]: "Japanese, Chinese, Filipino—same thing!"

PART II

IMMIGRANTS

MY FAMILY'S SLAVE

Introduced by JEFFREY GOLDBERG,
editor in chief of *The Atlantic* magazine

*W*hen Alex Tizon came to us with the mesmerizing, horrible, and beautiful story of Eudocia Pulido—a woman he called "Lola," who was enslaved in his family's household for fifty-six years—we immediately understood that this was the sort of journalism The Atlantic was made for. At once a tribute and a confession, "Lola's Story" provides a painfully intimate and searing look at the persistence of slavery in modern America.

"Lola's Story" was also an important piece for Alex: He had built his journalism career on the margins of society, giving voice to the anonymous, to the otherwise silenced, to the ostensibly insignificant. As Melissa, Alex's wife, later told me, his core belief was that all people, no matter how modest, had within them an epic story. The secret of Lola, and her tortured relationship with the Tizon family, was Alex's own epic story.

Alex had been working on the story with his editor at The Atlantic, Denise Wills, for nearly a year before he died. Reckoning with what his family had done—and his own complicity—was a slow and difficult process. Alex died right before we could tell him that we had decided to put his story on the cover of our magazine. Thanks to Melissa, and his siblings, we were able to finalize the story for publication. The response was overwhelming. "Lola's Story" became one of the most read articles in The Atlantic's history; by one authoritative measure, it was the most read story in the world that year. It inspired scores of responses from readers around the globe; Alex won, posthumously, a National Magazine Award, our industry's highest honor. Our great sadness is that he didn't get

to witness the reach and influence of the epic story, the one he had
waited his entire life to tell.

·   ·   ·

THE ASHES FILLED a black plastic box about the size of a toaster.
It weighed three and a half pounds. I put it in a canvas tote bag and
packed it in my suitcase this past July for the transpacific flight to
Manila. From there I would travel by car to a rural village. When I
arrived, I would hand over all that was left of the woman who had
spent 56 years as a slave in my family's household.

Her name was Eudocia Tomas Pulido. We called her Lola.
She was 4 foot 11, with mocha-brown skin and almond eyes that
I can still see looking into mine—my first memory. She was 18
years old when my grandfather gave her to my mother as a gift,
and when my family moved to the United States, we brought her
with us. No other word but *slave* encompassed the life she lived.
Her days began before everyone else woke and ended after we
went to bed. She prepared three meals a day, cleaned the house,
waited on my parents, and took care of my four siblings and me.
My parents never paid her, and they scolded her constantly. She
wasn't kept in leg irons, but she might as well have been. So many
nights, on my way to the bathroom, I'd spot her sleeping in a corner, slumped against a mound of laundry, her fingers clutching a
garment she was in the middle of folding.

To our American neighbors, we were model immigrants, a
poster family. They told us so. My father had a law degree, my
mother was on her way to becoming a doctor, and my siblings and
I got good grades and always said "please" and "thank you." We
never talked about Lola. Our secret went to the core of who we
were and, at least for us kids, who we wanted to be.

After my mother died of leukemia, in 1999, Lola came to live
with me in a small town north of Seattle. I had a family, a career,
a house in the suburbs—the American dream. And then I had a
slave.

At baggage claim in Manila, I unzipped my suitcase to make
sure Lola's ashes were still there. Outside, I inhaled the familiar

smell: a thick blend of exhaust and waste, of ocean and sweet fruit and sweat.

Early the next morning I found a driver, an affable middle-aged man who went by the nickname "Doods," and we hit the road in his truck, weaving through traffic. The scene always stunned me. The sheer number of cars and motorcycles and jeepneys. The people weaving between them and moving on the sidewalks in great brown rivers. The street vendors in bare feet trotting alongside cars, hawking cigarettes and cough drops and sacks of boiled peanuts. The child beggars pressing their faces against the windows.

Doods and I were headed to the place where Lola's story began, up north in the central plains: Tarlac province. Rice country. The home of a cigar-chomping army lieutenant named Tomas Asuncion, my grandfather. The family stories paint Lieutenant Tom as a formidable man given to eccentricity and dark moods, who had lots of land but little money and kept mistresses in separate houses on his property. His wife died giving birth to their only child, my mother. She was raised by a series of *utusans*, or "people who take commands."

Slavery has a long history on the islands. Before the Spanish came, islanders enslaved other islanders, usually war captives, criminals, or debtors. Slaves came in different varieties, from warriors who could earn their freedom through valor to household servants who were regarded as property and could be bought and sold or traded. High-status slaves could own low-status slaves, and the low could own the lowliest. Some chose to enter servitude simply to survive: In exchange for their labor, they might be given food, shelter, and protection.

When the Spanish arrived, in the 1500s, they enslaved islanders and later brought African and Indian slaves. The Spanish Crown eventually began phasing out slavery at home and in its colonies, but parts of the Philippines were so far-flung that authorities couldn't keep a close eye. Traditions persisted under different guises, even after the U.S. took control of the islands in 1898. Today even the poor can have *utusans* or *katulongs* ("helpers") or *kasambahays* ("domestics"), as long as there are people even poorer. The pool is deep.

Lieutenant Tom had as many as three families of *utusans* living on his property. In the spring of 1943, with the islands under Japanese occupation, he brought home a girl from a village down the road. She was a cousin from a marginal side of the family, rice farmers. The lieutenant was shrewd—he saw that this girl was penniless, unschooled, and likely to be malleable. Her parents wanted her to marry a pig farmer twice her age, and she was desperately unhappy but had nowhere to go. Tom approached her with an offer: She could have food and shelter if she would commit to taking care of his daughter, who had just turned 12.

Lola agreed, not grasping that the deal was for life.

"She is my gift to you," Lieutenant Tom told my mother.

"I don't want her," my mother said, knowing she had no choice.

Lieutenant Tom went off to fight the Japanese, leaving Mom behind with Lola in his creaky house in the provinces. Lola fed, groomed, and dressed my mother. When they walked to the market, Lola held an umbrella to shield her from the sun. At night, when Lola's other tasks were done—feeding the dogs, sweeping the floors, folding the laundry that she had washed by hand in the Camiling River—she sat at the edge of my mother's bed and fanned her to sleep.

One day during the war Lieutenant Tom came home and caught my mother in a lie—something to do with a boy she wasn't supposed to talk to. Tom, furious, ordered her to "stand at the table." Mom cowered with Lola in a corner. Then, in a quivering voice, she told her father that Lola would take her punishment. Lola looked at Mom pleadingly, then without a word walked to the dining table and held on to the edge. Tom raised the belt and delivered 12 lashes, punctuating each one with a word. *You. Do. Not. Lie. To. Me. You. Do. Not. Lie. To. Me.* Lola made no sound.

My mother, in recounting this story late in her life, delighted in the outrageousness of it, her tone seeming to say, *Can you believe I did that?* When I brought it up with Lola, she asked to hear Mom's version. She listened intently, eyes lowered, and afterward she looked at me with sadness and said simply, "Yes. It was like that."

Seven years later, in 1950, Mom married my father and moved to Manila, bringing Lola along. Lieutenant Tom had long been haunted by demons, and in 1951 he silenced them with a .32-caliber slug to his temple. Mom almost never talked about it. She had his temperament—moody, imperial, secretly fragile—and she took his lessons to heart, among them the proper way to be a provincial *matrona*: You must embrace your role as the giver of commands. You must keep those beneath you in their place at all times, for their own good and the good of the household. They might cry and complain, but their souls will thank you. They will love you for helping them be what God intended.

My brother Arthur was born in 1951. I came next, followed by three more siblings in rapid succession. My parents expected Lola to be as devoted to us kids as she was to them. While she looked after us, my parents went to school and earned advanced degrees, joining the ranks of so many others with fancy diplomas but no jobs. Then the big break: Dad was offered a job in Foreign Affairs as a commercial analyst. The salary would be meager, but the position was in America—a place he and Mom had grown up dreaming of, where everything they hoped for could come true.

Dad was allowed to bring his family and one domestic. Figuring they would both have to work, my parents needed Lola to care for the kids and the house. My mother informed Lola, and to her great irritation, Lola didn't immediately acquiesce. Years later Lola told me she was terrified. "It was too far," she said. "Maybe your Mom and Dad won't let me go home."

In the end what convinced Lola was my father's promise that things would be different in America. He told her that as soon as he and Mom got on their feet, they'd give her an "allowance." Lola could send money to her parents, to all her relations in the village. Her parents lived in a hut with a dirt floor. Lola could build them a concrete house, could change their lives forever. *Imagine.*

We landed in Los Angeles on May 12, 1964, all our belongings in cardboard boxes tied with rope. Lola had been with my

mother for 21 years by then. In many ways she was more of a
parent to me than either my mother or my father. Hers was the
first face I saw in the morning and the last one I saw at night. As
a baby, I uttered Lola's name (which I first pronounced "Oh-ah")
long before I learned to say "Mom" or "Dad." As a toddler, I refused to go to sleep unless Lola was holding me, or at least nearby.

I was 4 years old when we arrived in the U.S.—too young to
question Lola's place in our family. But as my siblings and I grew
up on this other shore, we came to see the world differently. The
leap across the ocean brought about a leap in consciousness that
Mom and Dad couldn't, or wouldn't, make.

Lola never got that allowance. She asked my parents about it
in a roundabout way a couple of years into our life in America.
Her mother had fallen ill (with what I would later learn was dys-
entery), and her family couldn't afford the medicine she needed.
"Pwede ba?" she said to my parents. Is it possible? Mom let out
a sigh. "How could you even ask?," Dad responded in Tagalog.
"You see how hard up we are. Don't you have any shame?"

My parents had borrowed money for the move to the U.S., and
then borrowed more in order to stay. My father was transferred
from the consulate general in L.A. to the Philippine consulate in
Seattle. He was paid $5,600 a year. He took a second job cleaning
trailers, and a third as a debt collector. Mom got work as a technician in a couple of medical labs. We barely saw them, and when
we did they were often exhausted and snappish.

Mom would come home and upbraid Lola for not cleaning
the house well enough or for forgetting to bring in the mail.
"Didn't I tell you I want the letters here when I come home?"
she would say in Tagalog, her voice venomous. "It's not hard na-
man! An idiot could remember." Then my father would arrive
and take his turn. When Dad raised his voice, everyone in the
house shrank. Sometimes my parents would team up until Lola
broke down crying, almost as though that was their goal.

It confused me: My parents were good to my siblings and me,
and we loved them. But they'd be affectionate to us kids one mo-

ment and vile to Lola the next. I was 11 or 12 when I began to see Lola's situation clearly. By then Arthur, eight years my senior, had been seething for a long time. He was the one who introduced the word *slave* into my understanding of what Lola was. Before he said it I'd thought of her as just an unfortunate member of the household. I hated when my parents yelled at her, but it hadn't occurred to me that they—and the whole arrangement—could be immoral.

"Do you know anybody treated the way she's treated?," Arthur said. "Who lives the way she lives?" He summed up Lola's reality: Wasn't paid. Toiled every day. Was tongue-lashed for sitting too long or falling asleep too early. Was struck for talking back. Wore hand-me-downs. Ate scraps and leftovers by herself in the kitchen. Rarely left the house. Had no friends or hobbies outside the family. Had no private quarters. (Her designated place to sleep in each house we lived in was always whatever was left—a couch or storage area or corner in my sisters' bedroom. She often slept among piles of laundry.)

We couldn't identify a parallel anywhere except in slave characters on TV and in the movies. I remember watching a Western called *The Man Who Shot Liberty Valance*. John Wayne plays Tom Doniphon, a gunslinging rancher who barks orders at his servant, Pompey, whom he calls his "boy." *Pick him up, Pompey. Pompey, go find the doctor. Get on back to work, Pompey!* Docile and obedient, Pompey calls his master "Mistah Tom." They have a complex relationship. Tom forbids Pompey from attending school but opens the way for Pompey to drink in a whites-only saloon. Near the end, Pompey saves his master from a fire. It's clear Pompey both fears and loves Tom, and he mourns when Tom dies. All of this is peripheral to the main story of Tom's showdown with bad guy Liberty Valance, but I couldn't take my eyes off Pompey. I remember thinking: *Lola is Pompey, Pompey is Lola.*

One night when Dad found out that my sister Ling, who was then 9, had missed dinner, he barked at Lola for being lazy. "I tried to feed her," Lola said, as Dad stood over her and glared. Her feeble defense only made him angrier, and he punched her just below the shoulder. Lola ran out of the room and I could hear her wailing, an animal cry.

"Ling said she wasn't hungry," I said.

My parents turned to look at me. They seemed startled. I felt the twitching in my face that usually preceded tears, but I wouldn't cry this time. In Mom's eyes was a shadow of something I hadn't seen before. Jealousy?

"Are you defending your Lola?," Dad said. "Is that what you're doing?"

"Ling said she wasn't hungry," I said again, almost in a whisper.

I was 13. It was my first attempt to stick up for the woman who spent her days watching over me. The woman who used to hum Tagalog melodies as she rocked me to sleep, and when I got older would dress and feed me and walk me to school in the mornings and pick me up in the afternoons. Once, when I was sick for a long time and too weak to eat, she chewed my food for me and put the small pieces in my mouth to swallow. One summer when I had plaster casts on both legs (I had problem joints), she bathed me with a washcloth, brought medicine in the middle of the night, and helped me through months of rehabilitation. I was cranky through it all. She didn't complain or lose patience, ever.

To now hear her wailing made me crazy.

In the old country, my parents felt no need to hide their treatment of Lola. In America, they treated her worse but took pains to conceal it. When guests came over, my parents would either ignore her or, if questioned, lie and quickly change the subject. For five years in North Seattle, we lived across the street from the Misslers, a rambunctious family of eight who introduced us to things like mustard, salmon fishing, and mowing the lawn. Football on TV. Yelling during football. Lola would come out to serve food and drinks during games, and my parents would smile and thank her before she quickly disappeared. "Who's that little lady you keep in the kitchen?," Big Jim, the Missler patriarch, once asked. A relative from back home, Dad said. Very shy.

Billy Missler, my best friend, didn't buy it. He spent enough time at our house, whole weekends sometimes, to catch glimpses of my family's secret. He once overheard my mother yelling in the kitchen, and when he barged in to investigate found Mom red-faced and glaring at Lola, who was quaking in a corner. I came in a few seconds later. The look on Billy's face was a mix of embarrassment and perplexity. *What was that?* I waved it off and told him to forget it.

I think Billy felt sorry for Lola. He'd rave about her cooking, and make her laugh like I'd never seen. During sleepovers, she'd make his favorite Filipino dish, beef *tapa* over white rice. Cooking was Lola's only eloquence. I could tell by what she served whether she was merely feeding us or saying she loved us.

When I once referred to Lola as a distant aunt, Billy reminded me that when we'd first met I'd said she was my grandmother.

"Well, she's kind of both," I said mysteriously.

"Why is she always working?"

"She likes to work," I said.

"Your dad and mom—why do they yell at her?"

"Her hearing isn't so good. . . ."

Admitting the truth would have meant exposing us all. We spent our first decade in the country learning the ways of the new land and trying to fit in. Having a slave did not fit. Having a slave gave me grave doubts about what kind of people we were, what kind of place we came from. Whether we deserved to be accepted. I was ashamed of it all, including my complicity. Didn't I eat the food she cooked, and wear the clothes she washed and ironed and hung in the closet? But losing her would have been devastating.

There was another reason for secrecy: Lola's travel papers had expired in 1969, five years after we arrived in the U.S. She'd come on a special passport linked to my father's job. After a series of fallings-out with his superiors, Dad quit the consulate and declared his intent to stay in the United States. He arranged for permanent-resident status for his family, but Lola wasn't eligible. He was supposed to send her back.

Lola's mother, Fermina, died in 1973; her father, Hilario, in 1979. Both times she wanted desperately to go home. Both times my parents said "Sorry." No money, no time. The kids needed her. My parents also feared for themselves, they admitted to me later. If the authorities had found out about Lola, as they surely would have if she'd tried to leave, my parents could have gotten into trouble, possibly even been deported. They couldn't risk it. Lola's legal status became what Filipinos call *tago nang tago*, or TNT—"on the run." She stayed TNT for almost 20 years.

After each of her parents died, Lola was sullen and silent for months. She barely responded when my parents badgered her. But the badgering never let up. Lola kept her head down and did her work.

My father's resignation started a turbulent period. Money got tighter, and my parents turned on each other. They uprooted the family again and again—Seattle to Honolulu back to Seattle to the southeast Bronx and finally to the truck-stop town of Umatilla, Oregon, population 750. During all this moving around, Mom often worked 24-hour shifts, first as a medical intern and then as a resident, and Dad would disappear for days, working odd jobs but also (we'd later learn) womanizing and who knows what else. Once, he came home and told us that he'd lost our new station wagon playing blackjack.

For days in a row Lola would be the only adult in the house. She got to know the details of our lives in a way that my parents never had the mental space for. We brought friends home, and she'd listen to us talk about school and girls and boys and whatever else was on our minds. Just from conversations she overheard, she could list the first name of every girl I had a crush on from sixth grade through high school.

When I was 15, Dad left the family for good. I didn't want to believe it at the time, but the fact was that he deserted us kids and abandoned Mom after 25 years of marriage. She wouldn't become a licensed physician for another year, and her specialty— internal medicine—wasn't especially lucrative. Dad didn't pay child support, so money was always a struggle.

My mom kept herself together enough to go to work, but at night she'd crumble in self-pity and despair. Her main source of comfort during this time: Lola. As Mom snapped at her over small things, Lola attended to her even more—cooking Mom's favorite meals, cleaning her bedroom with extra care. I'd find the two of them late at night at the kitchen counter, griping and telling stories about Dad, sometimes laughing wickedly, other times working themselves into a fury over his transgressions. They barely noticed us kids flitting in and out.

One night I heard Mom weeping and ran into the living room to find her slumped in Lola's arms. Lola was talking softly to her, the way she used to with my siblings and me when we were young. I lingered, then went back to my room, scared for my mom and awed by Lola.

Doods was humming. I'd dozed for what felt like a minute and awoke to his happy melody. "Two hours more," he said. I checked the plastic box in the tote bag by my side—still there—and looked up to see open road. The MacArthur Highway. I glanced at the time. "Hey, you said 'two hours' two hours ago," I said. Doods just hummed.

His not knowing anything about the purpose of my journey was a relief. I had enough interior dialogue going on. *I was no better than my parents. I could have done more to free Lola. To make her life better. Why didn't I?* I could have turned in my parents, I suppose. It would have blown up my family in an instant. Instead, my siblings and I kept everything to ourselves, and rather than blowing up in an instant, my family broke apart slowly.

Doods and I passed through beautiful country. Not travel-brochure beautiful but real and alive and, compared with the city, elegantly spare. Mountains ran parallel to the highway on each side, the Zambales Mountains to the west, the Sierra Madre Range to the east. From ridge to ridge, west to east, I could see every shade of green all the way to almost black.

Doods pointed to a shadowy outline in the distance. Mount Pinatubo. I'd come here in 1991 to report on the aftermath of its eruption, the second-largest of the 20th century. Volcanic mud-flows called *lahars* continued for more than a decade, burying ancient villages, filling in rivers and valleys, and wiping out entire ecosystems. The *lahars* reached deep into the foothills of Tarlac province, where Lola's parents had spent their entire lives, and where she and my mother had once lived together. So much of our family record had been lost in wars and floods, and now parts were buried under 20 feet of mud.

Life here is routinely visited by cataclysm. Killer typhoons that strike several times a year. Bandit insurgencies that never end. Somnolent mountains that one day decide to wake up. The Philippines isn't like China or Brazil, whose mass might absorb the trauma. This is a nation of scattered rocks in the sea. When disaster hits, the place goes under for a while. Then it resurfaces and life proceeds, and you can behold a scene like the one Doods and I were driving through, and the simple fact that it's still there makes it beautiful.

A couple of years after my parents split, my mother remarried and demanded Lola's fealty to her new husband, a Croatian immigrant named Ivan, whom she had met through a friend. Ivan had never finished high school. He'd been married four times and was an inveterate gambler who enjoyed being supported by my mother and attended to by Lola.

Ivan brought out a side of Lola I'd never seen. His marriage to my mother was volatile from the start, and money—especially his use of her money—was the main issue. Once, during an argument in which Mom was crying and Ivan was yelling, Lola walked over and stood between them. She turned to Ivan and firmly said his name. He looked at Lola, blinked, and sat down.

My sister Inday and I were floored. Ivan was about 250 pounds, and his baritone could shake the walls. Lola put him in his place with a single word. I saw this happen a few other times, but for the most part Lola served Ivan unquestioningly, just as Mom wanted her to. I had a hard time watching Lola vassalize herself to another person, especially someone like Ivan. But what set the stage for my blowup with Mom was something more mundane.

She used to get angry whenever Lola felt ill. She didn't want to deal with the disruption and the expense, and would accuse Lola of faking or failing to take care of herself. Mom chose the second tack when, in the late 1970s, Lola's teeth started falling out. She'd been saying for months that her mouth hurt.

"That's what happens when you don't brush properly," Mom told her.

I said that Lola needed to see a dentist. She was in her 50s and had never been to one. I was attending college an hour away, and I brought it up again and again on my frequent trips home. A year went by, then two. Lola took aspirin every day for the pain, and her teeth looked like a crumbling Stonehenge. One night, after watching her chew bread on the side of her mouth that still had a few good molars, I lost it.

Mom and I argued into the night, each of us sobbing at different points. She said she was tired of working her fingers to the bone supporting everybody, and sick of her children always taking Lola's side, and why didn't we just take our goddamn Lola, she'd never wanted her in the first place, and she wished to God she hadn't given birth to an arrogant, sanctimonious phony like me.

I let her words sink in. Then I came back at her, saying she would know all about being a phony, her whole life was a masquerade, and if she stopped feeling sorry for herself for one minute she'd see that Lola could barely eat because her goddamn teeth were rotting out of her goddamn head, and couldn't she think of her just this once as a real person instead of a slave kept alive to serve her?

"A slave," Mom said, weighing the word. "A *slave?*"

The night ended when she declared that I would never understand her relationship with Lola. *Never.* Her voice was so guttural and pained that thinking of it even now, so many years later, feels like a punch to the stomach. It's a terrible thing to hate your own mother, and that night I did. The look in her eyes made clear that she felt the same way about me.

The fight only fed Mom's fear that Lola had stolen the kids from her, and she made Lola pay for it. Mom drove her harder. Tormented her by saying, "I hope you're happy now that your kids hate me." When we helped Lola with housework, Mom would fume. "You'd better go to sleep now, Lola," she'd say sarcastically.

"You've been working too hard. Your kids are worried about you." Later she'd take Lola into a bedroom for a talk, and Lola would walk out with puffy eyes.

Lola finally begged us to stop trying to help her.

Why do you stay? we asked.

"Who will cook?" she said, which I took to mean, *Who would do everything?* Who would take care of us? Of Mom? Another time she said, "Where will I go?" This struck me as closer to a real answer. Coming to America had been a mad dash, and before we caught a breath a decade had gone by. We turned around, and a second decade was closing out. Lola's hair had turned gray. She'd heard that relatives back home who hadn't received the promised support were wondering what had happened to her. She was ashamed to return.

She had no contacts in America, and no facility for getting around. Phones puzzled her. Mechanical things—ATMs, intercoms, vending machines, anything with a keyboard—made her panic. Fast-talking people left her speechless, and her own broken English did the same to them. She couldn't make an appointment, arrange a trip, fill out a form, or order a meal without help.

I got Lola an ATM card linked to my bank account and taught her how to use it. She succeeded once, but the second time she got flustered, and she never tried again. She kept the card because she considered it a gift from me.

I also tried to teach her to drive. She dismissed the idea with a wave of her hand, but I picked her up and carried her to the car and planted her in the driver's seat, both of us laughing. I spent 20 minutes going over the controls and gauges. Her eyes went from mirthful to terrified. When I turned on the ignition and the dashboard lit up, she was out of the car and in the house before I could say another word. I tried a couple more times.

I thought driving could change her life. She could go places. And if things ever got unbearable with Mom, she could drive away forever.

Four lanes became two, pavement turned to gravel. Tricycle drivers wove between cars and water buffalo pulling loads of bamboo. An occasional dog or goat sprinted across the road in front of our truck, almost grazing the bumper. Doods never eased up. Whatever didn't make it across would be stew today instead of tomorrow—the rule of the road in the provinces.

I took out a map and traced the route to the village of Mayantoc, our destination. Out the window, in the distance, tiny figures folded at the waist like so many bent nails. People harvesting rice, the same way they had for thousands of years. We were getting close.

I tapped the cheap plastic box and regretted not buying a real urn, made of porcelain or rosewood. What would Lola's people think? Not that many were left. Only one sibling remained in the area, Gregoria, 98 years old, and I was told her memory was failing. Relatives said that whenever she heard Lola's name, she'd burst out crying and then quickly forget why.

I'd been in touch with one of Lola's nieces. She had the day planned: When I arrived, a low-key memorial, then a prayer, followed by the lowering of the ashes into a plot at the Mayantoc Eternal Bliss Memorial Park. It had been five years since Lola died, but I hadn't yet said the final goodbye that I knew was about to happen. All day I had been feeling intense grief and resisting the urge to let it out, not wanting to wail in front of Doods. More than the shame I felt for the way my family had treated Lola, more than my anxiety about how her relatives in Mayantoc would treat me, I felt the terrible heaviness of losing her, as if she had died only the day before.

Doods veered northwest on the Romulo Highway, then took a sharp left at Camiling, the town Mom and Lieutenant Tom came from. Two lanes became one, then gravel turned to dirt. The path ran along the Camiling River, clusters of bamboo houses off to the side, green hills ahead. The homestretch.

I gave the eulogy at Mom's funeral, and everything I said was true. That she was brave and spirited. That she'd drawn some short straws, but had done the best she could. That she was radiant when she was happy. That she adored her children, and gave us a real home—in Salem, Oregon—that through the '80s and

'90s became the permanent base we'd never had before. That I wished we could thank her one more time. That we all loved her.

I didn't talk about Lola. Just as I had selectively blocked Lola out of my mind when I was with Mom during her last years. Loving my mother required that kind of mental surgery. It was the only way we could be mother and son—which I wanted, especially after her health started to decline, in the mid-'90s. Diabetes. Breast cancer. Acute myelogenous leukemia, a fast-growing cancer of the blood and bone marrow. She went from robust to frail seemingly overnight.

After the big fight, I mostly avoided going home, and at age 23 I moved to Seattle. When I did visit I saw a change. Mom was still Mom, but not as relentlessly. She got Lola a fine set of dentures and let her have her own bedroom. She cooperated when my siblings and I set out to change Lola's TNT status. Ronald Reagan's landmark immigration bill of 1986 made millions of illegal immigrants eligible for amnesty. It was a long process, but Lola became a citizen in October 1998, four months after my mother was diagnosed with leukemia. Mom lived another year.

During that time, she and Ivan took trips to Lincoln City, on the Oregon coast, and sometimes brought Lola along. Lola loved the ocean. On the other side were the islands she dreamed of returning to. And Lola was never happier than when Mom relaxed around her. An afternoon at the coast or just 15 minutes in the kitchen reminiscing about the old days in the province, and Lola would seem to forget years of torment.

I couldn't forget so easily. But I did come to see Mom in a different light. Before she died, she gave me her journals, two steamer trunks' full. Leafing through them as she slept a few feet away, I glimpsed slices of her life that I'd refused to see for years. She'd gone to medical school when not many women did. She'd come to America and fought for respect as both a woman and an immigrant physician. She'd worked for two decades at Fairview Training Center, in Salem, a state institution for the developmentally disabled. The irony: She tended to underdogs most of her professional life. They worshipped her. Female colleagues became close friends. They did silly, girly things together—shoe shopping, throwing dress-up parties at one another's homes, exchanging gag gifts like penis-shaped soaps and calendars of half-naked men, all while laughing hysterically. Looking through their party pictures reminded me that Mom had a life and an identity apart from the family and Lola. Of course.

Mom wrote in great detail about each of her kids, and how she felt about us on a given day—proud or loving or resentful. And she devoted volumes to her husbands, trying to grasp them as complex characters in her story. We were all persons of consequence. Lola was incidental. When she was mentioned at all, she was a bit character in someone else's story. "Lola walked my beloved Alex to his new school this morning. I hope he makes new friends quickly so he doesn't feel so sad about moving again. . . ." There might be two more pages about me, and no other mention of Lola.

The day before Mom died, a Catholic priest came to the house to perform last rites. Lola sat next to my mother's bed, holding a cup with a straw, poised to raise it to Mom's mouth. She had become extra attentive to my mother, and extra kind. She could have taken advantage of Mom in her feebleness, even exacted revenge, but she did the opposite.

The priest asked Mom whether there was anything she wanted to forgive or be forgiven for. She scanned the room with heavy-lidded eyes, said nothing. Then, without looking at Lola, she reached over and placed an open hand on her head. She didn't say a word.

Lola was 75 when she came to stay with me. I was married with two young daughters, living in a cozy house on a wooded lot. From the second story, we could see Puget Sound. We gave Lola a bedroom and license to do whatever she wanted: sleep in, watch soaps, do nothing all day. She could relax—and be free— for the first time in her life. I should have known it wouldn't be that simple.

I'd forgotten about all the things Lola did that drove me a little crazy. She was always telling me to put on a sweater so I wouldn't catch a cold (I was in my 40s). She groused incessantly about Dad and Ivan: My father was lazy, Ivan was a leech. I learned to tune her out. Harder to ignore was her fanatical thriftiness. She threw nothing out. And she used to go through the trash to make sure that the rest of us hadn't thrown out anything useful. She washed and reused paper towels again and again until they disintegrated in her hands. (No one else would go near them.) The kitchen became glutted with grocery bags, yogurt containers, and pickle jars, and parts of our house turned into storage for—there's no other word for it—garbage.

She cooked breakfast even though none of us ate more than a banana or a granola bar in the morning, usually while we were running out the door. She made our beds and did our laundry. She cleaned the house. I found myself saying to her, nicely at first, "Lola, you don't have to do that." "Lola, we'll do it ourselves." "Lola, that's the girls' job." Okay, she'd say, but keep right on doing it.

It irritated me to catch her eating meals standing in the kitchen, or see her tense up and start cleaning when I walked into the room. One day, after several months, I sat her down.

"I'm not Dad. You're not a slave here," I said, and went through a long list of slavelike things she'd been doing. When I realized she was startled, I took a deep breath and cupped her face, that elfin face now looking at me searchingly. I kissed her forehead. "This is *your* house now," I said. "You're not here to serve us. You can relax, okay?"

"Okay," she said. And went back to cleaning.

She didn't know any other way to be. I realized I had to take my own advice and relax. If she wanted to make dinner, let her. Thank her and do the dishes. I had to remind myself constantly: *Let her be.*

One night I came home to find her sitting on the couch doing a word puzzle, her feet up, the TV on. Next to her, a cup of tea. She glanced at me, smiled sheepishly with those perfect white dentures, and went back to the puzzle. *Progress*, I thought.

She planted a garden in the backyard—roses and tulips and every kind of orchid—and spent whole afternoons tending it. She took walks around the neighborhood. At about 80, her arthritis got bad and she began walking with a cane. In the kitchen she went from being a fry cook to a kind of artisanal chef who created only when the spirit moved her. She made lavish meals and grinned with pleasure as we devoured them.

Passing the door of Lola's bedroom, I'd often hear her listening to a cassette of Filipino folk songs. The same tape over and over. I knew she'd been sending almost all her money—my wife and I gave her $200 a week—to relatives back home. One afternoon, I found her sitting on the back deck gazing at a snapshot someone had sent of her village.

"You want to go home, Lola?"

She turned the photograph over and traced her finger across the inscription, then flipped it back and seemed to study a single detail.

"Yes," she said.

Just after her 83rd birthday, I paid her airfare to go home. I'd follow a month later to bring her back to the U.S.—if she wanted to return. The unspoken purpose of her trip was to see whether the place she had spent so many years longing for could still feel like home.

She found her answer.

"Everything was not the same," she told me as we walked around Mayantoc. The old farms were gone. Her house was gone. Her parents and most of her siblings were gone. Childhood friends, the ones still alive, were like strangers. It was nice to see them, but . . . everything was not the same. She'd still like to spend her last years here, she said, but she wasn't ready yet.

"You're ready to go back to your garden," I said.

"Yes. Let's go home."

Lola was as devoted to my daughters as she'd been to my siblings and me when we were young. After school, she'd listen to their stories and make them something to eat. And unlike my wife and me (especially me), Lola enjoyed every minute of every school event and performance. She couldn't get enough of them. She sat up front, kept the programs as mementos.

It was so easy to make Lola happy. We took her on family vacations, but she was as excited to go to the farmer's market down the hill. She became a wide-eyed kid on a field trip: "Look at those zucchinis!" The first thing she did every morning was open all the blinds in the house, and at each window she'd pause to look outside.

And she taught herself to read. It was remarkable. Over the years, she'd somehow learned to sound out letters. She did those puzzles where you find and circle words within a block of letters. Her room had stacks of word-puzzle booklets, thousands of words circled in pencil. Every day she watched the news and listened for words she recognized. She triangulated them with words in the newspaper, and figured out the meanings. She came to read the paper every day, front to back. Dad used to say she was simple. I wondered what she could have been if, instead of working the rice fields at age 8, she had learned to read and write.

During the 12 years she lived in our house, I asked her questions about herself, trying to piece together her life story, a habit she found curious. To my inquiries she would often respond first with "Why?" Why did I want to know about her childhood? About how she met Lieutenant Tom?

I tried to get my sister Ling to ask Lola about her love life, thinking Lola would be more comfortable with her. Ling cackled, which was her way of saying I was on my own. One day, while Lola and I were putting away groceries, I just blurted it out: "Lola, have you ever been romantic with anyone?" She smiled, and then she told me the story of the only time she'd come close. She was about 15, and there was a handsome boy named Pedro from a nearby farm. For several months they harvested rice together side by side. One time, she dropped her *bolo*—a cutting implement— and he quickly picked it up and handed it back to her. "I liked him," she said.

Silence.

"And?"

"Then he moved away," she said.

"And?"

"That's all."

"Lola, have you ever had sex?," I heard myself saying.

"No," she said.

She wasn't accustomed to being asked personal questions. *"Katulong lang ako,"* she'd say. *I'm only a servant.* She often gave one- or two-word answers, and teasing out even the simplest story was a game of 20 questions that could last days or weeks.

Some of what I learned: She was mad at Mom for being so cruel all those years, but she nevertheless missed her. Sometimes, when Lola was young, she'd felt so lonely that all she could do was cry. I knew there were years when she'd dreamed of being with a man. I saw it in the way she wrapped herself around one large pillow at night. But what she told me in her old age was that living with Mom's husbands made her think being alone wasn't so bad. She didn't miss those two at all. Maybe her life would have been better if she'd stayed in Mayantoc, gotten married, and had a family like her siblings. But maybe it would have been worse. Two younger sisters, Francisca and Zepriana, got sick and died. A brother, Claudio, was killed. What's the point of wondering about it now? she asked. *Bahala na* was her guiding principle. *Come what may.* What came her way was another kind of family. In that family, she had eight children: Mom, my four siblings and me, and now my two daughters. The eight of us, she said, made her life worth living.

None of us was prepared for her to die so suddenly.

Her heart attack started in the kitchen while she was making dinner and I was running an errand. When I returned she was in the middle of it. A couple of hours later at the hospital, before I could grasp what was happening, she was gone—10:56 P.M. All the kids and grandkids noted, but were unsure how to take, that she died on November 7, the same day as Mom. Twelve years apart.

Lola made it to 86. I can still see her on the gurney. I remember looking at the medics standing above this brown woman no bigger than a child and thinking that they had no idea of the life she had lived. She'd had none of the self-serving ambition that drives most of us, and her willingness to give up everything for the people around her won her our love and utter loyalty. She's become a hallowed figure in my extended family.

Going through her boxes in the attic took me months. I found recipes she had cut out of magazines in the 1970s for when she would someday learn to read. Photo albums with pictures of my mom. Awards my siblings and I had won from grade school on, most of which we had thrown away and she had "saved." I almost lost it one night when at the bottom of a box I found a stack of yellowed newspaper articles I'd written and long ago forgotten about. She couldn't read back then, but she'd kept them anyway.

Doods's truck pulled up to a small concrete house in the middle of a cluster of homes mostly made of bamboo and plank wood. Surrounding the pod of houses: rice fields, green and seemingly endless. Before I even got out of the truck, people started coming outside.

Doods reclined his seat to take a nap. I hung my tote bag on my shoulder, took a breath, and opened the door.

"This way," a soft voice said, and I was led up a short walkway to the concrete house. Following close behind was a line of about 20 people, young and old, but mostly old. Once we were all inside, they sat down on chairs and benches arranged along the walls, leaving the middle of the room empty except for me. I remained standing, waiting to meet my host. It was a small room, and dark. People glanced at me expectantly.

"Where is Lola?" A voice from another room. The next moment, a middle-aged woman in a housedress sauntered in with a smile. Ebia, Lola's niece. This was her house. She gave me a hug and said again, "Where is Lola?"

I slid the tote bag from my shoulder and handed it to her. She looked into my face, still smiling, gently grasped the bag, and walked over to a wooden bench and sat down. She reached inside and pulled out the box and looked at every side. "Where is Lola?" she said softly. People in these parts don't often get their loved ones cremated. I don't think she knew what to expect. She set the box on her lap and bent over so her forehead rested on top of it, and at first I thought she was laughing (out of joy) but

I quickly realized she was crying. Her shoulders began to heave, and then she was wailing—a deep, mournful, animal howl, like I once heard coming from Lola.

I hadn't come sooner to deliver Lola's ashes in part because I wasn't sure anyone here cared that much about her. I hadn't expected this kind of grief. Before I could comfort Ebia, a woman walked in from the kitchen and wrapped her arms around her, and then she began wailing. The next thing I knew, the room erupted with sound. The old people—one of them blind, several with no teeth—were all crying and not holding anything back. It lasted about 10 minutes. I was so fascinated that I barely noticed the tears running down my own face. The sobs died down, and then it was quiet again.

Ebia sniffled and said it was time to eat. Everybody started filing into the kitchen, puffy-eyed but suddenly lighter and ready to tell stories. I glanced at the empty tote bag on the bench, and knew it was right to bring Lola back to the place where she'd been born.

FOR SEATTLE'S CAMBODIAN REFUGEES, TIME AND DISTANCE CAN'T BURY MEMORIES OF THE KILLING FIELDS

Seattle Times, January 23, 1994

STRANGERS IN A STRANGE LAND: THE HMONG ORPHANS OF HISTORY

Seattle Times, March 12, 1996

Introduced by **DAVID BOARDMAN**, dean of the Klein College
of Media and Communication at Temple University and
former executive editor of the *Seattle Times*

*T*omas Alex Tizon emigrated from the Philippines to the United
States with his parents as a four-year-old.

As he chronicles in his magnificent memoir, Big Little Man, *he
spent much of the next two decades struggling to sever those roots:
Hanging from trees to stretch his vertebrae and make himself taller.
Pinching his nose with a clothespin to make it narrower. Sealing
his lips with masking tape overnight in the hope of making them
thinner. Dropping "Tomas" to become "Alex."*

By Alex's late twenties, though—just as he came to the Seattle
Times, *where I would work with him as an editor for seventeen
years—he was determined not only to reconstruct his ties to the
Philippines and to Asia but also to deconstruct them, to try to understand how they shaped who he was and would become.*

*This exploration also compelled Alex to tell the stories of other
immigrants, particularly those from such places as Cambodia and
Laos, whose collective histories were in peril of being lost in less
than a single generation. The passion and compassion he brought
to that task are on full display in these two pieces.*

*Also manifest here is the alchemy that made Alex unique among
the hundreds of fine journalists with whom I worked during three
decades at the* Times*—melodious prose and arresting revelation,*

the ability to extract raw and often painful material from vulnerable subjects and to weave it into elevated, purposeful gold.

. . .

FOR SEATTLE'S CAMBODIAN REFUGEES, TIME AND DISTANCE CAN'T BURY MEMORIES OF THE KILLING FIELDS

PATIENT A has a stomach ache. It never goes away. It keeps her awake at night and tired during the day. She can't work or play or enjoy sex. For three years she goes from doctor to doctor, subjecting herself to tests. The tests find nothing. She insists on the pain.

The doctors are baffled.

One doctor, acting on a hunch, refers her to Asian Counseling and Referral Service in Seattle's International District. "What for? I'm not chakourt!" says the patient, a 26-year-old Cambodian refugee. Chakourt is the Cambodian word for "crazy." Chakourt is anathema among Cambodians. The pain persists and she heeds her doctor's direction.

After a month of counseling, her story starts to come out: One day in Cambodia, Khmer Rouge soldiers took her family to a field.

They ordered them to dig a hole and line up at the edge. A soldier shot several family members in the head. The soldier ran out of bullets. He hit the others with a rifle butt. He stabbed Patient A.

The family—mother, father, seven children—crumpled one by one into the hole. Some were still alive. The soldiers covered the hole with dirt. Patient A survived. She crawled out of the hole. On foot she crossed the border into Thailand. She was raped by Thai soldiers.

Eventually, she came to America. She now lives in a cramped, government-subsidized apartment in West Seattle.

Like so many of her people, the most brutalized of all Southeast Asian refugees, Patient A left the killing fields, but the killing fields did not leave her.

Fifteen years after the end of Khmer Rouge leader Pol Pot's

murderous regime, Cambodian refugees still live as a wounded people.

An estimated 2 million died out of a population of 7 million, the result of Pol Pot's campaign to wipe out dissidents and to re-make the country, starting at "Year Zero." Memories of slaughter, compounded by upheaval and uprootedness and culture shock, continue to take a toll on survivors.

Patient A's counselor finds that her stomach ache is a physical symptom of an incomprehensible emotional trauma.

The trauma is still working its way through her psyche, just as the trauma of genocide is still working its way through the collective psyche of the Cambodian people.

Cambodians represent 4 percent of King County's Asian population but make up 20 percent of the clientele, the largest client group, at the Asian counseling service. It is a scenario found in communities all over the country where Cambodians have settled.

A Department of Mental Health study says that two out of three Cambodian refugees in the U.S. have experienced the violent death of a close family member—the highest percentage of any refugee group.

Furthermore, studies done within the past year show that at least half of adult Cambodian refugees in the U.S. suffer from depression or post-traumatic stress; a quarter have severe difficulty functioning in society. Many will never recover.

Yet they suffer in almost complete obscurity, their plight hardly a blip in American mainstream consciousness.

Unlike the Jewish holocaust (6 million were killed in Nazi concentration camps) which has been given its historical due, the stories of its survivors chronicled and documented, even celebrated, the Cambodian holocaust has only seemed to dim in memory, even as survivors live and struggle in our midst.

The dimming is evident in the dwindling of federal aid for refugees.

The Refugee Act of 1980 originally provided 36 months of financial support to refugees as part of a transitional period. That was cut to 18 months in 1982, to 12 months in 1989, to eight months in 1992.

It's evident in the way Cambodians are routinely unacknowledged as a separate people with a distinct story, but are lumped together with Laotians and Vietnamese in contradictory stereotypes: as clinging parasites and overachieving threats, today's welfare grunts and tomorrow's nuclear physicists.

Cambodians, one doctor says, are an "invisible people."

PATIENT B is a Cambodian widow. She has been in the U.S. for several years. One day she goes to a psychiatric clinic because she is "feeling sad day and night."

The doctor's inquiries unearth nothing extraordinary. Then after six months of therapy, she reveals that Khmer Rouge soldiers had disemboweled her parents in front of her.

The doctor is stunned, and later writes in a medical journal: "Our traditional American psychiatric training left us totally unprepared to deal with these tragedies."

The psychiatric care of survivors of mass violence is a nascent field, but one fact is clear: the trauma can and often does remain alive in the survivor, often manifesting as a constellation of complaints known as post-traumatic stress disorder: recurrent nightmares, depression, flashbacks, sweats, distress and paranoia.

"There are long-term effects that our society is going to have to deal with," says Jennifer White-Baughan, a psychologist at the University of California, San Diego, who works with Cambodian refugees.

"Who knows how long it will take? It's not just the generation that experienced the holocaust but also the children who are living with these shattered adults."

Clinicians say many refugees carry their wounds and memories dormant inside them for years before something awakens them. The trigger could be anything: a loud noise, an image, a face, a scene in a movie. This latency period may last years or even decades.

Says Sandy Lew, the clinical supervisor at the Asian counseling service: "We have Cambodian clients who've been here 10 years and are just now starting to tell their stories."

For many Americans who did not watch the 1984 movie "The Killing Fields," what happened in Cambodia blurs with all the internecine fighting in Southeast Asia during the 1960s and '70s.

From 1975 to the end of 1978 the communist Khmer Rouge, a heavily armed peasant group of ideologues, galvanized in part by years of U.S. bombing during the Vietnam war, tried to turn Cambodia into a giant agrarian commune.

They forced city-dwellers to the countryside and systematically killed anyone who might pose a threat to their ideology: intellectuals, professionals, religious and civic leaders, indeed, anyone wearing glasses, which was considered a mark of a thinker. In the Cambodian capital of Phnom Penh, 40 percent of the population of 2 million either died or disappeared, the bodies of victims later unearthed from hundreds of mass graves outside the city.

In the countryside, people died of disease, starvation and executions.

"Under the mango trees, the skulls and bones of the old and young lay in an obscene carpet of death," writes Cambodian author Nayan Chanda.

Cambodians flooded out of the country starting in late 1978, when a Vietnamese invasion ousted the Khmer Rouge. Most fled to Thailand, whose initial response was tragic: Thai soldiers pushed back some 40,000 Cambodians through mined slopes and shot those who tried to return. Thousands died.

After an international outcry, Thailand granted haven.

Nisay Nuth, 39, was one of those forced through the mine fields. He is now an outreach counselor for the Khmer Community of Seattle–King County (Khmer is the dominant ethnic group in Cambodia). He recalls walking through forests for two days before reaching the minefields. Twenty people began the journey with him.

Five survived.

"I was one of them," says Nuth, who, like other survivors, wonders with some guilt why he made it while so many others did not.

Nuth eventually made it to a Thai refugee camp, where tens of thousands of Cambodians languished for five years or longer before being resettled in a new country.

About 150,000 Cambodian refugees came to the United States between 1975 and 1992, settling in such disparate communities as San Diego, Minneapolis, New York City, Raleigh, N.C., Portland and Seattle. (Cambodian immigration to the United States has dropped to near zero in the past year, since a U.N.-supervised election last May has allowed repatriation of refugees.) The largest number settled in California.

About 15,000 Cambodian refugees live in Washington state, including 7,000 to 8,000 in King County, mostly in the Rainier Valley, West Seattle and White Center.

About 4,000 Cambodians live in Pierce County; 1,000 in Snohomish County, and about 600 in Olympia. Most live in government-subsidized housing and receive public assistance.

Unlike the Vietnamese, the vast majority of Cambodian refugees come from subsistence farming backgrounds with no formal education.

Many cannot read or write in their own language and do not know the basics of language structure, making it doubly hard to learn a complex language such as English.

The leap in consciousness required of Cambodians and other Southeast Asian refugees from preliterate, preindustrial backgrounds is possibly greater than that of any group in history.

The Cambodian story is not part of the active memory of the American people partly because Cambodians themselves have not fully articulated it. Most of those who would be spokesmen and spokeswomen—teachers, intellectuals, writers, artists—were killed by the Khmer Rouge.

But another reason for the silence has to do with a world view that sees nothing beneficial in dredging up painful memories, a view contrary to the Western psychiatric tenet that remembering is one of the first steps toward healing.

PATIENT C, a 40-year-old Cambodian man, is typical: "Why talk? You can't do anything. . . . Sometimes I have nightmares. Soldiers burying people. Dead or not dead, they would bury them. I don't like to think of that. I don't think it would help to remember. When I think of my brother, how he was killed, I get in trouble. Sometimes it makes me crazy. So I try to forget."

Cambodia's culture of fear also fostered a "societal silence." The Khmer Rouge killed dissidents without hesitation, but also killed were people who simply used the wrong word at the wrong moment. Grief was not allowed, nor anything that could be interpreted as dissatisfaction.

"The best way to survive was to shut up," says Lee Lim, a 31-year-old Cambodian who works as an Asian liaison for King County police.

Clinicians agree that the majority of Cambodian refugees suffering from depression or post-traumatic stress have not sought psychiatric help. And the relatively few who do must learn a whole new way of understanding mental health, a concept that has no equivalent in the Cambodian language.

Likewise, clinicians must work toward understanding the Cambodian world view, a largely pantheistic view that does not make easy separations between spirit, body and mind; natural and supernatural; past and present lives. Ask Cambodians if they have had conversations with dead relatives and many, perhaps the majority, will answer yes.

One remarkable characteristic documented by clinicians is the almost total absence of anger in Cambodian refugees toward their antagonists, be it Pol Pot or the Khmer Rouge or the Thai.

It was the anger of Jewish survivors of the Nazi holocaust that fueled the telling and re-telling of their story to the rest of the world.

Not so with Cambodians. And the reason is revealed in the way Cambodians understand terms such as "trauma" and "torture."

The English derivation of the word "torture," for example, is from the Latin root torquere, which means to cause to twist or turn, or to cause physical pain.

The Cambodian term, in contrast, is associated with the Buddhist concept of karma, or fate.

"The way they fit it into their consciousness is that they believe they must have done something in their past that brought this suffering on them," says Dr. David Kinzie, who runs an Indochinese mental health clinic in Portland.

"The idea is, 'Maybe we deserve this. . . .'"

ON A RECENT SATURDAY, members of the Cambodian community congregate at the Boys & Girls Club at White Center for a celebration and prayer.

The celebration marks the age-old Cambodian tradition of canoe racing under a full moon, the memory of which harkens back to the long, tranquil time before war.

Food is prepared in the back of the room. Rattan mats are spread on the floor, and the crowd of about 70 seat themselves facing the Buddhist monks in orange robes at the front of the room.

Presently, a prayer begins, the crowd joining with hands clasped.

"It is a prayer to God for people who have died," says Buntha Cheam, interpreting in a whisper.

Cheam is a refugee assistance counselor who has helped organize this gathering. "It is a prayer asking for peace for the people who have died. We offer food to the monks, the monks offer the food to God and to the dead."

The prayer lasts a half-hour.

The hope for the future of Cambodians can be found in certain aspects of this gathering. In the shattered families who have rallied around one another, creating new families: A young person who has lost her parents, for example, is simply taken in by another family. There are no orphans.

Cambodians bring with them a dedication to community rarely found now in Western cultures, according to Dr. Evelyn Lee, a psychiatry professor at the University of California, San Francisco who works with refugee populations. The definition of "self" in Cambodian includes community.

It can be found in their emphasis on devotion and discipline, as well as in their unshakable belief in fate, which helps in the acceptance of cataclysmic events.

Cambodians and other Southeast Asian refugees, Lee says, are products of one of the oldest cultures, cultures that emphasize trust in neighbors, gratitude for the smallest gestures, and patience with hardship—characteristics that, Lee says, Westerners would be wise to learn from.

Finally, it can be found in the children and young adults. Some of the older Cambodians, too tired to forge a new life in a strange world, only hope for their children and grandchildren.

Children like Bunthoen Rim, 15, a sophomore at Evergreen High School in White Center. Rim was only four when she left Cambodia, too young to be scarred by the horrors of the old country.

Rim's father was killed and four of her siblings starved to death, facts that she recalls now without heavy emotion. In school, she is a top student, not content with her 3.8 grade-point average.

"My goal is to be a 4.0," she says with a Western candor and confidence. "I want to try my best because I look forward to the future. It's just me and my mother now, and I want a good life for us."

But Rim and her peers have other, newer obstacles in front of them. Many Cambodian teenagers, inheriting some of their parents' transcultural disequilibrium as well as absorbing the ethos of the housing projects, are finding their niches in street culture.

Cambodian youth gangs have emerged in cities throughout the West Coast.

The young are moving on to an American future, problems and all, while the old still grieve the past. This generational gap, too, is evident at the Boys & Girls Club, where, during the prayer, some of the teenagers disengage from the proceedings and begin wandering and chatting in the lobby.

Even after the group prayer ends, a few of the older Cambodians continue to pray silently as the others move to the banquet table.

"Still praying for the dead," Cheam whispers, looking over at them. They chant and pray near a corner, their bodies forming figures of grief inconsolable and permanent.

. . .

STRANGERS IN A STRANGE LAND:
THE HMONG ORPHANS OF HISTORY

BLIA XIONG, a small, soft-spoken woman with a radiant face, says she's been writing a letter in her head for years that goes something like this:

Dear American People,

Some of you know who we are. Most of you don't. We are called the Hmong. We have existed for thousands of years. In the last two centuries, we have lived in the mountains of Laos, in a place called The Plain of Jars.

Your CIA recruited us to fight in your war against the communists in Laos and Vietnam. More than 10,000 of us died in that war. There is no memorial for our dead. When we came to America as refugees, hardly anyone knew of our involvement in your war. Most of you still don't.

Hmong means "Free people." But we are not free. These are the things that bind us: We have no country. We have little money. We have a disintegrating culture. We have an epic story, but few listeners.

We invite you to know our story.

It's an undercurrent in the lives of Hmong young and old, this desire to be known, says Xiong. It's the legacy of having been driven out of China, chased out of Laos, rejected by Thailand and resettled like scatter-shot all over the United States.

Their transformation from hilltribe people in Asia to urban refugees in America is chronicled in a new exhibit at the University of Washington's Burke Museum called "Hmong in America: Refugees From A Secret War."

Xiong, a language interpreter in UW's Medical Center, is co-curator of the exhibit, along with local anthropologist Nancy Donnelly, author of several books on Southeast Asian refugees.

"The Hmong don't like the term 'secret war,'" said Donnelly. "It wasn't secret to them."

The Hmong were living in isolated, self-sufficient mountain villages when the Central Intelligence Agency recruited them to fight against communist Lao and Vietnamese forces. For years, the Hmong's involvement was intentionally kept secret from the American people.

For many of the estimated 1,000 Hmong who've settled in Western Washington, the exhibit is an all-important acknowledgement not only of their involvement in the war but of their plight in the United States.

More than 115,000 Hmong now live in this country, with the largest concentration in Fresno, Calif., where Hmong worldwide gather annually to celebrate the Hmong new year.

In Washington, they have settled in clusters in South Seattle, Burien, Kirkland and Carnation.

Most live on public support. The old, worn down by years of war and dislocation, have resigned themselves to living as strangers in a strange land. The young, though, are forging a new identity—part Hmong, part American, with the latter slowly supplanting the former.

It's a struggle to keep the Hmong heritage alive, said Choua Yang, 25, a senior at the University of Washington and one of only a handful of Hmong students at the UW. Yang has volunteered as a tour guide for the Burke exhibit.

"I want to do whatever I can to preserve our history," Yang said. "People know so little about us. We're always mistaken for Vietnamese or Chinese. Growing up, in school, we had to show our teachers on a map where we came from. Even our own people, the young ones, don't know about our past. They're starting to lose our language, our customs."

Part of the reason, said Kia Lee, 20, a sophomore at the UW, is that the Hmong story is almost always left out of history texts. Lee said she herself didn't know about her people's involvement in the Vietnam War until college. "When I found out," she said, "I was so happy. Our people were mentioned. It made me feel proud. It made me want to learn more. Now I want to be a teacher so I can teach about our people. In the future, I'd like to be able to say, 'I am Hmong' and not have to explain it every time."

DEATH OF A DREAMER: A YOUNG BRIDE FROM THE PHILIPPINES IS MURDERED

Seattle Times, April 21, 1996

Introduced by **TERRY MCDERMOTT**, colleague of Tizon's
at the *Seattle Times* and the *Los Angeles Times*

I first met Alex Tizon sometime in the late 1980s, not long after we
had both signed on at the Seattle Times. We worked together for
the next ten years. Alex did a lot of good work during that time—
nice, but not exceptional. It was clear from the beginning that he
had talent and ambition, two traits that were like brothers who
spent most of their time beating each other up. It took a while to
teach them how to get along. One big problem, one common to
younger writers, was that Alex wanted his ambition to show on the
page. He hadn't yet learned to relax. His sentences were grave, serious, full of portent. Too much so.

This piece, written in 1996, marks, I think, the first appearance
of Tizon as a mature writer. The piece is ambitious and concerns
issues close to Alex's heart—his ethnicity, the utter poverty of his
home, the effects of that poverty and dreams of what might erase
it, the complicated geography of desire. None of this is announced.
The prose is unaffected, almost casual; he doesn't say what he's
about but lets his detailed and careful reporting carry the load.
The subjects here are big, ambitious, maybe a bit unwieldy. Tizon
handles them with control, with deliberation.

Look at the close observation here: "She looks like a doll from a
department-store showcase, a sleeping beauty, by some mortician's
magic made perfect and remote." Here: "The whole town has a
lean-to feel about it, as if blown together by a strong Pacific wind.
Nothing appears quite squared, from the lazy angles of ramshackle
buildings to the carefree plats of streets and power lines." And here:
"Susana, eight months pregnant, was shot three times in a straight

*vertical line—head, chest and abdomen—killing her unborn child,
as well."*

Putting the reporting front and center does not forbid writerly
expression. Look at this: *"If she couldn't be a traveler, she could at
least be near those who were. In her eyes, and in the eyes of many
in developing countries, every foreigner is a messenger from a world
of dreams."*

If there is one thing above others to learn here, it is that when
you build the bones of a story on great reporting, you can take the
reader anywhere.

· · ·

CATAINGAN, PHILIPPINES—There's no sign marking the entrance to the cemetery. It isn't necessary; everyone here knows
where it is. At the end of a long muddy trail, it just appears, a city
of tombstones in the middle of a mango grove.

Susana Blackwell's tomb is a simple block of concrete about
elbow high. There's a man resting an elbow on it right now. It's
Susana's father, Zucino Remerata. He's 65, with sweat on his forehead and thick knotty fingers that have spent a lifetime grasping
tools. He spends his days here, building a cover for Susana's tomb.

There are others with him on this sweltering afternoon,
townspeople who knew Susana, and who are now using her final
resting place as a tabletop for an informal discussion.

The men are talking tough. The women fan themselves and
speak of regrets. The group, on this occasion, has decided to pick
on Timothy Blackwell. In this insular town of 39,000, where the
only news medium is the nearest neighbor, he—Timothy Blackwell, U.S. citizen, Montana native, Seattle resident, estranged
husband, triple-murder suspect, bearded burly white man in
his 40s, and whatever else he may be—isn't called anything but
Blackwell.

"Blackwell is a coward. I wish he were here. He would not last
long," says one man, lifting his shirt to expose the grip of a .45.
"He likes guns. I would show him one."

Susana's mother, Marcella, is crying. "Never mind Blackwell," she says. "Leave Blackwell to God. God will know what to do with him."

The gathering at the cemetery lasts the better part of an afternoon. Once in a while, somebody breaks off to look at Susana's picture framed at the head of her tomb. It's a school photo. She radiates warmth and earnestness and a certain awareness of her own allure.

It isn't unlike her photo in Asian Encounters, the bride catalog published 7,000 miles away in Bellingham, which promised subscribers access to "pretty single Asian women who want to meet you!" and from which Blackwell chose Susana, out of dozens of other smiling Filipinas, as his future mate.

A final picture is passed around by the people leaning on her tomb. It was taken just before Susana's casket was sealed. The bullet hole on her forehead is gone. She looks like a doll from a department-store showcase, a sleeping beauty, by some mortician's magic made perfect and remote.

It's a long journey to Susana's world, but it doesn't equal the distance she traveled. She went from village girl in that school photo to young woman for sale in a bride catalog to young wife shot dead in a second-floor hallway of a courthouse across the ocean in a remote place called King County.

She would have turned 27 next month.

Parts of her story are common to a great number of people here, and parts particular only to her. The common parts tell a sad story of this tattered nation. But Susana was not pure victim. Friends describe her as a dreamer, not of the wishy adolescent kind, but a serious one, someone inclined to take the necessary steps. She wanted to marry an American.

The opportunity came; she took some chances.

Susana was known first as the daughter of Zucino and Marcella, sister of Alex, best friend to Edith. She was known by a wider circle of people as the pretty cashier at her parents' mercantile store. She was petite and effusive; everyone seemed to like her, a girl from the neighborhood, but not exactly the girl next door.

She was smart. An honor student at Cataingan National High

School, she studied nursing then, later, hotel and restaurant management at a college in Cebu, 12 hours away by ferry. Susana moved to Cebu and ferried home almost every weekend.

She had means. By American standards, her parents would be poor, but here the Remeratas are better off than many. They own two small stores and one of the nicest homes in Cataingan, a concrete house with a green, corrugated-steel roof. They have no car, stove, flush toilet or telephone, but do have several "katulongs," or helpers, to do the menial chores around the house.

"Susana never had to wash clothes or clean house. She was a señorita," says her friend Liza Orbiso, who runs a contracting business on the island. "Whatever she wanted, she got—a meal served on a tray, or a trip to Cebu or Manila. All she had to do was ask."

She was a local beauty queen—Miss Cataingan, Miss Masbate, a contestant for Miss Cebu. In the Philippines, home of the most infamous former beauty queen of all, Imelda Marcos, beauty queens hold a revered status. They turn into movie stars, marry powerful politicians or become politicians themselves. (Marcos is now a congresswoman in a northern province.)

Susana's pageant titles, judging from the framed pictures on her bedroom wall and throughout her parents' house, were important to her and her parents.

Her friends called her Miss Madaldal, which means talkative. A chatterbox, that Susana. Sweet, but don't get her started. Movie stars, romance, adventure—these fueled her talk. Even in quiet moments, said lifelong friend Edith Villamor, Susana seemed occupied by a world of concerns far removed from here.

Cataingan is a town of fishermen, farmers and miners; of barefooted children chasing goats, and young women washing clothes at a river's edge; of dusty roads, nipa huts, small concrete storefronts and one very large, almost cathedral-like, Catholic church. There's no sign outside the church, but everyone knows it's St. Vincent's.

Susana was baptized, married and eulogized there.

Except for the church, the whole town has a lean-to feel about it, as if blown together by a strong Pacific wind. Nothing appears quite squared, from the lazy angles of ramshackle buildings to the carefree plats of streets and power lines.

Electricity reached the town 12 years ago. Phone service and cable TV are on the way. Meanwhile, cockfighting remains the top entertainment in town.

Cataingan is situated in the southeast corner of the island of Masbate, a mound of land shaped like an arrowhead, about two-thirds the size of King County. Masbate is the main beef supplier to the rest of the Philippines. Three-fourths of the island is grassland.

Half a million people live here, segmented into six dialects, living in or around 21 scattered towns connected by one main road. It isn't a good road. It's 2 1/2 hours of rough riding from the airport to Cataingan, a distance of 35 miles.

They've been working on improving the road for years, but there's always one disruption or another, lack of money being the most constant. Masbate is visited regularly by two other disruptive forces: typhoons and elections.

Typhoons hit a dozen times a year, sometimes leveling entire towns. Elections aren't as frequent but wreak as much havoc. People die at election time. Since 1980, five prominent leaders, including a former governor and a congressman, have been assassinated. Three barrio captains have been missing since the last election. Nobody bothers to count minions who have disappeared.

The bodyguard of a local congressman, the Hon. Fausto Seachon Jr., said, as he showed off his arsenal of weapons: "Elections are a good time to take a holiday off the island."

Masbate is one of the 7,100 islands that make up the Philippines. It's one of the poorer provinces of one of the poorest nations in Asia. The average urban worker in the Philippines earns the equivalent of $140 a month. In farming regions—which is to say, most of the country—that amount would be closer to a year's earnings.

It's why the lines in Manila for visas to other countries never end; why 600,000 Filipinos go abroad each year to work as domestic helpers and laborers; why thousands of Filipinos go to extraordinary lengths to attract foreign spouses. The national obsession is to change nationalities.

An estimated 20,000 Filipino women leave the country each year as wives or fiancees of foreigners. The largest number, 5,000, marry Americans; 2,000 marry Australians; the rest go to Europe, Canada, Japan, Hong Kong and Taiwan. Many of the relationships begin by mail.

As widespread as the term has become, "mail-order bride" is a misnomer. Women aren't ordered or delivered like appliances from Sears, as was done on the American frontier in the 19th century.

Nowadays, women are made accessible to men through agencies that provide the women's names and addresses for a fee. It's up to the man to initiate a correspondence and up to the woman to respond. Some agencies arrange "tours" in which men travel to meet prospective brides in person. In these ways, agencies are no different from the legal introduction services that have come into vogue all over the Western World in the past decade.

More than 100 agencies in the United States specialize in international matchmaking, and the Philippines is only one of a host of target countries. The entire developing world, including much of Latin America, Eastern Europe and the former Soviet republics, is seen as a bargain bin of accessible women.

Cherry Blossoms, of Honolulu, one of the oldest and largest mail-bride agencies in the United States, used to market only Asian women. Now, roughly half its prospective brides come from Russia and Poland. Cherry Blossoms publisher Bob Burrows says his agency gets 2,500 orders a month for his catalog.

For whatever reasons, Burrows says, there's a strong pull among many Americans to marry foreigners, and government statistics bear that out. U.S. Immigration reports that 200,000 Americans—men and women—marry foreigners every year. These couples meet while on vacation, business or exchange programs—and sometimes through mail-order catalogs.

Men are the exclusive users of the mail-order method, and it's the catalogs that most often elicit protest. They, in fact, do have the feel of a Sears catalog, with pages and pages of smiling women as the commodities along with the requisite captioned enticements:

"Beautiful Latin Ladies Ready to Meet You!" "Gorgeous Pacific Women! Pearls of the Orient—Beautiful Ladies Known for their Beauty, Charm, Grace and Hospitality!" "Russian Beauties Looking for American Friends!"

In a very real sense, the men who get wives through this route are "buying" their way into marriage. Their affluence is a primary appeal, which isn't to say there aren't other attractions. Motives are usually a confluence of desires, not the least of which may be a want for companionship and family.

Still, the man buys the catalog, the address, the airline ticket to the woman's country, and then pays for the wedding and travel expenses to bring the new wife home. The whole process, according to Jerry Davis, the Bellingham matchmaker who brought Susana and Blackwell together, costs $4,000 to $6,000 if done efficiently. Blackwell claimed to have spent $10,000.

The asymmetry strikes at the heart of what's perverse about the business of matching First World men to Third World women. The two groups are driven by completely different imperatives: the men by the luxury of choice and desire, the women by the more urgent need to escape a life of fixed poverty.

The men enter into a power relationship in which it's easy for them to be the absolute power. The women leave their communities, land in a foreign culture often with no money or contacts, and are, at least in the beginning, totally dependent on their new spouses.

Certainly in some cases, the men are counting on a certain kind of inequality. Many buy into the image of Asian women as exotic and submissive, and some men fully expect it. It's what the catalogs promise.

Susana was a small-town girl looking for a bigger life, always talking about finding an American husband and settling down in a land across the ocean where she didn't sweat day and night, and maybe there'd even be snow.

She told her friend Liza Orbiso she wanted an American husband "so they could have beautiful children. . . . Everyone knows that children of Filipino and American parents are handsome. It's that American blood. It makes us stronger."

"Mangangarap" is the word Orbiso used to describe Susana. Dreamer. It comes from the Tagalog word "pangarap," one definition of which is "ambition."

The reason she went into hotel management, friends say, is because she was drawn by romantic visions of travelers coming from distant places, bringing with them the mystique of lands she'd seen only in magazines. If she couldn't be a traveler, she could at least be near those who were. In her eyes, and in the eyes of many in developing countries, every foreigner is a messenger from a world of dreams.

This is the story Susana told her mother and best friend Edith Villamor:

While at college in Cebu, Susana and a group of her friends found out about an older Filipino woman who knew how to find American pen pals. The woman, it turned out, worked for Jerry Davis, the Bellingham matchmaker who published Asian Encounters. Davis paid the woman a small finder's fee—one source said 10 pisos (about 40 cents)—for every Filipina she recruited.

It all seemed so easy. Susana and her friends filled out an application, had some pictures taken and went back to their boarding house and laughed about it. They did it to see what would happen. They had no idea.

Sometime afterward, Susana and her friends visited a palm reader on a whim. The palmist told Susana that her future husband would not be a Filipino; he would come from another country. The presage confirmed her own wish, and she was excited by it.

In the April-May-June 1990 issue of Asian Encounters, Susana's picture appeared with this unprepossessing caption:

Susana (age 21) 5'3," 105 lb. Philippines.
Roman Catholic. Hotel & Restaurant Management.

Hobbies: dancing, reading, cooking.

Susana was surprised when the letters started pouring in. Never did she expect this. By the time she got her first letter from Timothy Blackwell in the summer of 1991, she was getting an average of 13 letters a day from some 100 American pen pals. It was a lot of work keeping up with the correspondence. What began as a fanciful idea became a serious project.

She kept a photo album of her pen pals, pages and pages of captioned pictures of American men in various poses:

Here is Mark fishing. Here is Ronnie flexing his muscles. Here is Alex with his pet frog. Here is Donald standing next to his house. Here is Donald next to his swimming pool. Here is a close-up of Donald's swimming pool.

There were at least 30 names. Many were obviously trying to do their own image-selling, banking on the allure of The Wealthy American. It could be said that she had her own catalog to choose from.

Blackwell, then in his mid-40s, working as a handyman and eventually as a lab technician, was living in a small studio apartment in North Seattle. He was engaged in his own serious project. He'd written as many as 24 women from Asian Encounters; half responded to his letters.

Not much research has been done on the men who shop for wives through catalogs, but the little information available isn't flattering.

An informal survey done by a Filipino women's group found that a large number of the men were "socially or physically unattractive in their own culture." A significant number had chauvinistic attitudes, histories of abuse, or physical disabilities.

One Filipina declared more pointedly: "Your losers come here to get wives."

A study at the University of Texas found the men came from all socio-economic backgrounds but tended to be older and divorced, and many had gone through at least one traumatic experience with a previous partner.

An Everett man with a Filipino wife had this to say:

"You go through a couple of divorces in this country, you get a bellyful of American women and their liberated ways. Then you go over there (the Philippines), and these girls have a serving attitude—everyone does. It's part of the culture. They believe the man is the head of the home."

Despite what many critics want to believe, there isn't a great body of evidence showing that marriages-by-mail are more prone to trouble than other kinds of marriages—the state of marriage being what it is.

The men in mail-order marriages face some risk, too. So eager to fall in love, some have been tricked by Third World brides into sending large amounts of money or being used to gain entry into a First World country. U.S. Immigration says it's a common scam.

Among bar girls in Manila, there's an inside joke regarding what characteristics they seek in foreign men: Mabait, Mayaman, Matanda, Malapit nang Mamatay. They're referred to as "The Four Ms," which translate into Kind, Rich, Old and About To Die.

It's clear, however, that women in mail-arranged marriages face the graver risks. Immigrant counselors say men risk broken hearts and broken bank accounts; women often risk life and limb.

The sense of "purchase" in the men can lead to a feeling of "ownership" of the women, says Ninotchka Rosca of GABRIELA, a women's advocacy group based in Quezon City. "A paid-for wife," Rosca says, "is a slave for life."

GABRIELA has documented stories of Filipina brides in Germany, Norway, Sweden, Holland, the Netherlands and Japan who were forced into isolation, slave labor, prostitution or suicide. Australia is unanimously singled out as the worst offending country, with 18 Filipino wives killed by Australian husbands since 1985. GABRIELA, though, has seen a recent rise in mail-order abuse by other Asian countries, Japan and Thailand in particular.

One 21-year-old Filipina told the story of how her Thai fiance confined her in a room, repeatedly raped her, allowed his friends to rape her, and fed her only rice and water for a month. She was then placed in jail for a year on charges never made clear to her.

She was eventually freed and forced to earn her own fare back to the Philippines.

Rosca: "It's just unconscionable what's being done to our women."

The brutality of some of the cases pushed the Philippine government in 1990 to pass a law prohibiting the practice of matching Filipinas for marriage to foreigners through the mail. Republic Act 6955, though, is largely regarded as symbolic.

To get around the law, marriage brokers simply changed their label to "pen-pal clubs." Ads for pen-pal clubs can be found in any number of magazines in the Philippines. Not all of these clubs are fronts for mail-order operations.

If there's an attraction, people will find a way, and despite the horror stories, there's still an attraction among Filipinos to Americans and America in particular that goes beyond need to something resembling idolatry.

British-born writer Pico Iyer, in his travelogue of Southeast Asia, came close to the heart of it when he wrote: "American dreams are strongest in the hearts of those who have seen America only in their dreams."

A year after receiving her first letter from Timothy Blackwell, Susana stopped writing the other men. She testified in her annulment trial that she'd decided, "It would be Tim."

She told her friend Orbiso: "The palmist was right!"

Susana and Blackwell exchanged more than 40 letters, a few cassette tapes, and occasionally talked on the phone over an 18-month period before Blackwell decided to fly to Cataingan. He arrived in Cebu on March 3, 1993, met Susana in person for the first time in Cataingan on March 6, and the two got married at St. Vincent's on March 31.

It was a big Filipino wedding that was videotaped by a local professional filmmaker. Her mother replayed the tape, along with tapes of the wedding reception and Susana's "despedida," or farewell party.

Susana said she was in love with Blackwell, although the videos of both the wedding and reception didn't indicate overflowing affection from either Susana or Blackwell for each other. They appeared ill-at-ease, like two people from opposite ends of the Earth who'd just met, and who still didn't know how to act around one another.

He spent six weeks in the Philippines and, by most accounts, including his own, wasn't comfortable in Cataingan. He later complained of the heat and sanitation, and that he sometimes had to share a bed with two other people.

Susana's family did their best to keep him comfortable, preparing American meals for him, constantly offering cold drinks, and borrowing all the neighbors' electric fans to keep him cool.

Communication also was a problem. Susana's family spoke very little English, and Blackwell spoke none of the island dialects. He also said Susana, who spoke broken, halting English, was not as attentive to him as he was led to expect from her amorous letters, preferring to talk with her friends over him.

Meanwhile, money seemed to be flying out of his pockets. He said he spent $2,000 on the wedding, which included expenses to bring in a high-priced beautician from Cebu, another $2,000 on the reception and, later on, $600 for a TV and VCR for Susana's parents. Blackwell later complained of Susana's spending, but townspeople said Blackwell offered to pay for everything and acted as if he had money to spare.

He later testified that he broke off the wedding plans while in Cataingan and was trying to book a flight back to the United States when Susana persuaded him to stay and the two had sex for the first time.

"I spent a year-and-a-half corresponding with this woman," he said in court. "I felt I loved her very much."

Still, he preferred to spend most of his time in Cebu, where more people spoke English and where he could eat familiar foods and stay in an air-conditioned hotel room.

This might explain why he lost his temper the day after the wedding when he and Susana missed a ferry to Cebu. He blamed

Susana for making them late to the ferry dock. Blackwell admitted he raised his voice to her. Susana said he raised his voice and choked her.

Susana told her mother what happened. Marcella said she didn't want her daughter to go to America with this man, but Susana told her she was willing to take a chance with him. She said she still loved him.

Blackwell returned to the United States in mid-April. It took Susana almost a year to get the necessary papers to join her husband in his newly rented apartment in Kirkland. She arrived Feb. 5, 1994.

Based on her court testimony and that of people who came in contact with her, Susana was as disoriented in Blackwell's world as Blackwell was in hers.

Blackwell later testified that his new wife was cold, distant, uncommunicative and slept fully clothed. Susana's attorney, Mimi Castillo, argued that what Blackwell mistook for remoteness was really culture shock and homesickness, not to mention the kind of dissonance to be expected in a new marriage of virtual strangers.

As far as Susana sleeping clothed, she went from Philippine tropic to Seattle winter, the equivalent of moving from the Northwest to the North Pole. She never imagined the land of dreams could be so cold, Castillo said.

The couple spent exactly 13 days together.

The final parting happened after Susana claimed Blackwell choked and struck her, and pushed her head into a sink. She called the police. Blackwell, who told officers he was assisting Susana in washing her face, was arrested and charged with misdemeanor assault. The charge was dropped when Susana failed to appear in court.

Blackwell has said her accusations of assault, including the alleged ferry incident on Masbate, were simply not true. He contends Susana, with cold calculation, used him for money and passage to the United States, and that she had no intention of staying married to him.

In retaliation 10 days after she left him, he started the annulment process that would have forced her to be deported back to the Philippines. Shortly before the trial, records show, he offered to drop his annulment claim if she agreed to pay him $17,000 — the amount he said he'd spent on her, including court costs, since their first encounter four years earlier.

Susana didn't have that kind of money and had no prospects of getting it. Her attorneys, using a battered-wife clause in immigration law, were working to keep her from being deported. The clause is the only protection against deportation if an immigrant doesn't remain married at least two years to an American spouse. In other words, if Susana could prove she was battered, she could get permanent-resident status.

The trial got ugly.

Susana said her new husband was not only cruel and brutal, but that he was impotent and possibly gay. Blackwell in court said his wife was a money-hungry con artist, and that deporting her would be "a small amount of justice."

"I feel very responsible," he said, "because I feel like I brought a disease into this country."

The details of Susana's life during the trial are sketchy. She lived with another Filipina from the same region in the Philippines. She worked full-time at O Boy! Oberto in Kent. She sent her parents and friends in Cataingan regular shipments of stuffed animals, perfumes, cosmetics and costume jewelry.

She got pregnant, she said, by someone who raped her during a party. She said she couldn't identify the man who raped her. Jerry Davis claims he has information indicating that a Filipino boyfriend impregnated her, possibly as another attempt to keep from being deported.

On March 2, 1995, minutes before closing arguments in the annulment trial, Susana and two friends who testified on her behalf, Phoebe Dizon and Veronica Johnson, were sitting on a bench in a second-floor hallway of the courthouse. Police say Blackwell calmly removed a 9-mm semiautomatic handgun from his briefcase, approached the women and shot them from a distance of one foot.

Susana, eight months pregnant, was shot three times in a straight vertical line—head, chest and abdomen—killing her unborn child, as well.

When he was subdued by security guards, Blackwell had an extra ammunition clip in his other hand. Inside his briefcase was an envelope containing $650—he'd just closed his bank account—and a last will and testament that read in part:

"I am of sound mind and body and take full responsibility for my actions. I wish to thank the many friends and family members I have and others who have given me support. . . . I regret not being able to contact them and say goodbye as I want to very much. I believe they will understand my feelings."

He faces three counts of aggravated first-degree murder, and one count of manslaughter for the death of the unborn child. Blackwell has pleaded not guilty to all of the charges. Because he has no criminal record, court observers say, his defense likely will be some form of temporary insanity.

The Remeratas don't plan to attend the trial. It's too far away, and that world across the ocean too strange. "I don't speak English. I don't know how anything works," says Zucino Remerata. Besides, he says, "whether I go or not, my daughter will still be dead."

In the minds of her family, Susana left the island in white and returned in white. They videotaped her memorial service and entombment. They were eerily similar to her wedding and reception—the same church, same crowd, with her parents looking equally lost in the proceedings, and Susana dressed in elegant white, the center of it all.

At the end of the memorial service, only a pane of glass separated her from the people who stood in a long, sweltering line to get one last look. A parent who attended the service spoke of her young child's reaction: "How come she's not sweating?" the child asked.

The mother said, "She's in a cold place now."

Everyone here knows what she meant. In Cataingan on most

days, cold is a thing to wish for. Cold happens in places far from here, better than here.

Susana made it to one of those places, at least for a short time. So many others want a taste of that other, dreamed-of life—risks be damned. The vast majority won't get past just thinking about it; then there are some who'll take their chances, and a few who'll find a cold unlike any other.

(Many of the quotes in this story have been translated from Masbateneo, Cebuano and Tagalog.)

A DEATH IN GAZA: PEACE ADVOCATE
AND "A HEART TOO BIG TO HOLD"

Los Angeles Times, March 18, 2003

Introduced by LYNN MARSHALL, national desk researcher
for the *Los Angeles Times*, for whom it was a privilege to play a role
in Tizon's work for three of the nine years of her tenure—
even on breaking-news days

*T*his piece is one of the first daily stories that Alex and I worked
on together. It was on deadline, Alex's least favorite way to write
a story and his least favorite part of being the Northwest Bureau
chief for the* Los Angeles* Times. *But it was the day's job. He worked
the phones in Seattle, and I drove to Olympia for the dateline and
anything extra I could get.*

*In those days a story like this, where the national media ran a
day behind, could be just an easy rewrite of a wire piece, with a
few extra quotes and color. But that wasn't what Alex wanted. He
was determined to do justice to the life behind the headline. Prep-
ping me for what he needed out of a news conference with Rachel
Corrie's college friends, he said he wanted to know who she was as
an artist.*

"You've got to be kidding," I thought.

*But reading the story now, I see that this framework is what
elevates the piece from a daily to a profile of a passionate young
woman, who deliberately moved outside her comfort zone and died
for it. While Alex avoids directly rehashing the volatile politics surrounding Corrie's death, by conjuring historical scenes in Manila
and Tiananmen Square, he gives her heroic status. Capturing
the details of her passions and her artistic aspirations mattered
far more to Alex than a tick-tock of a short life and sudden brutal
death. And he was right. It is impossible to read this story and not
wonder who Rachel Corrie could have become as an artist.*

. . .

OLYMPIA, WASH.—At 23, Rachel Corrie was the kind of person many people dream of becoming someday: passionate, creative, giving, courageous to the point of risking her life for a just cause. One-on-one, friends say, she was as soft as a petal.

Which makes the circumstances of her death—crushed by an Israeli army bulldozer on Sunday—all the more brutal for the stunned circle of family and friends she leaves behind in this liberal patch of woods known as Washington's capital.

Although her supporters stop short of calling her a martyr, some said her death will only fuel the peace movement at a time when war with Iraq looms.

Corrie was outside the town of Rafah, in the southern part of the Gaza Strip, acting the part of a human shield. She stood in the way of a bulldozer that was about to wreck a Palestinian home. Depending on whose version you believe, the bulldozer was either digging out bombs (Israel's version) or razing neighborhoods for a new wall that Israel wants to build (the Palestinian version).·

Corrie and other peace activists from a group called the International Solidarity Movement, a Palestinian-led group, believed that the bulldozer would stop.

Just as military vehicles did in Manila when, during the 1986 "people's revolution," nuns handed out flowers to the machine-gunners. Just as the column of tanks did in Tiananmen Square in 1989, when a lone man, broadcast worldwide on television, stood in the path and brought the war machines to a standstill.

On Sunday, the armored, super-sized bulldozer, called a D-9, did not stop. It inched forward, lurched and caused the ground to give way, causing Corrie to fall into the path and underneath the vehicle. The bulldozer, witnesses said, moved forward and then backward over Corrie's body. Her head and chest were crushed.

The Israeli military called it "a regrettable accident," but blamed the activists for behaving recklessly in a dangerous zone. The U.S. government has asked for an investigation.

Fellow activists in the hundreds gathered for a candlelight vigil Sunday night, and again Monday afternoon at a downtown park to honor their fallen colleague, and to rally the community to continue the work that Corrie died for.

"Rachel was filled with love and a sense of duty to her fellow man," said her parents, Craig and Cindy Corrie, in a statement. "She gave her life trying to protect those that are unable to protect themselves."

Friends describe Corrie as athletically slender with blond hair and thoughtful, intelligent eyes. She was attractive in a plain-spoken way, the opposite of flashy, not working to call attention to herself. She was reserved in large crowds but intimate one-on-one. She played soccer, gardened and loved the poems of Pablo Neruda.

She was a leader not from charisma but quiet doggedness. In the peace organizations around Olympia, she was known as the organizer behind the scenes, the "heart and soul," said friend Phan Nguyen, of an umbrella group called the Olympia Movement for Justice and Peace.

Corrie had a playful side—one childhood photo shows her mugging with a cigar in her mouth—but she was profoundly serious about helping the people she viewed as the underdogs of the world.

Those who have known her the longest say Corrie was one of those rare people who was born with an altruistic heart. Linda Young, a cousin, remembers one night at the family dinner table when Corrie was in third grade: "She kept talking about hungry people," Young said, "and how we need to figure out a way to feed them. She was in elementary school and she was worried about world hunger."

Much of it, Young said, had to do with being part of a family that was creative and generous and viewed itself as citizens of the world rather than simply Americans. The Corries, in Olympia since 1975, hosted a number of international students and supported exchange programs. Corrie traveled to Russia on a school exchange program.

Her father, Craig, is an insurance executive; her mother, Cindy, a volunteer in schools and an accomplished flutist. The parents moved to Charlotte, N.C., a few years ago. Corrie, the youngest and who family members called the most idealistic of three children, was said to have a dreamer's ambition.

John McGee, a computer specialist at Evergreen State College, said his daughter went to elementary school with Corrie. He has known her since she was six. McGee said in the fifth-grade yearbook, everyone in class listed what they wanted to be when they grew up. All the other kids named one or two things.

Said McGee: "Rachel had a list of at least 20 things."

According to her closest friend, Colin Reese, who shared an apartment with her for the last four years, Corrie wanted most to become a writer and artist. He said all over their apartment lay journals of poems and reflections, and sculptures she was working on. She wasn't the most punctual or tidy person in the world, but when it came to peace work, she "would work harder and longer than anybody else."

She was a college senior, needing only one quarter to graduate from Evergreen, where she focused on International Studies and Art. She left for the Gaza Strip at the end of January and was scheduled to return at the end of this month to enroll for the spring quarter.

"No amount of reading, attendance at conferences, documentary reading and word of mouth could have prepared me for the reality of the situation here," Corrie wrote in a Feb. 7 e-mail to her friends and family.

She got involved with the International Solidarity Movement in the last year. The group is devoted to stopping, through nonviolent means, Israeli encroachment on Palestinian territory. Her main mission was to create a sister-city relationship between Olympia and Rafah, a town of 140,000 Palestinians, mostly refugees.

According to her e-mails, she had laid the groundwork for a pen pal program between children in both cities. She was there with five to eight fellow peace activists, all of them Americans or

Europeans. The group increasingly took to being human shields for Palestinians who were, she said, constantly being harassed, fired upon and even bombed.

One of her most basic jobs entailed walking with Palestinian children to and from school to protect them from gunfire. Israeli soldiers, she said, would go far out of their way not to harm an American or European.

Nguyen, who is active in the International Solidarity Movement and who has twice traveled to Israel, said Corrie was most urgently concerned about the fresh-water wells in Rafah. Corrie said the Israeli army had destroyed three out of the four wells and was using bulldozers to clear out entire neighborhoods to create a wall separating Israeli settlers and Palestinian refugees.

In another e-mail, Corrie described an earlier standoff in which an army bulldozer made lurches toward protesters, even using the front of the machine to push the activists aside. She seemed acutely aware of the danger involved in the tactic.

"She had a heart too big to hold," said her former high school advisor, Carolyn Keck. "A lot of us think of doing the kinds of things she did, but she actually did them. I'm sorry that she's gone. I'm sorry for the world, because we need people like her."

PART III

NATIVES

ON EDGE: 9/11, A MUSLIM FAMILY
AND A WYOMING TOWN

Seattle Times, September 21, 2001

Introduced by **JACQUI BANASZYNSKI**, editor of Nieman Storyboard
and Tizon's assigning editor at the *Seattle Times* for two years—
including for the series "Crossing America" and its sequel, traveled
in reverse, a year later—who went on to travel, teach, and debate
the value of journalism awards with Tizon after they both
left the newspaper

*T*he Seattle Times *newsroom sits twenty-four hundred miles
by air—almost twenty-nine hundred miles by the most direct
ground route—from what has come to be known as Ground Zero in
Manhattan. Yet for all that distance, the 9/11 terrorist attacks were
intensely local no matter the zip code, striking through the heart of
Americans' sense of security and identity.*

*But how could we tell a story, in the face of such harsh and
demanding breaking news, that is more about feelings than facts?*

*The solution came from a political reporter who had the grace to
offer it to the room: Go on the road—that classic American ritual—
to chronicle the story of a changed nation. The idea was as simple as
it was profound. To bring it to life, it would take a reporter who could
divine a destination and write an emotional journey onto Page One.*

That reporter was Alex Tizon.

*In partnership with photographer Alan Berner, he climbed into
one of the last available rental vehicles in Seattle and headed east
with no clear assignment beyond some vague and vast notion of
finding America.*

*In a month on the road, Tizon filed thirteen stories from thir-
teen places on an unmapped journey we called, simply, "Crossing
America." He wrote from Oklahoma City, where a domestic terrorist had bombed the federal building six years earlier; from Pennsylvania, where 9/11 terrorists had been brought to the ground by
valiant passengers; and, of course, from Ground Zero.*

But he also dared to write from places that live outside the usual reach of headlines: an elementary school in Eastern Washington, a diner in rural Kansas, a military school in Missouri. And from Sheridan, Wyoming, where Tizon found Zarif Khan Jr., the patriarch of the only Muslim family in town:

> If you have three or four hours to hear what it's like to be Muslim in a town that's 98 percent white, conservative and Christian, especially as war looms with Muslim extremists, he'll tell you in a long, elliptical way that the town has been kind.

Tizon approached stories as journalist and essayist. The questions that intrigued him were unanswerable in any traditional definition of news and dwelled in the more amorphous worlds of philosophy, spirituality, and human nature. His own quest becomes the through-line in "Crossing America," so he writes in a personal, reflective voice:

> My skin is as brown as mocha and most everybody I met here over two days was friendly and helpful.
>
> But part of the ethos of the wide-open West is a tolerance for the maverick, friendly cousin to the rogue. There's room to veer from the politically correct path, space for the unconventional and weird. Ideas can ferment in isolation behind a mountain or in the inner sanctums of a thousand-acre ranch, and sometimes those ideas aren't very nice.

Tizon had an instinct for finding people who represented the complexity of life as it is really lived and a gentle, lean-forward way of listening that invited those people to give voice to that reality.

. . .

SHERIDAN, WYO.—You know just by looking at his face that the past 10 days have been much different for him than for most of us.

He has brown skin, thick eyebrows, a handsomely aquiline nose over a dark mustache that curls around the corners of his mouth. His name is Zarif Khan Jr., a Pakistani-American and the head of the only Muslim family in town.

He has a lot on his mind. You get the impression he's a gabber anyway, but now his gabbing has new purpose, not to mention that he's the kind of guy who must begin every story from the very beginning, in pre-history. For context.

So if you have three or four hours to hear what it's like to be Muslim in a town that's 98 percent white, conservative and Christian, especially as war looms with Muslim extremists, he'll tell you in a long, elliptical way that the town has been kind.

"These are my friends. This is my town. I'm an American. I love America," he says. "I wouldn't want to live anywhere else."

Not that he isn't nervous, or that the past week-and-a-half hasn't been a wrecking ball to his gut.

There have been a few minor incidents, which Khan shrugs off. A few nights ago, someone called the house and asked if he had Osama bin Laden's e-mail address. There was laughter on the other end. It sounded like a group of youngsters huddled around a phone.

No, Khan said.

How about his cell-phone number?

Khan hung up. Kids!

In the past few days, an old pickup has been seen chugging though town with a message made up of masking tape on the back fender: "Nuke the Diaper Heads." It took a lot of strips of tape. Someone worked at it. Later, I found the truck parked outside an electronics store but couldn't find the driver. Was it an adolescent trying to be patriotic or a patriot with anger to vent?

The biggest employer in town is the Veterans Affairs hospital. A lot of retired military live in the area. But it could easily have been someone nonmilitary, a rancher or miner, of which there are plenty in town, or just someone with lots of time and tape on his hands.

Sheridan lies on the eastern foothills of the Bighorn Mountains in the state's northeast corner. It was named after a fearsome

U.S. general named Phil Sheridan, whose most famous quote was "The only good Indian is a dead Indian."

That was 140 years ago. The general long ago retired to the big Quonset hut in the sky, and the town, like most of the American West, has moved well beyond its wildness to something approaching tolerant, even enlightened, civility.

My skin is as brown as mocha and most everybody I met here over two days was friendly and helpful.

But part of the ethos of the wide-open West is a tolerance for the maverick, friendly cousin to the rogue. There's room to veer from the politically correct path, space for the unconventional and weird. Ideas can ferment in isolation behind a mountain or in the inner sanctums of a thousand-acre ranch, and sometimes those ideas aren't very nice.

You can be creative and eccentric, and say what you want. You can drink a half-pint of Jack Daniels and shoot marmots till you're cross-eyed. You could say out loud, as someone did in a tavern here the other day, "the little faggot" Matthew Shepard—killed a few hundred miles south of here, outside Laramie, three years ago—got what he deserved, and no one will protest.

Encountering a rogue and his buddies is what concerns Khan.

"It only takes one wacko to get drunk and do something stupid," he says.

He's noted, since Sept. 11, the only two suspected fatal hate crimes against Muslims or people who look Muslim have happened in the West and Southwest: A Sikh was killed in Mesa, Ariz., and an Arabic man was shot in Dallas.

But it would be an exaggeration to say Khan lived in fear. He's been a wrestling coach for half his life and knows how to take a big man down, even at age 45 and with a belly that smothers his belt buckle. He worries more for his four kids and extended family. That family numbers around 80 in the region. They own a dozen roadside motels, with a 13th—a Motel 6—being built.

The family is prosperous; the family name, one of the best-known around. He heads the second generation of Khans in Sheridan County.

His father, an uneducated laborer, left Pakistan in 1908, wandered by ship and rail into Sheridan, sold hamburgers, first from a cart, then out of his own restaurant, saved his money, did well in the stock market and fulfilled the American Dream the present-day Khans continue to build on.

It's a mini-empire built on beef patties and top-secret sauce. Khan's father, though nearly illiterate, knew that living well wasn't only the best revenge but also the best defense against small-minded people.

The Khans have lived well and made a lot of friends.

After the terror attacks, Khan's phone line was jammed with townspeople calling to offer support and protection. One was a town councilman. Another came from the family's Jewish pediatrician. The principal where his two teenage boys attend school told them if anybody as much as said anything mocking, he would take care of it.

Next door to his Sundown Motel, where he and his family live, sits the new headquarters of the Sheridan police department; some of the officers were once teenage drinking buddies of Khan's.

Nevertheless, the past week-and-a-half have been emotional for the Khan family. He's been riveted to the TV like the rest of us, but no doubt his experience has been more complex, if not more painful because it's cut in two directions.

Along with his grief for the victims came a sinking realization that strangers would be looking at him and his family and all Muslims differently for a long time.

He refers to the terrorists as "sickos," and yet skittering around in his private thoughts is a fraternal sympathy for the plight of Muslims around the world, and a nagging question that, once squeezed out, is best expressed like this:

"If America is the policeman of the world, why can't it be a policeman for Muslims, too?"

Given the opportunity with the right person, he would ask this question plaintively, with no rage, and with the expectation that a good answer, or a good change, would come.

He believes in America, he says: the idea, and the wide, sweeping, democratic, mass of it. Last week, he took out an old flag, climbed to the top of his motel and stuck it where it could be plainly seen, above the front entrance. It was no Iwo Jima moment or anything, and it's a droopy, wrinkled flag that's seen better days, but it's his flag, and every day since, walking out into the parking lot, he's glanced up to make sure the wind hadn't knocked it down.

As I left him, he was waving and scratching his belly. President Bush made the dead-or-alive comment and was winding up the machine for battle. War was creeping close, and I feared that harder times lay ahead for the Khans of our country.

A MATTER OF JUSTICE AND HONOR:
THE FIGHT TO CLEAR CHIEF LESCHI'S NAME

Los Angeles Times, December 28, 2004

Introduced by SCOTT KRAFT, managing editor and former
national editor of the *Los Angeles Times*, who hired Tizon to join the
national staff as Northwest Bureau chief

*W*hen a writer pitches a story on an execution that occurred
*nearly a century and a half before, an editor's natural instinct
is to demur. When Alex was doing the pitching to us, though, we
always paid attention. We had learned, early on, to place a lot of
confidence in his eye for a story and, in particular, his ability to find
universal themes and lessons in everything he saw, read, or reported.*

*One thing I love about this piece is how Alex sets it up in his
introduction as, essentially, a deathbed request to the protagonist.
What follows is part detective story, part history—and, overall, a
fascinating look at a modern-day mission to correct a past wrong.*

*There are so many lyrical, narrative touches in this piece. But
I particularly like Alex's ending, fashioned here as an epilogue,
which can be such an effective device. In it, Alex takes us along
with Cynthia Iyall as she returns to the site of her ancestor's hanging. One of the most difficult challenges for any writer is creating
an ending that is poignant but not heavy-handed or—gasp—syr-
upy. Alex handles it beautifully, bringing us full circle, from Iyall's
meeting with her grandfather and his challenge to her, to the very
site of the terrible wrong he wanted her to right. The last words of
the piece strike the perfect note:*

*She hoped the ancestors were happy, though, that drums
of celebration were beating somewhere.*

What a powerful walk-off line from a master narrative writer.

. . .

TACOMA, WASH.—On a winter's morning 146 years ago, a posse of lawmen brought a squarely built, dark-skinned man in his late 40s to a spot on the prairie that formed a natural bowl. The sides had filled with spectators, nearly all white. At the bottom was a crude gallows.

The man was led up the ladder. He bowed, then recited a prayer in a language few in the crowd understood. According to one translation, he said he'd made peace with God and no longer wanted to live. He thanked his jailer for his kindness.

At 11:35, the man, who had spent his last two years in prison, was hanged. His name was Leschi (pronounced lesh-eye), the last chief of the Nisqually tribe and the first man to be legally executed in the territory that would become Washington state.

He had been convicted of murdering a white militiaman. Leschi denied any involvement in the killing. A number of people, including high-ranking Army officers who refused to execute him, and even, in the end, his executioner, believed Leschi was railroaded.

The execution, on Feb. 19, 1858, was the finishing blow in the subjugation of Indian tribes in the Puget Sound. The Nisqually Indians, who had lived in the region for thousands of years, lost their land, much of their freedom and their leader. The last humiliation was that Leschi, who tried to protect his people, would go down in state records as a convicted murderer.

"That would make us the descendants of a murderer," said Cynthia Iyall, whose lineage traces back six generations to Leschi's sister. The tribe, with roughly 500 members, occupies a small, forested reservation east of Tacoma.

"So many generations of Nisqually people have had to live with this," said Iyall (pronounced eye-yal). She is 43, small and trim, with brown hair and light blue eyes inherited from her non-Indian mother. "For the older people, it was hard to even talk about. You could see the pain in their faces. You could see the anger."

Iyall had grown up, in nearby Tumwater, hearing Leschi's story. Her grandfather used to take her to places in the hills where

Leschi used to camp. But it wasn't until Iyall moved onto the reservation as an adult that she began to take a deep interest.

She devoured every account of the story, and the more she learned of Leschi—that he was an orator rather than a warrior, that he helped the area's first white settlers and tried twice to make peace with the Army—the deeper she felt the wound.

After her grandfather died, Iyall became close with another elder, Sherman Leschi.

Sherman was the last living male descendant with the Leschi name. He lived alone all his life, never had children, never married. He bore an uncanny resemblance to Chief Leschi, whose image was captured by an artist's sketch. Iyall said visitors familiar with the sketch would see Sherman and gasp, "Leschi!"

One Sunday morning in June 2000, Iyall and Sherman, 68, sat in his living room. Sherman was consumed by the Leschi story. It came up in every conversation. But he was more pensive this time.

"I have something I want you to do," Iyall recalled him saying.

She looked closer into his face.

"I want you to clear Leschi's name."

Six months later, Sherman fell ill and died.

ON THE DAY Leschi was hanged, Indian drums from several tribes could be heard in the distance, sounding their protest. Talk of reversing the injustice "began the day after he was executed," said Larry Seaberg, 65, a direct descendant.

But the Nisqually tribe, besieged by hardship for most of the previous 1 1/2 centuries, was too busy trying to survive to put any serious effort into legally clearing Leschi's name.

Iyall recalled leaving Sherman's home dazed that Sunday morning.

She held a full-time job as a development planner for the tribe and had few connections outside of Indian Country. She wanted to honor Sherman's wish. It was her wish, too, but she was afraid—until one spring morning.

Four months after Sherman's death, Iyall was walking on a

trail in the woods when an owl landed on a branch just above her face. She stopped in her tracks. The owl stared. She walked farther, and the owl flew past and again landed above her and looked into her eyes.

"We must have stared at each other for two minutes," Iyall said.

She ran home, shaken, told others about it and, despite a lifelong aversion to superstition, came to believe the owl carried a message from Sherman and other Nisqually ancestors, perhaps Leschi himself. The message:

"You've been given something to do. Do it. We will be with you."

Over many months, Iyall reached out to various people. Two years later, she was leading a core group of three women of Indian ancestry, ages 40 to 80: a tribal historian, a museum curator and a lawyer.

There were so many avenues to investigate. About the time Iyall and her three allies began meeting in earnest, in 2002, the state of Massachusetts exonerated five women convicted of witchcraft and put to death by colonial authorities three centuries earlier.

Nothing like that had ever happened in Indian Country, but the word "exoneration" resonated. Iyall's group named itself the Committee to Exonerate Chief Leschi. They wanted something amounting to more than just a clique of Indians sounding yet more drums. But they needed help from the outside.

AN ACCIDENTAL MEETING brought the group in contact with John Ladenburg, the Pierce County executive. With Ladenburg's help, the group recruited a couple of state lawmakers, and in March, the Legislature passed a resolution asking the state Supreme Court to overturn Leschi's conviction and "right a gross injustice."

There was one problem: The high court could not do it. Chief Justice Gerry Alexander said no one would have legal standing to petition the court on behalf of a man dead for nearly 150 years.

He also said a state court did not have jurisdiction to overturn a ruling by a Territorial Supreme Court, which was a federal entity and the region's highest court in the days before statehood.

But Alexander came up with an idea: How about convening a one-time "historical court" that would reexamine Leschi's case? A panel of the state's highest-ranking judges would, as in any trial, hear both sides and come up with a verdict.

At least one member of Iyall's group, the lone Nisqually elder, Cecilia Svinth Carpenter, 80, was against the idea. "What if they convict him again?" she asked.

Carpenter wanted a guaranteed outcome.

Alexander refused. He said the court had to be "straight-up."

The Nisqually tribe and Iyall's group agreed, with trepidation, and the court date was set for Dec. 10 in the auditorium of the Washington State History Museum.

The judges would include two state Supreme Court justices, two appellate judges, two county judges and one tribal judge, all of whom would review in advance what records existed of the case.

Leschi's defense would be argued by Ladenburg and a tribal attorney. The government's case would be made by two Pierce County prosecutors. Leschi was jailed and initially tried in Pierce County, which encompasses Tacoma and the Nisqually Reservation.

It would be called a Historical Court of Inquiry and Justice. The verdict would not be legally binding but would carry the moral weight of the state's highest arbiters of law.

On court day, about 200 people filled the auditorium, which was shaped like a partial bowl, with sloping sides and a small stage area at the lowest point. Many spectators, from local tribes, wore colorful coats and beads. Near the front, Iyall and friends nervously held hands and awaited the start.

A gavel fell. "All rise," the bailiff said.

ELEVEN WITNESSES TESTIFIED. They were historians, tribal elders and experts in military and Indian law. Two witnesses, both

Leschi descendants, broke down crying. Some in the audience also wept.

Attorneys on both sides questioned the witnesses, who, one by one, pieced together a picture of life in the Puget Sound in the mid-1850s.

In those years, a stump-sized, single-minded dynamo, Territorial Gov. Isaac Stevens, working on behalf of the U.S. government, negotiated treaties with the region's Indians, ostensibly to keep the peace between Indians and white settlers who were arriving in great numbers. The underlying objective was to separate the Indians from their land.

Through six treaties in two years, the Indians lost nearly all of what is now Washington. The Nisqually, who had lived in villages along 78 miles of the Nisqually River, were consigned to 1,280 acres of rocky bluff far from the river.

"We are a salmon people, a fishing people," testified elder Billy Frank. Without access to the river, the tribe was doomed.

The two tribal leaders of the time, Leschi and his brother, Quiemuth (pronounced kway-mooth), led a resistance. There were raids and counterraids, with killings on both sides. A climate of fear and hatred permeated the region.

Stevens formed a territorial militia to help the Army. He sent a detachment of militiamen to capture Leschi and his brother.

One day in October 1855, members of that detachment were ambushed along a trail that threaded through Connell's Prairie, near what is now Bonney Lake. A militia colonel named A. Benton Moses was shot in the back and killed. A soldier identified Leschi as the shooter.

Army officers who knew Leschi promised him amnesty to end the war. The chief was turned in by one of his nephews. Quiemuth turned himself in, and was stabbed to death in the governor's office. No charges were filed in Quiemuth's murder.

Betraying the Army's promise, Leschi was tried twice for Moses' killing.

The first trial ended in a hung jury, with one of the hold-out jurors, Ezra Meeker, eventually writing an account of the case.

Leschi was tried a second time, convicted by a jury of 12 white men, and sentenced to death. The Territorial Supreme Court upheld the decision.

These were the facts, not disputed by either side of Chief Justice Alexander's court.

The government's case, argued by prosecutors Carl Hultman and Mary Robnett, took a couple of approaches.

Robnett argued that Leschi's trials followed the laws of the day, and there was no evidence to show the verdict was motivated by politics or race. In fact, she suggested, the current hearing was more politically motivated than Leschi's trials. Hultman said the Territorial Supreme Court had reviewed the verdict and decided there was "sufficient evidence" to support it.

"How can we go against that decision?" Hultman said, explaining the scant, handwritten records that survive. "We know less than they do."

The attorneys for Leschi said the chief was tried under an undeveloped judicial system, and the verdict came in a racially charged atmosphere.

Testimony brought up some little-known facts:

The sole witness in both trials, militiaman A.B. Rabbeson, was part of the grand jury that indicted the chief. Rabbeson was also the jury foreman in the second trial. The judges in both trials were members of the Territorial Supreme Court, which, in effect, meant they reviewed their own decisions and decided to uphold the verdict.

Evidence that Rabbeson mistook another Indian for Leschi, and an Army report that showed Leschi was not at Connell's Prairie that day, were never presented at trial. Perhaps the most significant omission was that the judge in the second trial, unlike the first, did not instruct the jury to consider Leschi, as the Army did, an "enemy combatant."

Telling testimony came from the witness most sympathetic to Gov. Stevens, retired history professor Kent Richards, author of a Stevens biography.

"Stevens believed that executing Leschi would bring closure

to the war," Richards said. At the end of every war, "someone must be held accountable, and in the Indian wars of the 1850s in western Washington, Leschi was held accountable."

Testimony in Alexander's court lasted 4 1/2 hours.

The judges deliberated for half an hour. As they reentered the auditorium, Iyall sat up in her chair and reached over to grasp Billy Frank's hand.

The verdict was unanimous. In the summation, Alexander said a state of war existed between the U.S. Army and the region's Indians, and as a legal combatant, "Chief Leschi should not, as a matter of law, have been tried for the crime of murder."

Alexander declared Leschi exonerated.

The crowd erupted in applause. Even the prosecutors applauded. Iyall stood and hugged friends and family members, some weeping with joy.

But Carpenter, the elder, sat in her chair expressionless. This was the outcome she had wanted, but a part of her seemed unwilling to be appeased.

"It doesn't change the legal record," she said. "This was really a way for white people, for the state of Washington, to say, 'We're sorry.' And I accept it. It's the best we can do."

On a cold morning, a few days after the exoneration, Iyall got in her pickup and drove the 10 or so miles to the place where Leschi was hanged.

The bowl in the prairie had long been filled in and forgotten. In the parking lot of a strip mall in what is now the working-class town of Lakewood, a boulder sits under a leafless oak tree. An inscription on it says the last chief of the Nisqually tribe was hanged 300 yards southeast of that spot.

As Iyall stood, hands in her coat pocket, scanning the words, an elderly woman with a cane strolled by and stopped.

She read the inscription, too.

"They cleared him, you know," the woman said. "I walk past this every day, and it always hurt. I was so happy when I heard."

"Me, too," Iyall said.

Iyall had come here once with Sherman Leschi, shortly before his death.

More than four years had passed since their conversation in his living room. She left his house in a daze that day, and was now in a different kind of fog, the kind that came after chasing something for so long and finally catching it, but then having no energy left to celebrate.

She hoped the ancestors were happy, though, that drums of celebration were beating somewhere.

A WORLD AWAY IN NAVAJO NATION:
FAR FROM THE SEPT. 11 FALLOUT

Seattle Times, September 1, 2002

Introduced by **ALAN BERNER,** photographer for the *Seattle Times*,
who worked with Alex on both of the "Crossing America" series
for the newspaper

*Y*ou don't go knocking on the door to a hogan.
*You don't drive up in a Ford Expedition as big as the ho-
gan—an eight-sided hut made from earth and logs—and expect
someone to come out and welcome and talk to two strangers who
have driven up a dirt road ignoring a sign that said, "No Trespass-
ing."*

*Alex and I had dirty laundry, so we drove thirty miles south to
Kayenta, Arizona, from Gouldings Trading Post.*

*It was late in the day, after we'd stopped by Monument Valley
High School, where a Navajo tribal member was shooting baskets
against a backdrop of the "Mittens," those formations seen in so
many John Ford films—and Marlboro ads.*

*At the laundromat we ran into David and Sarah Clark, a Na-
vajo couple with a pickup full of laundry.*

*He said he'd take us up to a friend's hogan the next day—Rose
Yazzie's home.*

We said we'd pay him to be a guide and translator.

*We were at Rose's home for only an hour or two. She spoke spar-
ingly, not uncaring about 9/11, but apart.*

*The fall of the Twin Towers was another world away. She had
never been.*

Alex bought a small Navajo rug from her sister.

I bought a bunch of greasewood stirring sticks used in cooking.

I paid David Clark with American Express Travelers Cheques.

He stared at them and asked, "What are these?"

. . .

MONUMENT VALLEY, ARIZ.—There might not be a place on
Earth farther from the events of September 11 than Rose Yazzie's
heart. It isn't a haughty or angry distance, but a simple sense of
apartness summed up in the words:

"That is your world; this is ours."

Yazzie is a Navajo. She is small and imperial, like a miniature
queen, 58 years old but with the demeanor of an ancient. An
ancient who wears Reeboks. They were a gift.

The outside world has tried, with pinhole success, to infiltrate
her earthen hut, where she spends her days weaving rugs from
the wool of her sheep. She speaks no English and has no desire
to learn. Yazzie has never left the reservation.

Only a few dozen people live in this valley of magnificent
spires, the spiritual center of the Navajo Nation, a place where
the Earth bleeds a rusty umber, and the blood, it is said, gives
life to the tribe.

The landscape might be familiar. Marlboro used it as a backdrop for its cigarette ads. John Wayne filmed his signature West-
erns here. It isn't likely they trespassed on Yazzie land.

Rose Yazzie lives at the end of a long dirt road closed to outsiders without permission. A sign at the entry says so. How we got
past the sign was a matter of luck and dirty laundry.

The road out of Las Vegas led from desert to plateau, from
dusty brown to a baked terra cotta, the land slowly climbing into
the region known as Four Corners, the intersection of Arizona,
Utah, New Mexico and Colorado. A lonely highway sign marked
the entrance into the Navajo Nation. It read simply: "Indians."

Navajos encourage a spare, some would say concise, kind of
communication: You say what needs saying and no more. You
do not laugh if there is nothing funny. You do not smile for no
reason. Most important, you do not ask too many questions.

For us, it meant numerous short conversations.

Until we met David Clark at the laundromat. He and his wife,
Sarah, hauled in a pickup-load of dirty clothes. Almost 60 percent

of Navajos live below the poverty line; half live in homes with no electricity or plumbing. Eighty percent of the roads on the nation's largest reservation—as big as West Virginia—are not paved. For David and Sarah, it was a long, dusty journey to Best Laundry in Kayenta, 30 miles away.

"We're used to it," David says. It's better than washing clothes in a river.

He is 49, solid as a sandstone boulder with dark, leathery skin and deep black eyes that seem, from the first moment, to be welcoming. When he was a boy, a couple of Mormon missionaries made friends with his family, and David went off to school in Utah for a few years. They tried, but the Mormons never converted him.

Today, David raises sheep and grows corn, and when the opportunity arises, he works as a guide. There hasn't been much guide work this year, he says, not since September 11.

Navajo leaders, in their reserved, understated way, have encouraged tourism. A tribe with 255,000 members and no casino has to adapt, has to open up even if it hurts.

This year, the absence of tourists has been an economic bust. Only 60,000 visitors have come through the valley this year, compared with 400,000 last year. Lodges and gift shops brim with unsold blankets that are the Navajos' main trading commodity.

But there is no gnashing of teeth over this. It's simply the hand of fate, like a drought or a flash flood. And there are many in the tribe, secretly or otherwise, who prefer the reservation to themselves.

Three kinds of Navajo live on the reservation, David says. The young ones who no longer speak Navajo, who buy rap music and aspire to play in the NBA. The realists, like David, Sarah and most of the official tribal leaders, who've accepted that Navajos are also Americans and must therefore try to live some semblance of the American way. And individualists like Rose Yazzie, who is first and only a Navajo.

Her kind is a fast-vanishing species.

David brought us to Yazzie's hogan, an eight-sided hut made

of earth and juniper logs. The two are old friends. At first she appeared interrupted, imposed upon. David explained us. She sighed and then nodded as if to say, "Proceed."

With David translating, we asked her about September 11.

Yazzie said she heard about what happened, holding up two fingers of her left hand, and then crashing into them with the index finger of her right. She knew nothing of al-Qaida and the war on terrorism. She said she felt bad for the children.

What children, we asked. The children who died, the children whose parents were killed? The children of the terrorists? The children on the reservation who now fear airplanes?

"The children," she said, and looked away.

Aside from that, the attacks meant little to her, other than a piece of news from a faraway land that she will never see, a land that will never see her.

"It is a sad thing, but it is not our world," she said.

If there was one place in the universe she would like to see before she died, it would be a strange and exotic land to the east, a place relatives have told her about. It is called Albuquerque.

Albuquerque? That's only a few hours away, we said. Why not go there this weekend? We could take you!

"Far," she said, laughing softly, almost to herself, as if we crazy outsiders had asked her to go to Jupiter. "Someday."

We visited for an hour, and at the end, she walked us out into the sunshine, her Reeboks leaving little tread marks on the dirt floor. She sighed a queenly exhalation.

She waved and nodded, and then looked up, hands on her hips, at the red-rock monuments that towered over her hogan. In the sunshine, the rock formations took on a glow, as if fire lit them up from the inside. A distance away, her sheep wandered the same trails that her parents walked, and her grandparents before that, all the way back, according to the Navajo story, to the beginning of time.

Her back yard was a red valley of everlastingness. This was her world.

THE FISH TALE THAT
CHANGED HISTORY

Seattle Times, February 7, 1999

Introduced by **FLORANGELA DAVILA**, managing editor
of Seattle-based *Crosscut*, who was a reporting colleague
of Tizon's at the *Seattle Times*

*izon was never afraid to look at someone and tell us what he
saw: A meaty brown hand. A leathery face. A hell-raiser of a
man. Tizon loads his stories with physical descriptions that sing;
his eye for detail is unrivaled, but he also has such a beautiful ear.
Consider his choice of verbs: skulk, roar, pop—verbs with attitude.
Consider the rhythm he crafts with his word choices, sentence pair-
ings, sequencing of paragraphs.*

*It's also classic Tizon to get conversational in a story—it's you,
the reader, right here with me, and I'm going to let you into a world
and in on a moment so you can understand the importance of
whom I'm writing about. And, can you hear the person's voice?
In addition to admiring the hell-raising accomplishments of Billy
Frank Jr., I'm certain Tizon enjoyed meeting and writing about him
because (1) he preferred to be called Billy and (2) he swore. Swear
words are muscle words, and Tizon delighted in their sound; the
second he heard Frank's cursing, Tizon would have calculated how
smartly they would sum up Frank for the reader, and he would have
smiled. Score! (Side note: Tizon would have made a tremendous
radio reporter with that discriminating ear for "good tape.")*

*I sat one cubicle row away from Tizon at the Seattle Times.
The more anguished he looked while typing—he'd be the first to
admit that writing is hard—the more I anticipated seeing the final
published piece. (I sometimes cheated by reading it in the system as
the story was making its way to the copy desk, because I was that
excited to read it.)*

Tizon's writing was never thin or bland or simple, because he had already deeply considered the purpose of his story before ever typing his first word. He always kept the reader in mind, and nothing would have horrified him more than if he presented a story to someone and the reaction was "Meh, well, that was a total waste of time."

He obsessed over his work, and it pays off in a story such as this one: an examination of a twenty-five-year court decision through the story of a squarely built, scruffy-wool-cap-wearing Indian fisher. Look at how Tizon takes us out onto the water with Frank. Look at the efficiency and impact of his quotes. Look at that ending. God-damn.

. . .

BILLY FRANK JR. may be the most distinguished person you'll ever call Billy. He'll insist on it. Call him Mr. Frank and he'll look around for someone else. Say "Hi Billy," and a meaty brown hand will be instantly extended to you.

He's got fisherman's hands. At 67, he's considered an elder statesman for his people, with governors and U.S. senators among his friends. He's collected awards for humanitarianism. Above all, though, Billy Frank is a Nisqually Indian, which is to say, a fisherman.

If you're a newcomer—one of the 2 million people who've come to Washington since the mid-1970s—you may not know this old fisherman's story.

It's a fish tale, except it's all true and involves more than catching a fish. The fate of Indian tribes and the future of a once-rich industry hung in the balance. Race, politics and Marlon Brando came into play. In the end, a major shift in power took place, permanently changing the status of Indians in the United States.

In the middle of it all was a conservative, white, bespectacled judge named George Hugo Boldt who, 25 years ago this week, handed down the mother of all fish decisions. The ruling shocked the region, and the repercussions—and resentments—continue still.

"The fishing issue was to Washington state what busing was to the East," says former U.S. Congressman Lloyd Meeds of Everett. "It was frightening, very, very emotional."

As in any good tale, there were good guys and bad guys, and for most of the story, Billy Frank was considered a bad guy. He was arrested more than 40 times over three decades. He was branded a renegade by then-Gov. Dan Evans.

His whole tribe was viewed as a band of outlaws, as were all Indians who dared defy the state.

For most of this century, white society did not look kindly upon Indians, when they looked upon them at all. They were viewed as a nuisance, a hindrance to progress. In the Northwest, tribes were widely seen as poaching communities—lawless, primitive, skulking around in the dark.

"The Indian was a child and a dangerous child," wrote a Washington state Supreme Court justice in 1916. "Neither Rome nor Britain ever dealt more liberally with their subject races than we with these savage tribes, whom it was generally tempting and always easy to destroy."

This was the world Billy Frank grew up in.

OF COURSE, he never saw himself as a poacher. To be an Indian in the Puget Sound was to have salmon swimming in your veins. If you let Billy Frank tell the story, he might go back a few thousand years through a hundred generations of Nisqually fishers.

"For context."

He's squarely built with gray hair pulled back under a scruffy wool cap. He wears bifocals. His face is lined and leathery with the look of history about it. And the man can talk. Stories spill out easily, and those meaty hands always seem to be expressing something.

He swears a lot, mostly out of exuberance. "Goddamn, it's a beautiful day!" he might say. When he talks about "the mountain," he's referring to Mount Rainier. "The river" means the Nisqually River.

He's lived his whole life in the 78 miles between the mountain and the river's mouth, and that's where he's headed now, with two guests, in his 17-foot aluminum boat.

The trip from his house to the mouth of the river takes 20 minutes. Harbor seals and sea lions pop their heads out of the water as the boat passes. Three-quarters of a mile upriver, just before the old Pacific Highway bridge, Billy Frank points to a gravel bar on the opposite bank.

"The first time, I was cleaning fish right there," he says.

He recalled it was a cold December night, just before Christmas 1945. He was 14. He had just emptied his net of a load of chum salmon and was working on his knees in the dark when two bright lights flashed on him.

"You're under arrest," a voice said. The boy ran and stumbled.

Two game wardens took him by the arms.

"I told them to leave me alone. I live here!"

Today he can point to dozens of spots along the river and tell like stories: of having boats and nets confiscated, of being chased and tear-gassed, tackled, punched, pushed face-first into the mud, handcuffed and dragged soaking wet to the county jail.

Like his father before him, Billy Frank lived like an outlaw, fishing at night and always on the lookout for men in uniforms.

Indians all over the Northwest lived the same way.

When brought to court, their sole defense was that they had a right to fish according to century-old treaties signed with the U.S. government.

"Most of them didn't have lawyers," said Al Ziontz, a Seattle attorney who came to represent several Northwest tribes. "The Indians would cite the treaties, and the state would brush them aside, acting like the treaties were just pieces of paper that somebody found in a trunk."

The irony was that those pieces of paper were never the Indians' idea; they were imposed by a fair-skinned people too powerful to fight. Eventually, the squiggly words on those pages would be the Indians' only weapons.

BILLY FRANK MANEUVERS his boat into a muddy creek just west of the river. Carcasses of spawned-out salmon line the banks. A quarter-mile up the creek, he points to an isolated Douglas fir, now a snag, rising a hundred feet into the air. Interstate 5 roars a short distance away.

"Treaty Tree," he says, expressionless.

Under that tree, in 1854, the process began ending life as the 6,000 Indians of the region had lived it for thousands of years.

Billy Frank's grandfather, Kluck-et-suh, was a boy at the time, and played under that tree and fished this water, then called Medicine Creek.

Working on behalf of the U.S. government, Territorial Gov. Isaac Stevens, a stump-sized, single-minded dynamo of a man, negotiated a rapid-fire series of treaties with the region's Indians for the sole purpose of taking their land so white settlers could move in.

Starting with the Medicine Creek treaty signed under that 100-foot Douglas fir, Stevens pushed through six treaties in two years. The Indians lost most of Western Washington seemingly overnight. They were forced onto reservations, some as small as a few hundred acres.

"Isaac Stevens saw treaty-making as a command-and-obey process, not a negotiation," writes author and University of Colorado law professor Charles Wilkinson in an upcoming book, "Messages From Frank's Landing." "He knew what he wanted going in and did not plan on departing from his script."

The treaty at Medicine Creek was typical.

The two-page document was written in advance, in English, and presented to the Nisquallys, Squaxins and Puyallups, who knew little English. Stevens then insisted the talks be conducted in Chinook jargon, a mixed tongue of English, French and Indian words used for trade.

Asks Wilkinson: How could the Indians possibly know the transcendent meaning of what they were signing?

One interpreter at Medicine Creek, asked by Stevens whether he could get the Indians to sign, assured the governor, "I can get these Indians to sign their death warrant."

The treaties might have been that for the Indians had it not been for a clause in each of them guaranteeing tribes the right to fish ". . . at all usual and accustomed grounds and stations."

Stevens had no qualms about Indian fishing. Fish and game were abundant to the point of seeming limitless. What did it matter? If anything was to become extinct, it would be the Indians themselves.

"Essentially, they hoped we'd all die off," said Joe Waterhouse, a Jamestown S'Klallam Indian and a student of treaty history.

Many tribes came close. Smallpox, random violence and relocation devastated Billy Frank's tribe. Nisqually numbers fell from 2,000 in 1800 to fewer than 700 by 1880. Their chief, Leschi, a charismatic leader who led a rebellion against Stevens, was hanged at Fort Steilacoom.

And their reservation grew smaller and smaller as the needs of the new state of Washington expanded.

BY THE TURN OF THE CENTURY, the Nisquallys, like other Puget Sound tribes, clung to the single-most-important thing they had left from their ancient culture: their relationship to the salmon of the rivers.

The salmon fed them physically and spiritually and brought in what little money they had. Access to the rivers meant everything.

In the first year of statehood, 1889, legislators, in the name of conservation, closed six rivers to salmon fishing. All were Indian fishing grounds. The state eventually banned net fishing in all rivers, except the Columbia, effectively outlawing the Indians' main way of catching fish.

Over the next 50 years, the number of white commercial fishermen exploded, industrializing the fisheries and prodding the state to come down harder on the Indians, now seen as competitors.

Non-Indian commercial fishers caught salmon by the millions of tons in the Pacific and Puget Sound, but the state blamed declining fish runs on Indian netting and lawlessness. The Indians didn't follow state-mandated seasons, didn't get licenses or heed catch limits.

Tribes claimed the real culprits in the salmon's decline were commercial fishing, dam-building and logging. Decades of research would eventually corroborate this.

In reality, Indians, still river-fishers, caught only what was left over. According to the state's own figures, Indians were catching less than 5 percent of the harvestable salmon in the region at the height of the fish wars.

Even to catch that, "we had to go underground," Billy Frank says. "To survive, to continue our culture, we had to become an underground society."

By the 1960s, the state's sporadic arrests turned into a relentless series of raids and stings, much of it focused on the Nisqually River. The river had become the locus of Indian protests.

Revolution was in the air all over the country, and Northwest Indians, seizing the "sit-in" tactics of civil-rights activists elsewhere, began staging "fish-ins," in which protesters would openly fish in defiance of state laws.

One of the "renegade leaders," as the state labeled him, was a crew-cut, hell-raising Nisqually Indian named Billy Frank, son of Billy Frank Sr., himself a veteran of the fish wars. Many fish-ins took place on the family's 6-acre riverfront parcel known as Frank's Landing.

The Landing became the moral center of the resistance.

BILLY FRANK WAS no longer the frightened 14-year-old arrested upriver in 1945. He'd worked all over, struggled with and overcome a drinking problem, married and fathered children. He'd spent two years in the Marine Corps and saw enough of the world to know right from wrong. But with only a ninth-grade education, he didn't see himself arguing fine points of law.

"I wasn't a policy guy. I was a getting-arrested guy," he likes to say.

The state responded to the fish-ins with a military-style campaign, using surveillance planes, high-powered boats and radio communications. At times, game wardens resorted to tear gas and billy clubs. And guns.

The confrontations were telecast nationwide.

Soon a parade of celebrities came to support the Indians, the most famous among them, Marlon Brando and Jane Fonda. When Brando was arrested during a 1964 fish-in on the nearby Puyallup River, he told reporters he was just "helping some Indian friends fish."

The violence escalated. The state became more aggressive, and Indians fought back, using fists and stones.

Billy Frank recalls an incident in which a state boat rammed his prized canoe—carved by an Indian friend up river, Johnny Bob—dumping him in the water. Billy almost drowned. The state confiscated the canoe.

Indian activist Hank Adams was shot in the stomach while fishing, but survived. He claimed the assailants were white vigilantes, but police never pursued the case.

"It was a frightening time," said former Congressman Meeds, whose district included Everett and the San Juans, white fishing strongholds.

Meeds, 71, once highly popular, saw his constituency turn against him for his early support of the tribes. He decided not to run for a seventh term when it became clear he would lose. Other lawmakers felt similar pressure.

In one of the most dramatic raids of the fish wars, this one in September 1970, a squadron of helmeted Tacoma police used tear gas and clubs to arrest 59 protesters camped on the Puyallup. Gunshots were fired, and Indians were beaten and brutally manhandled.

That same month, the U.S. government finally intervened. The government, on behalf of the tribes, filed suit against the state of Washington. After all, it was the government's own documents—those pieces of paper pushed by Isaac Stevens and ratified by Congress—the Indians constantly invoked.

Assigned to hear the case was U.S. District Court Judge George Hugo Boldt.

BILLY FRANK REMEMBERED the name. Six years earlier, Billy and five friends had spent 30 days in jail for staging a fish-in. Their attorney tried to free them on grounds of illegal arrest but failed.

One of the judges who denied their release was George Boldt.

What else was known of Boldt was not encouraging for the tribes. He was in his late 60s, an Eisenhower appointee and a conservative with no background in Indian law. Most worrisome was the native Montanan's reputation as an avid sport fisherman.

Sport-fishers as a group blamed Indians for the drop in steelhead runs.

Over the next three years, Boldt presided over a highly complex trial with a law-and-order firmness, but not without charm. Retired *Times* reporter Don Hannula, who followed the trial, tells of a witness who described the thrill of landing a steelhead trout:

"If you've ever made love—that's the nearest I can express it," the witness told the judge. Asked where he fished, the witness clicked off a long list of rivers. Judge Boldt, peering above his horn-rimmed glasses, replied: "That doesn't leave you much time for making love, does it?"

Make Love, Not War was the slogan of the times, but what followed both in and out of Boldt's courtroom was a classic Western showdown.

Outside were pickets and hangings in effigy. Inside, lawyers debated the central question: Could the state of Washington regulate the fishing practices of Indians who signed treaties with the U.S. government?

But the underlying question was more far-reaching: To what extent could tribes, as separate nations within a nation, rule their own people and control their own destinies?

Both sides relied on the treaty clause that read, "The right of taking fish at usual and accustomed grounds and stations is further secured to said Indians in common with all citizens of the territory."

The state interpreted the words "in common with all citizens" to mean that Indians, like all other residents of the state, must be subject to state control. The Indians argued the treaties entitled them to fish unimpeded at any of their "usual and accustomed places."

Testifying at the trial were Indians young and old, like Billy Frank and his father, who told stories passed on to them by their fathers and grandfathers. They talked of the time before white people came, and of the generations of Indian fishers that went back, according to their view, to the beginning of time. For context.

"He listened to us," Billy Frank says of the judge, in what may be his highest praise. "He listened very carefully."

ON FEB. 12, 1974, Judge Boldt handed down his 203-page decision.

The Indians won. Overwhelmingly.

Boldt, relying on an 1828 edition of Webster's American Dictionary, interpreted "in common with" to mean the Indians were entitled to half the harvestable salmon running through their traditional waters. Fifty percent! The ruling shocked even the Indians, who made up only 1 percent of the state's population.

Furthermore, Boldt made the tribes co-managers of the state's fisheries. With the drop of a gavel, tribes transformed, in the eyes of the law, from underground poaching societies to at-the-table equals with the state authorities that had persecuted them for so long.

The ruling stuck. It withstood years of sometimes-violent protest by non-Indian fishermen. It withstood state appeals argued doggedly by then state Attorney General Slade Gorton. The Court of Appeals and eventually the U.S. Supreme Court upheld Boldt's decision.

A decade of tumultuous adjustments passed before the Indians started harvesting their 50 percent. The state and the tribes
eventually learned to work together, the tribes represented by the
Northwest Indian Fisheries Commission, of which Billy Frank
has been chairman for almost 20 years.

The 50-50 formula was extended to shellfish and game, but
not without rancorous opposition.

Many non-Indian fishermen still resent Boldt, still curse him
and the tribes. And a whole new group, waterfront property owners—angered by court-approved Indian harvesting of shellfish on
their tidelands—have joined the campaign to roll back what Boldt
unfurled.

"Boldt made a bad decision," said Tom Nelson, 61, of Renton,
and a leader in the sport-fishing community. "Most people in the
state—and I go around speaking to a lot of groups—think Boldt
made a bad decision."

Nelson's sport-fishing group wants to put a "Ban All Nets"
initiative on the November ballot. Though it wouldn't immediately affect tribes, observers say tribes are the ultimate target. Up
to 80 percent of all net-fishing in Puget Sound is done by Indian
fishers.

Salmon continue to decline. Despite its mandate to better
manage the state's fisheries, Boldt didn't save them. No court
decision could. Fisheries all over the world are in crisis for the
same reason: too many people fishing, polluting and destroying
habitat. Or simply too many people.

"The number of fish dropped while we were in the courtroom
arguing over who got the fish," said David Getches, lead tribal
attorney in the Boldt case.

Most tribes are still poor.

But the Boldt decision reverberated throughout Indian country because, in symbol, it had less to do with allocation of fish
than with allocation of power. It elevated tribal treaties to at least
the level of state law, and gave Indians a new political status.

Boldt was a great boost in the direction of tribes ruling themselves. It coincided with a Nixon-era infusion of federal money intended to strengthen tribal governments.

The result has been both a political and economic awakening, seen in arenas as divergent as tribal casino resorts in Connecticut, tribal police powers in New Mexico and online tribal lotteries in Idaho.

Tribes nationwide have become a force to be reckoned with.

In Washington, the Muckleshoot tribe held up a city of Tacoma plan to build a pipeline along the Green River, ancestral fishing grounds. The project went through but only after Tacoma agreed to pay the tribe $20 million, build a tribal fish hatchery and hand over 100 acres.

In Utah, the Goshute Indians, over the vitriolic objections of its non-Indian neighbors, plan to lease part of their reservation for nuclear-waste storage. The tribe, hoping for a multimillion-dollar boon, says it's their right as a sovereign nation.

In New Mexico, the city of Albuquerque has agreed to spend $300 million on cleaning up the Rio Grande River to meet the water-quality requirements of the Isleta Pueblo, which manages part of the watershed.

"Without question, the Boldt decision is among the one, two or three most-significant decisions in the history of Indian law. It was that profound," said author Wilkinson.

"And Billy Frank was the heart and soul of it. He was the image of the defiant Indian standing up for something that was right and true."

AFTER A LONG DAY of showing his two guests around the river, Billy Frank's boat runs out of gas. It stalls, and is carried swiftly downstream on a powerful current. The boat spins once, twice. And from out of Billy's mouth comes a noise that sounds like "Yee-haaaaw!"

He grabs a paddle, and eventually guides the boat steadily downriver to Frank's Landing. "We made it," he says with mock drama.

"We're safe!"

For him, it was just another hairy ride on the river, as his whole life has been. He's traveled an extraordinary distance.

From skulking in the rivers, he and his people have come to oversee them. Instead of arrest warrants, he gets invitations to speak—to this congressional panel or that Senate committee, to the world conference of Amnesty International.

He's been awarded the Albert Schweitzer Prize for Humanitarianism, joining past winners, former President Jimmy Carter and former U.S. Surgeon General Dr. C. Everett Koop.

But his most prized acquisition has been the old shovel-nosed canoe that his friend Johnny Bob carved 40 years ago and for which Billy paid him 15 salmon—the one state wardens confiscated after ramming him in the river in 1964.

In a gesture of reconciliation, the state gave it back to him for his birthday in 1980. Then, a few years ago, a massive flood carried it away, and Billy lost it again. But it came back, this time returned by a niece who found it downriver.

The canoe now hangs ceremoniously from the ceiling at the new We He Lut Indian school on the Landing. Billy Frank and his two guests study it.

He tells its story and unwittingly sums up his own life. He says it was formed by old hands in the backwoods of the Nisqually, that it began in the river and will end there, and that it's surprised everyone with its resilience.

"There it is," he says, "still here."

ALASKA BY WAY OF KATRINA: AT THE FAR EDGE OF A NEW ORLEANS DIASPORA

Los Angeles Times, March 7, 2006

Introduced by **DEAN BAQUET**, former editor in chief
of the *Los Angeles Times* and current executive editor
of the *New York Times*

*P*art of most national correspondents' jobs is to spot "trends," to come up with stories about something that more and more people are doing. Alex didn't particularly like trend stories, however; as we learn in this collection, he was drawn to stories about lone wolves and eccentric amateur scientists and conspiracy theorists and all manner of other people who march to the unique beat of their own drums in life. He liked opposite-of-trend stories. And that made him, however counterintuitively, a terrific national correspondent.

Alex, like every other reporter on the national staff of the Los Angeles Times, covered the Katrina disaster and its aftermath in New Orleans. But in this story, written half a year after the floods, he is drawn to a highly unusual aspect of the diaspora spawned by the tragedy. It is the tale of an African American woman from New Orleans who has wound up resettling in Alaska, about as far away from home as she could possibly get and still be in the United States.

With humor and empathy, he lets Patti Tobias tell us about her particular odyssey. In a deft humorous touch, he portrays her phone as a beacon: Every time it rings, it seems, she has a new adventure to tell a faraway friend or family member. Yet Alex also subtly suggests here a larger theme of American generosity. A couple in Anchorage takes this woman and her family into their home, sight unseen; an Idaho man donates his mileage points to buy all the airline tickets. Patti Tobias may never get used to the frozen diaper

wipes in her new home in icy Alaska, but she will also never forget
the warmth of the total strangers who helped her get there.

. . .

ANCHORAGE—She didn't know diaper wipes could freeze so
fast. One moment they were a stack of moist towelettes, next they
were an icy white brick.

Patti Tobias had left her infant's wipes in the back seat of the
car on a morning when the temperature dipped to 7 degrees below zero. "Huh," she said, inspecting the block and grinning.

Her relatives in New Orleans would get a kick out of this.

She would share it as part of the chronicle of "a little black girl
in Alaska," the story of her new life as told to friends and family in
daily long-distance phone conversations. Her dispatches included
stories of moose and mountains and white people. Patti, 39, had
never been around so many white people. Most have been quite
nice.

No one refers to her as a little black girl; it's Patti's tag for herself, partly a joke and partly a declaration of her exile. She is a
Hurricane Katrina evacuee, as far from home as she could be in
the continental United States.

"This is me," she says, "a little black girl with three kids and
three suitcases, in Alaska, wearing three layers of clothing!"

Most Katrina evacuees stayed within a day's drive of their
hometowns in the Gulf Coast. A few ventured to the West and
East coasts. The Red Cross counted about 90 evacuee families
that made the 5,000-mile journey to the Last Frontier. They
came because of family and church connections; they came, as
in the Tobiases' case, because a stranger beckoned.

The evacuees scattered throughout the state, with the highest
concentration in Anchorage. Six months after Katrina, though,
many have returned to the Lower 48, leaving only the die-hards—
no one knows exactly how many. The Tobias family is one of
eight left in Anchorage public housing.

Patti says she would like to stay in Alaska for the adventure.

But some states need all four seasons to reveal themselves fully. Driving on ice, for example, has become a part of daily life. With a cold snap upon them, and more to come, Patti and her children are only now learning what it takes to be Alaskan.

PATTI WEARS A HAT inside her cottage. It's a Wednesday afternoon, and she's pacing the living room with a cellphone to her ear. Her 1-year-old, Ginsi, sleeps on the couch, so bundled she looks like a pillow.

Outside, son Tokobey, 12, pushes his 6-year-old sister's face in the snow. Her name is Gionni. She later reports that her brother did it three times that afternoon. Tokobey believes it to be an Alaskan pastime.

"It's supposed to be minus 10 tonight," Patti says. She's talking to someone in Texas. She makes and gets calls all day. "Oh yeah, you feel it. You feel it to your bones. I was bringing in the groceries and my knuckles were frozen."

She had never lived anywhere else but New Orleans, a place where people wear tank tops in winter. The family (Patti is divorced) occupied a duplex in New Orleans East, seven houses away from one of the broken levees. The floods took everything, including Patti's job as a receptionist.

She and her children fled to a Red Cross shelter in nearby Lake Charles, La., where a volunteer behind a computer asked where she wanted to go. "Alaska," Patti said. She had always fantasized about Alaska, seduced by pictures of glaciers and mountains; it seemed so exotic, so different from any place she had ever been.

The first listing that popped up on the computer was from an Anchorage couple willing to take in an evacuee family. A flurry of e-mails and phone calls followed. An Idaho man donated his mileage points to buy airline tickets.

Two weeks after the hurricane, the Tobias family landed in Anchorage at 1 A.M., dazed, ragged and wary.

"We didn't know [the host couple]," Patti said. "We didn't know if we were going into Jeffrey Dahmer's house," referring to the serial killer who ate some of his victims. Dahmer was white and most of his victims were black or Asian.

Their hosts, it turned out, were not cannibals.

Their names are Chantel Ayers-Kalish, 37, and Rob Kalish, 49. They are white and longtime Alaskans. She owns and operates a small pottery studio near the airport. He works as a geologist for an oil company. They have three children, ages 4, 6 and 7, and a big house with two vacant bedrooms and an extra bathroom.

The couple had been moved to tears by images of hurricane victims in the news. Their offer of temporary housing was, Chantel said, a kind of "karmic insurance: because you never know when you might be in the same situation."

THE TOBIAS FAMILY lived with the Kalish family for two months—a melding, Chantel said, "of two families, two cultures, two races." The kids dived right in, and within days were playing and fighting like siblings. The adults were more cautious.

Rob, a soft-spoken, easygoing man, got along with everybody. Chantel had never had a close black friend. Patti had never had a close white friend. One trait bonded them instantly: a knack for gabbing.

After some weeks, the women were comfortable enough for Chantel to call Patti "sweetie" and for Patti to call Chantel "Chan" or "white girl," as in: "What do you want to eat for breakfast, white girl?"

During the days, the children went to school, came home and played. Chantel and Rob went to work, while Patti stayed at the house, watching movies, baking cookies and occasionally cleaning house.

The families ate dinner together, except for Patti. While Chantel might prepare a turkey-breast meal with fruit and salad, Patti would stay in her room and later cook up some red beans and fried fish for herself.

Tokobey found a way to make Rob and Chantel crack up: He would talk like black comedian Dave Chappelle, spouting raw street language in a little-boy way. It worked every time, but

Chantel eventually told him the girls might overhear and start imitating him. Tokobey stopped.

There were bumps.

Chantel's 6-year-old, Olivia, once kicked Gionni in the back. The two girls had similar temperaments, theatrical and strong-willed—a couple of tiny drama queens. When they got along it was bliss; when they fought, it was no-holds-barred. Olivia was bigger.

Tokobey accidentally started a small fire in the kitchen, setting off an alarm that brought fire trucks. Chantel's other two children, Gabrielle and Gwyneth, looked on in glee, as they did for much of the two months.

All three adults came to parent all six children. One day, Patti yelled at Olivia for "being manipulative" after Olivia had started a group game in which she engineered a way to leave Gionni out. Another day, Chantel got furious at Tokobey for wearing his muddy boots in the house for "the ten-thousandth time."

Each mother resented the other's tone toward her children, but tolerated it.

By the middle of November, the Kalish family was ready to get their space back, and Patti and her children were ready to move into their own place. The parting was emotional and affectionate. The families keep in close contact.

"We would do it again in a heartbeat," Chantel said. There were challenges but nothing insurmountable. Race became irrelevant. She said she couldn't imagine not keeping in touch with Patti's three kids as they grew up.

For Patti, it was the end of her first phase of realizing that most of Alaska was inhabited by white people. "I didn't know," she said. "I thought Alaska would be full of Native Alaskans."

New Orleans was two-thirds black; Anchorage is about three-fourths white. Whites make up about 70% of the state's population, natives about 15% and blacks 3%.

Gionni and Tokobey attend a public elementary school where each is the only black child in class. The family attends a predominantly white church, whose members, Patti says, have been welcoming and generous.

But it's definitely not like her church in New Orleans—Greater St. Stephen Full Gospel Baptist Church—where the parishioners were black, the singing was raucous and the preaching was so fiery that members had to fan themselves after the service.

Patti says her new church is . . . "What's the word? Tamer."

THEIR APARTMENT—a narrow, two-story, three-bedroom cottage painted sunflower yellow—resembles a birdhouse in a row of birdhouses in a part of town called Jewell Lake. The back patio door looks out at a snow-covered field, and beyond that, to an evergreen forest. Above the trees loom the Chugach Mountains.

"I opened the blinds and there was a moose. He was looking at me, and I was looking at him," Patti says into her cellphone.

She's telling someone in New Orleans about a recent visitor on her patio. It was about 8 feet tall and 1,000 pounds. She took four close-up pictures of the largest nostrils she had ever seen and sent them to relatives.

"If I'd have opened the door, he would have walked right in," Patti says.

Every day brings something new, she says to another visitor, her cellphone tucked back in her pocket. The other day "they shot a bear in town." She took a boat ride in Cook Inlet and checked out some glaciers. The glaciers looked much grander before she and her kids all got seasick. She would like to learn how to ski.

She's also looking into nursing courses at the University of Alaska. Patti's housing is paid until the summer of 2007, thanks to a state emergency-assistance voucher. Between savings and child support from her ex-husband, she has enough to live on until she decides on school or work.

Day by day, Patti is learning about the one essential trait required to survive in Alaska: an independent spirit. It might even help to be a bit of a loner. Isolation from the rest of the country is one of the state's great offerings, but not everyone is cut out for it.

"It takes commitment to live in Alaska," Chantel once told Patti.

She's finding out what her friend meant. You can't just get in a car, drive to your hometown and shoot the breeze with old friends and family. A visit like that, if you can't afford airline tickets, amounts to an epic journey.

"I get a little lonely sometimes," Patti admits.

But she says she doesn't like to dwell on it. There's too much adventure waiting to waste time being glum.

Outside, Tokobey tinkers with a new all-terrain vehicle that someone gave him for his birthday. Gionni plays with Ginsi in the snow. Tiny flakes have begun falling, and the housing project has taken on a snowy glow.

"What does that look like to you?" Patti says, looking out at her neighborhood. "Doesn't that look like a picture of Christmas?" Here it is, months after the fact, and it still feels like the holiest day of the year.

Her family would get a kick out of that.

The cellphone rings. She grins.

Someone back home must have been reading her mind.

PART IV

LONERS

THOM JONES AND THE COSMIC JOKE: AUTHOR'S SURPRISE "SUCCESS" BREEDS MISERY

Seattle Times, April 2, 2000

Introduced by **NICOLE BRODEUR**, writer and
longtime columnist for the *Seattle Times*

*T*here's a line in Alex Tizon's "Thom Jones and the Cosmic Joke"
*that stopped me cold when I read it again, years after it appeared
in the* Seattle Times's *Pacific magazine:*

> *It takes a certain temperament to convert every experience
> into suffering.*

*Those words could have been written about Tizon himself. He
suffered mightily for his art, agonized over structure and adjectives
and rhythm. His stories were crafted, not banged out and turned
in. And even after he had done that, he still wanted the piece back
for one last polish.*

*What came easily to Alex was observing. Asking a question and
then waiting, watching. Letting the silence sit there like a dropped
dollar bill and refusing to snap it up.*

*Not all reporters do that. They ask a question, rephrase it, lead a
subject along like a toddler through a park. Was it like this? Like that?*

But Alex would ask a question and stop.

*From those moments came some of his most beautifully crafted
words and images. There are very few quotes, and the ones that are
included are telling, almost spoken under the subject's breath.*

*In "Thom Jones," he shows off his keen observations of the way
his subject walks, laughs, carries himself:*

> *His eyes can seem startled and blank, as if he'd just turned
> a corner and witnessed something inexplicable. He doesn't
> laugh often, but when he does, he gives in to it completely,*

closing his eyes and throwing back his head, sometimes laughing beyond the situation, as if reveling in a secret joke or like a man who has thrown the cosmic dice and won.

He moves and speaks slowly. Sometimes he slurs his words. That's partly from his years of boxing and also from overlapping ideas trying to get out of his mouth all at once.

I wondered what Alex asked to get that kind of reaction.

I have been on the receiving end of Alex's curiosity—been asked a single question that cut suddenly, quickly, and without much pain, like washing a sharp knife and seeing blood. He asked things that never occurred to me, that required a moment to think.

And Alex would just sit there, waiting, watching, and listening, never filling the moment himself.

That he would do later, on the page.

. . .

MAYBE THIS WAS SOMETHING that happened to ex-janitors, one of their secret compulsions. Maybe it was an epileptic seizure. In any case, he could not resist. The floor needed sweeping, and the dust-sweeper was there, leaning against a wall, seductively, and before he could be stopped, Thom Jones was sweeping the floor and evidently liking it.

"So quiet," he said, marching the length of the cafeteria, pushing that two-lane sweeper like a pro. "So peaceful."

Finished, he replaced the sweeper, dusted off his hands and resumed the tour of his old janitorial routine at North Thurston High School in Lacey. He was a night custodian here for almost a dozen years, B.P., or Before Pugilist.

"The Pugilist at Rest," his 1991 short story in The New Yorker, was a watershed event, the kind every writer dreams about. Pugilist won the O. Henry Award and was the top story in the Best American Short Stories 1992. He signed a two-book, $50,000 contract with Little, Brown and Co. His first book, of the same name, was a finalist for the National Book Award.

Before Pugilist, he was unknown and unpromising. Nine years

After Pugilist, the ex-Marine, ex-boxer, ex-janitor and 55-year-old Olympia resident is the author of three critically acclaimed books, including the recently released "Sonny Liston Was A Friend of Mine," a multiple award winner, a Guggenheim fellow and the heir apparent, some say, to Raymond Carver as the pre-eminent short-story writer in America.

He went from full-time custodian to full-time star instructor at the star-studded Iowa Writer's Workshop.

But doggone if he doesn't miss his old job. At least that's how he felt at the moment. Maybe it wasn't the old job exactly, but the old life that surrounded the old job. That life allegedly was simpler and therefore happier.

"Now my life is hell," he said.

IT TAKES a certain temperament to convert every experience into suffering, and Jones shows all the signs. He is ruggedly handsome in a squashed-face, elfin kind of way, morbidly funny and given to far-flung and contradictory digressions. He will reassure you that he doesn't suffer from multiple-personality syndrome. Diabetes, epilepsy, insomnia, yes, yes, yes. Alcoholism, depression, yes, yes. But not multiple personality.

His tone says, I may be messed up, but not THAT messed up.

His eyes can seem startled and blank, as if he'd just turned a corner and witnessed something inexplicable. He doesn't laugh often, but when he does, he gives in to it completely, closing his eyes and throwing back his head, sometimes laughing beyond the situation, as if reveling in a secret joke or like a man who has thrown the cosmic dice and won.

He moves and speaks slowly. Sometimes he slurs his words. That's partly from his years of boxing and also from overlapping ideas trying to get out of his mouth all at once.

The squashed face is also from the boxing. He could look pretty mean if he wanted—with his jutting forehead, block chin, bent-fender nose—but his overall bearing is gentle, almost soft. Even as he recounts twisted tale after twisted tale, one sorry-assed character after another, as he does in his books.

At 5-foot-10, he is 2 inches shorter than he used to be, a result of age and gravity, and, he might add, colossal pressure. That's what success brings, in case, like Jones, you didn't know. When your name is routinely uttered in the same breath as Carver, even Chekhov—that's pressure. Now everything he writes must be great. And there's all the attention, the offers from magazines and publishing houses and movie studios. And the money. Oh, what hell.

"I'm not happy if I don't suffer at least five hours a day," he said. "I have a quota."

He brings to mind that old rhyme: "Two men look out through the same bars, one sees mud, the other stars."

Jones is the guy checking out the mud.

ON THIS DAY, at the high school, Jones literally was spotting dirt. The carpet between the English department and the library was filthy. Stains everywhere. He shook his head in disapproval. It was never like this when he worked here, uh-uh.

He is a returning hero at North Thurston, a concrete-and-glass complex that sits in the middle of a leafy campus at the edge of town. The school was completely rebuilt in 1984, which, as schools go, still qualifies it as new. It's new enough that carpet stains still stand out.

Staff and students greet Jones with respect. The English and history teachers whose wastebaskets he used to empty now are his fans. They attend his readings. And he has a continuing connection to the place: His wife Sally works in the school's library, and his teenage daughter Jennifer is an honor student and cheerleader. Go Rams!

Three of his old janitor pals are still on the payroll. He ran into a couple of them on the tour. "Well if it isn't Satan's lieutenant," one of them said, shaking hands. They caught up and talked about the latest in vacuum cleaners.

It isn't a terrible stretch to draw a parallel between his old job and his new one. The quest was to seek out dirt in the deepest recesses and address it. This was something Jones seemed to come by naturally. His whole apparatus was drawn instinctively to the dark places of life and of the heart, particularly the male heart in its most wretched state. "The whole world," one of his characters says, "is a neurology ward, I guess."

His characters are boxers, grunts, drug addicts, drop-outs, janitors. Inevitably, they are doomed, dying or bewildered. At the very least they are aggrieved. Many are diseased. Others are stuck in existential funks, or, as he says, in "a kind of Bermuda Triangle of hard-ass reality."

You would not read Jones to get cheered up, unless neurosis makes you happy. You might read him to languish in the mud of life, which can be invigorating in its own foul sort of way. You might discover a poignant insight about your own base soul, or your roommate's. Or you might read him strictly for the prose, which leaps up and grabs you by the face like an angry pit bull.

He is working on his first novel, about a whacked-out advertising copywriter who gives up Madison Avenue to do humanitarian work in Africa. Leprosy comes into play, as does a journey into one heart of darkness or another. The story, like his others, is partly autobiographical.

Some 20 years ago, he was fired from an advertising job when, after being asked to write an ad for Jolly Green Giant garden peas, Jones turned in copy that quoted the Green Giant as saying, "These are the best (expletive expletive) peas I ever ate. These are great (expletive) peas."

Jones was told in no uncertain terms the Jolly Green Giant did not talk that way. He eventually threw a typewriter out a window, and somehow soon after ended up on the Dark Continent.

NOW HE WONDERED OUT LOUD how his novel would do. He wanted to consult the I-Ching, which is why at the moment he was headed to the school library. As a custodian, he was in charge of 13 classrooms and the library. Inevitably he spent most of his time in the latter, and not necessarily dusting shelves.

When he wasn't napping in the sound room or reading up on exotic diseases, he was consulting the I-Ching, which is an Asian form of divination in which you ask a question, shake some coins, and then consult the book of I-Ching for an answer.

Jones would ask questions like, "Will my stories ever be published?"

So often the book was right.

More than ever, he became a believer in fate. Things happened for a reason, and not always for the good, but often. There was a reason life allowed him to escape his dysfunctional family and hometown of Aurora, Ill., a reason he was discharged from the Marines in the mid 1960s after suffering a savage beating in the ring at the hands of a boxing champion. All but one of his recon unit was killed in Vietnam, as he almost certainly would have been had he not been discharged.

There was a reason he couldn't hold jobs and drifted from place to place, why he eventually married Sally and settled down in her hometown of Olympia in the mid 1970s and why he worked as a janitor even though he had an English degree from the University of Washington.

The janitor job, it turned out, gave him the freedom to read, a book a day at one point. It also gave him the time to do whatever it is that writers must do in their own heads to be able to write what they were meant to write.

"The Pugilist at Rest" was plucked from the massive slush pile at The New Yorker. Chance. The right editor read it at the right moment. And Thom Jones would never have to push a broom again. That is, unless he wanted to.

Inside the library, Jones knew exactly where the I-Ching sat, on a top shelf in the back. He took it down and reached in his pocket for some coins. He shook them and threw them on a desk like a gambler shooting craps. He opened the book to the right page and started to read. He paced. And then he began to laugh, his mouth open, his head thrown back.

He laughed and laughed.

SEEKING POETIC JUSTICE: A PACIFIST AUTHOR LEADS AN ONLINE ANTIWAR MOVEMENT ROOTED IN LANGUAGE AND IMAGERY

Los Angeles Times, March 3, 2003

AN IRAQ WAR ALL HIS OWN: AN EXEMPLARY SOLDIER GOES ON TRIAL FOR REFUSING TO FIGHT IN A WAR HE CALLS ILLEGAL

Los Angeles Times, February 5, 2007

Introduced by **KIM MURPHY**, who—on both ends of a reporting tour in Moscow and London—managed to precede and succeed Tizon as Seattle Bureau chief of the *Los Angeles Times*

*F*rom the deep forests and blue-collar port towns of the Pacific Northwest, Alex Tizon and his subjects were a world away from the war blazing across Iraq. In these two stories, he traces the far-away conflict's trail of moral outrage and political polarization through the longitudes of the American psyche. In both cases, he manages to paint one of the most divisive political issues of our lifetimes in intimately human terms.

Tizon's stories are almost always built on characters, and here we see two ordinary men wrestling with how to live their moral convictions in a society that does not uniformly share them. One is Sam Hamill, a poet who has been invited by First Lady Laura Bush to join a White House symposium on poetry in America—just as her husband is preparing, on dubious pretenses, an invasion of Iraq. We meet the other, First Lieutenant Ehren Watada, four years later, as he has become the first commissioned officer to face a court-martial for refusing to deploy in that war.

Tizon opens his sketchbook in both cases to deftly show us what they look like, in aspect and manner. I generally tell writers to avoid physical descriptions of their subjects; it most often is a superficial crutch that pretends to open doors but, in fact, imparts nothing *essential to character or story. A Tizon piece can almost always be held up to prove me wrong:*

> *Sitting at his desk at Copper Canyon, Hamill looks like a cowboy, wearing blue jeans and western shirt and vest. He is a trim, compact man with blue eyes that seem simultaneously sleep-deprived and mischievous. His hair is as white as the cigarette butts in the ashtray.*

Tizon weaves through his story the image of a poet, "a craggy white-haired introvert," who's turned back to chain-smoking as a response to the turmoil stirred up with his antiwar poetry; small tidbits of his bleary eyes and gravelly voice help drive home what it's like to have uncorked a genie bottle with his defiance of the war and of one of America's most popular first ladies.

Then, there's Watada:

> *In the middle of the room he stands in stocking feet, wearing baggy fatigues like pajamas, hands on hips. He's deciding where to begin the packing. When all the world seemed chaotic, it made sense to organize. Should he start with his barely mussed chemical suit or his spotless all-weather traction-control camouflage boots?*
>
> *His smooth brown face is boyish and devoted, like a child inspecting his most precious toys.*

Again, the physical image of Watada—the smooth-faced young warrior packing up his prized battle gear because his conscience wouldn't let him use it in this particular war—projects the story line powerfully.

Tizon pivots from these closely observed character studies, in both cases, to capture the wider debate both men represent. He turns the story about Hamill into a meditation on the power of poetry, bringing in the voices of other poets and their verses.

With Watada, the incorporation of the national conversation is more subtle. Instead of taking the easy route of interviewing other

*people for their opinions on the lieutenant's actions, Tizon cap-
tures the debate memorably with two unforgettable images: the two
majors who "accidentally" broke Watada's nose during a football
game and the numerous other soldiers who passed by him anony-
mously with quick signals of encouragement: "the approving nods,
the knowing glances, the subtle remarks about hanging in there
and keeping the chin up."*

*Finally, a word about narrative structure: Tizon grasps this par-
ticularly well in the poetry piece. Instead of laying out Hamill's
life story at the beginning, he parcels it out when needed to drive
the story line. We don't find out that Hamill spent time on the
streets and in jail until Tizon reveals, midway through the piece,
that his day job is teaching writing to convicts. "He knew them
well, because, as he put it, 'I used to be one of them.'" Likewise, we
don't find out until later in the story—as the degree to which this
campaign has been wearing on him becomes apparent—that he
receives stacks of emotional letters and e-mails.*

*Tizon closes with a rumination on poetry, and one can't help
but think that it's a reflection he must often have had about writing
in general in a world that can seem less than attentive:*

> *It's generally accepted that poetry, in this sprint-paced,
> digital age, no longer appeals to the masses as it once did.
> Reading poetry requires contemplation; it is an act of stop-
> ping and reflecting, neither of which, to many Americans,
> holds priority over climbing the corporate ladder or devel-
> oping buns of steel.*

Tizon, and we love him for it, made time for poets.

. . .

SEEKING POETIC JUSTICE: A PACIFIST AUTHOR LEADS AN ONLINE ANTIWAR MOVEMENT ROOTED IN LANGUAGE AND IMAGERY

PORT TOWNSEND, WASH.—The poet needs another cigarette.
He'd worked himself down to eight smokes a day, on pace to quit

before his 60th birthday, but now he's back up to a pack and not sleeping very much besides.

Sam Hamill—author of 13 volumes of poetry, pacifist ex-Marine, Buddhist, craggy white-haired introvert—once had a life he liked. It was lived in private. Then First Lady Laura Bush, in mid-January, invited him to take part in a White House symposium called "Poetry and the American Voice."

Hamill, so opposed to war with Iraq that he trembles with anger when discussing it, says the invitation created in him "a kind of nausea." He ran to the store and bought a carton of Parliaments, then got online and invited a few friends to submit antiwar poems to a new Web site he set up, www.poetsagainstthewar.org.

The collection of poems was to be Hamill's response to the first lady's invitation. But when word got out about the poems, the White House canceled the event. That's when one part of the story ended, and another began: The uprising of poets took on its own life.

Within days, there were 2,000 poems on the site. By the start of February, there were 9,000, and by last week, more than 13,000 and counting. The contributors, some of the most highly esteemed poets in the land, got organized and held antiwar readings coast to coast.

In short, Hamill sent an e-mail and started a movement. He says he had no idea he'd be tapping into such a deep and fiercely coursing vein, and that he'd be reviving the literary debate on whether poets and poetry still have relevance in 21st century America.

The culmination of the e-mail campaign, Hamill says, will take place Wednesday, when he and a group of fellow poets are to present the anthology to select members of Congress. The presentation will be followed by another wave of poetry readings across the country, and then, down the road, the anthology will be culled for a book.

"That will be the end," says Hamill, his voice coarsened by fatigue and smoke. "It will be the period at the end of the paragraph, and then I want to be done with it.

"I want to go back to my life."

THE LIFE to which he'd like to return is spent mostly in seclusion in a room full of books, abiding by some private vow to the poetic word.

He's arranged his home as a bulwark against interruption. His house, built one plank at a time with his own hands, is a two-level cedar cabin, which he shares with his wife, poet and artist Gray Foster. A few dozen feet down a wooded path sits a smaller cabin, his writing hut, where he spends most of his days. Inside the hut is a picture of a daughter, his only child, now a 38-year-old nurse in Vancouver, Canada.

Both house and hut hide in a grove of towering cedars and Douglas firs in a forest just outside this mossy port town at the northeast edge of the Olympic Peninsula. A life farther removed from the rat race would be hard to find.

Some mornings he spends at his other office, four miles down the road at Copper Canyon Press, which operates inside what used to be a blacksmith barn. It's nonprofit, and one of the oldest and most respected of the small poetry presses.

Hamill co-founded the press three decades ago and essentially ran it without pay for nearly 20 years. Nobody gets rich in the business of poetry. Nearly all poets need day jobs. For Hamill, it was teaching poetry to convicts.

For 14 years, in Alaska and Washington prisons, he taught the refinements of the poetic word to thieves, rapists, gang members and murderers. He knew them well, because, as he put it, "I used to be one of them."

His story in brief: battered as a child, homeless at 14, in and out of jail by 15 (for vagrancy and car theft), a street thug and heroin addict for the rest of his teen years. Then he joined the Marines. In the military, a doctor surgically removed some of the most visible of his blue jailhouse tattoos, namely the ones on his knuckles. One tattoo, "MOM," still peeks out from under his shirt cuff.

While stationed in Okinawa, Japan, Hamill became first a Buddhist and then a pacifist, neither of which made the Marines very happy. He squeaked through with an honorable discharge and a changed outlook.

His passion for Japanese and Chinese cultures profoundly affected him, his poems reflecting the spare and precise manner of Asian poetry. His topics alternate between the mystical and the mundane, the political and the self-deprecating.[1]

SITTING AT HIS DESK at Copper Canyon, Hamill looks like a cowboy, wearing blue jeans and western shirt and vest. He is a trim, compact man with blue eyes that seem simultaneously sleep-deprived and mischievous. His hair is as white as the cigarette butts in the ashtray.

"This is what it's become," he says, swiveling his chair and gesturing at three knee-high stacks of unopened mail. "I get up in the morning and there're 200 e-mails at home, another 120 at work, a stack of phone messages, the answering machine, and this."

He says he's been functioning on three hours of sleep a night.

Hamill and his colleagues have been roundly criticized by pundits and other poets for mixing poetry and politics, for grandstanding and, as one critic put it, "simply making noise." Critics say the first lady, a former librarian, was merely following her agenda of promoting literature and the arts, and look how rudely those poets responded. (The White House offered no explanation for canceling the event.)

By coincidence, the White House symposium that spurred the movement was also to be the occasion of introducing Dana Gioia, new chairman of the National Endowment for the Arts. Gioia, who lives in Sonoma County, is a literary critic and poet of some renown, though he is probably best known among fellow poets for his widely circulated 1992 book, "Can Poetry Matter?"

Gioia's answer was "no," at least not in the current state of American poetry, a world he describes as insular, esoteric and self-

---

1. A Sam Hamill poem originally followed this text.

marginalizing, populated by elitist literary snobs writing for other elitist literary snobs. Writing poetry for political purposes, some critics say, is just another way to further alienate the public.

"I don't feel poetry should be merely an expression of opinion. I cannot write a poem to order even if the order is a strong one," says John Hollander, author of 17 books of poetry and a professor at Yale University. "When asked to make a political statement, I say, 'As a citizen, I will; but as a poet, I will not.'

"My poetry is not a citizen of the United States. I am."

Maybe it's the Zen Buddhist ideal of living a single un-segmented life that compels Hamill to not separate his political views from his poetic expression. Hamill says the foremost reason for his protest against the war is his belief that killing is morally wrong, a belief that crystallized while he was in Japan. The documented horrors of the atomic bombs dropped on Hiroshima and Nagasaki, he says, left a potent impression on him.

Many of the most influential poets of the day have not only supported Hamill, but applauded him.

Philip Levine, a Pulitzer Prize winner in 1995, says if Hamill had not rallied other poets against the war, Levine himself would have. Levine was invited to the same symposium and was preparing to decline and make his own protest statement.

"We're talking about killing thousands of people, destroying a country and causing the entire Muslim population of the world to rise up," Levine says. "Of course we need to speak up, and poets have always spoken up. It's a long and powerful tradition."

As modern examples, poets Adrienne Rich, Susan Griffin and Robin Morgan became leaders in the feminist movement. Poet Robert Lowell, another Pulitzer recipient, boycotted a similar White House event to protest the Vietnam War and helped lead the 1967 march on the Pentagon. Norman Mailer, though primarily a novelist, also considers himself a philosopher-poet obligated to comment on the most vital issues of the day.

It's generally accepted that poetry, in this sprint-paced, digital age, no longer appeals to the masses as it once did. Reading poetry requires contemplation; it is an act of stopping and reflecting, neither of which, to many Americans, holds priority over climbing the corporate ladder or developing buns of steel.

But poetry still has a following—small, scattered and diverse. According to Poets House, a poetry archive in New York City, there were from 1,300 to 1,600 poetry titles published in the United States last year.

"Poets affect society in a much greater way than, say, people who build buildings," says Rep. Jim McDermott, a Democrat from Washington and a reader of poetry. Poets, he says, affect society indirectly, by instilling readers with ideas and images, and inspiring them to act, the notion behind Percy Bysshe Shelley's statement that "poets are the unacknowledged legislators of the world."

McDermott and Rep. Marcy Kaptur (D-Ohio) have made arrangements to officially receive Hamill and his 13,000-poem anthology. The two legislators, who hope to be joined by some of their colleagues in Congress, plan to enter some of the poems into the congressional record.

HAMILL'S ADVENTURE involves much irony, of course. All stories involving poets must have irony. The most obvious one has to do with why so much attention has been paid to protesting poets, and it's because—even Hamill wouldn't dispute this—of Laura Bush's invitation. Without the Bush name attached to the story line, www.poetsagainstthewar.org would be just another obscure lefty Web site.

The other irony has to do with the Internet, which even poets find mesmerizing and magical. Such a compilation would not have been possible in such a tiny span without the Internet, which was most comprehensively developed by the military. It would have been difficult to solicit such quick responses, and quick works of art, from such a wide range of literary luminaries.

The list of Pulitzer contributors includes W.S. Merwin, Carolyn Kizer, Galway Kinnell and Maxine Kumin. Former U.S. poet laureates include Rita Dove, Stanley Kunitz and Robert Pinsky.

Hamill himself is a former Guggenheim fellow.

"I just sent a letter to a few friends, and it turns out I have 13,000 friends, most of them I've never met," Hamill says, his voice scraping the air. "I didn't set out to start a movement. I certainly didn't set out to become the leader."

Now Hamill finds himself at the head of something that makes him cringe—a bureaucracy. An organization with layers. With memos and meetings. He oversees 25 editors across the country who are helping him edit the online poems. Those editors have sub-editors. He has three "spokespersons" in Washington, D.C. He must deal with computer and Web site experts, with publishers, critics.

Hamill swears a lot, and when talking about bureaucracy, the four-letter words spew out.

Amid it all, the sweetest irony is that Hamill is the happiest unhappy man in Port Townsend. Poets can do that—claim to feel two contradictory things at once. He's hated the hubbub of the last six weeks, but, he says, he's been "heartened" by the passion of his fellow poets. Levine says Hamill has also thoroughly enjoyed "goosing" the people in D.C.

Once it's all over, when the package has been delivered, Hamill says, it'll be time to push the mute button on all the noise, to slowly taper down his "to do" list until all that's left is reading, writing and editing poetry. He might sleep in now and then, and maybe he can quit smoking all over again.

THIS STORY RAN *with several excerpts of poems that appeared on www.poetsagainstthe war.org.*[2] *Among them was this from Hamill:*

> *I have not been to Jerusalem,*
> *but Shirley talks about the bombs.*
> *I have no god, but have seen the children praying*
> *for it to stop. They pray to different gods.*
> *The news is all old news again, repeated*

---

2. Permission for use of the Sam Hamill poem from www.poetsagainst thewar.org was granted by the Sam Hamill Estate.

like a bad habit, cheap tobacco, the social lie.
The children have seen so much death
that death means nothing to them now.
They wait in line for bread.
They wait in line for water.
Their eyes are black moons reflecting emptiness.
We've seen them a thousand times.
Soon, the President will speak.
He will have something to say about bombs
and freedom and our way of life.
I will turn the tv off. I always do.
Because I can't bear to look
at the monuments in his eyes.

. . .

AN IRAQ WAR ALL HIS OWN: AN EXEMPLARY SOLDIER GOES ON TRIAL FOR REFUSING TO FIGHT IN A WAR HE CALLS ILLEGAL

OLYMPIA, WASH.—The soldier stands in his living room eyeing all the cool soldier stuff he never got to use in a real fight. Like the helmet with not a single ding and the sleek body armor with not a scuff. The gear piles high on the carpet.

First Lt. Ehren Watada is giving it all back and, out of courtesy, packing it up. The Army had treated him with the utmost respect until the moment it decided to court-martial him. It was nothing personal. The Army does what it has to do.

Just as Watada himself did what he felt he had to do seven months ago when he became the first—and only—commissioned officer in the United States to publicly refuse deployment to Iraq.

His conscience, he said, had overtaken him. He told the world what he had privately told his superiors months earlier: that he believed the war was illegal and immoral, and he would play no role in it.

Watada tried to resign; the Army respectfully denied him. He said he was willing to fight in Afghanistan; the Army refused him again—a soldier can't pick and choose where he fights. As his unit shipped off to Iraq, Watada stayed to face the consequences.

Thousands of GIs have gone AWOL or voiced opposition to the Iraq war, but when an officer says he won't go, the whole military machine must take note. It means dissent has crept up the chain of command, potentially undermining the war effort.

The Army felt compelled to respond forcefully, charging Watada, 28, with one count of failure to deploy and four (later reduced to two) counts of "conduct unbecoming" for making public statements against the war and against the Bush administration. His court-martial begins today at Ft. Lewis, 15 miles north of here.

Watada ponders the prospect of spending four years in military prison, and he muses on his spiral from exemplary military man to reviled antiwar poster boy.

"Life has been . . ." He laughs nervously and shakes his head, searching for words. "A little abnormal."

His living room, like the rest of the apartment complex, feels boxy and new and unmistakably inexpensive—made for function rather than form. A balcony looks out at a parking lot crowded with pickups and SUVs.

In the middle of the room he stands in stocking feet, wearing baggy fatigues like pajamas, hands on hips. He's deciding where to begin the packing. When all the world seemed chaotic, it made sense to organize. Should he start with his barely mussed chemical suit or his spotless all-weather traction-control camouflage boots?

His smooth brown face is boyish and devoted, like a child inspecting his most precious toys. He's not a small man, but not big either. Certainly not as big as the Rushmore-sized symbol he's become to the antiwar movement, which hails him as nothing less than an American hero.

But he also bears no sign of the sniveling qualities ascribed him by pro-war groups that have branded him a coward. One syndicated columnist posted Watada's Army photo on her website with the caption "The face of a deserter."

With everyone judging him, he wants to make one thing clear. "I'm not afraid to fight," he says. "I'm not a pacifist. If our country needed defending, I'd be the first one to pick up a rifle. But I won't be part of a war that I believe is criminal."

Watada calls himself "an ordinary American" and a patriot who unwittingly found himself in a moral dilemma he could never have imagined when he first put on a uniform 18 years ago. That's when the story begins, according to his mother, Carolyn Ho, a high school counselor in Honolulu.

IT ALL STARTED because she thought Cub Scout uniforms were cute.

The uniforms also represented wholesome activity. Ho and her then-husband, Bob Watada, wanted to keep their two young sons out of the malls and out of trouble. Ehren was the thoughtful one; his older brother, Lorin, the rambunctious one.

Ehren thrived on the order and discipline, and the little rewards that marked one's ascension in the scouting ranks. "He was the sort who studied for every merit badge possible," Ho says.

Thus Watada's kinship with the uniformed life was born. He went from Cub to Boy to Eagle Scout, and he had an inkling as early as 15 that he would end up in the armed forces.

As an Eagle Scout, he got the idea of carving out a hiking trail on a hillside abutting a neighborhood park in Honolulu.

Neighbors privately snickered. Sure, kid. Go ahead. Good luck.

Ho says she still beams whenever she drives past the park today and she spots the trail zigzagging up the hill. That's my son's work, she thinks. It took many months. She'd never doubt his resolve again.

Ho tells one other story. At Kalani High School, where Watada was a four-sport athlete, he reported a fellow football player who had been stealing money from the cafeteria coffer. "He risked ostracism [as a snitch] in a very small, tight-knit community," Ho says. "But he's like that, very principled."

Ho is calling from a hotel in Indiana. Her ex-husband, Bob, is in a hotel in Washington, D.C. Both parents have spent the last six months speaking at schools and churches across the nation, telling their son's story and lobbying the government to acquit him.

The parents shudder at the thought of their son behind bars. Invariably, both Ho and Bob Watada entertain fleeting misgivings: Maybe joining Cub Scouts was a mistake. Maybe, Bob Watada says, he should have tried harder to persuade his son to simply go to Iraq and "lie low."

Lying low is better than prison.

But there's a counterpart to this parental protectiveness.

Rebecca Davis, head of a Maine-based group called Military Families Voice of Victory, prays every day for her son, Stuart, who is serving in Iraq. Davis has publicly called Watada a traitor. "What he's done," she says, "is embolden an enemy who is aiming for my son's head."

WATADA, KNEELING ON THE CARPET with an arm buried deep in an olive-green duffel, explains his epiphany about the war in Iraq. It was the slo-mo kind, not the brilliant flash of lightning in the night.

The way he tells it, the arc of his realization somewhat followed that of many Americans. That is, he believed at the beginning but grew disillusioned as the justifications for the war proved false and the strategy flawed.

In 2003, after graduating near the top of his class at Hawaii Pacific University, he walked into a recruiting station in Honolulu and hopscotched from Officer Candidate School to his first tour of duty in Korea, where his superiors rated him exemplary.

His battalion commander, whom Watada won't name so as not to drag him into his predicament, spoke long and often of the paramount importance of preparation.

"He told us, 'If you don't know all there is to know about your mission, you're failing yourself and you're failing your soldiers,'" Watada says, still kneeling. He folds his hands in front of him now and looks vaguely like someone pleading or about to propose. "I took the lesson to heart."

So when he was reassigned to Ft. Lewis in early 2005 in anticipation of deploying to Iraq, he did his job: He got to know everything there was to know about Iraq. He spent nights online, read books, talked to combat veterans, devoured media reports.

At the end of 2005, he was convinced that the Bush administration had purposefully manipulated intelligence to justify the invasion and that the congressional approval of the war therefore was based on lies.

He said he was so anguished by his conclusion and the knowledge that he would soon be "participating in the madness" that he grew deeply depressed. In December 2005, he sought guidance from a chaplain and a mental-health counselor. Neither helped. He considered filing for conscientious objector status but couldn't in good conscience, he says, because he does not oppose bearing arms.

"I was in this situation where I knew something was wrong," he says, still on his knees, "but I was being forced to do it anyway. It felt like I was in an invisible prison of my own making. It's a terrible place to be."

Then it occurred to him: He'd rather risk the other kind of prison. It would be difficult but ultimately easier to live with. In January 2006, he submitted a letter of resignation, he was refused, and the process rolled inexorably to where it is today.

The Army could have chosen to accept Watada's resignation. Court-martialing him, however, sends a clear message to other officers thinking about defying orders to deploy. During a preliminary hearing in August, Army prosecutor Capt. Dan Kuecker called Watada's actions "dishonorable" and "disgraceful."

For his part, Watada doesn't blame the Army as much as he blames the administration. The Army does what it must to function. Military culture has always presumed that individuals lose certain kinds of freedom when joining the armed forces.

"The idea is when you put on a uniform, you put your personal opinions to the side," says Kathleen Duignan, executive director of the National Institute of Military Justice in Washington,

D.C. A military could not be effective if soldiers had the option to choose which wars to fight and which to forgo.

Duignan says the best-known case that parallels Watada's occurred in 1965 during the Vietnam War, when 2nd Lt. Henry Howe was caught participating in an antiwar demonstration. The Army court-martialed Howe and sentenced him to two years of hard labor.

Watada's unit deployed to Iraq last summer. He has been doing administrative work ever since, barred from traveling farther than 250 miles from Ft. Lewis. His life settled into a workaday routine—going to work, coming home to his little apartment and wondering what the future holds.

Standing up, crossing his arms as if in defiance, he says he believes history will absolve him no matter what happens in court this week.

At the base, there have been no blatant acts of hostility. "But, yes," Watada says, "you can feel the seething just underneath."

During what was supposed to be a casual football scrimmage among officers late last year, two majors "accidentally" broke Watada's nose. One major shoved, the other smacked. Watada for weeks walked around with two black eyes, a crooked beak and a sneaking hunch it was no accident.

But what encourages him is how much quiet support he receives from individual soldiers. The support, he says, isn't showy. "Nobody wants any part of me officially," he says, laughing that nervous laugh again. There are the approving nods, the knowing glances, the subtle remarks about hanging in there and keeping the chin up.

"It happens almost every day," Watada says. And it makes him think that maybe, just maybe, a whole lot of other uniformed souls feel the same way he does and just haven't figured out a way to say so.

IN THE LAND OF MISSING PERSONS

Introduced by **Denise Kersten Wills**,
features editor at *The Atlantic* magazine

*W*hen I e-mailed Alex to tell him that we wanted to accept this
story, his first for The Atlantic, I heard back within minutes.
*He was in the hospital. He had just come out of knee-replacement
surgery. He was still in a drugged post-op haze. "If you don't mind
this," he wrote, "I will call you right now."*

*That was Alex. He had a boundless, contagious enthusiasm,
and he was tireless in his reporting, winning the trust of ordinary
people and telling their stories with remarkable depth and clarity.
Alex was an editor's dream: a wonderful stylist, a genius at drawing the emotion out of a scene, a humble and generous writer who
never let his ego interfere with his work.*

*"In the Land of Missing Persons" was more than a decade in
the making—a testament to the deep connections Alex was able to
develop with his subjects. The story centers on two men, Rick Hills
and Richard Bennett, whose families were brought together by a
tragic twist of fate after both disappeared in the Alaskan wilderness.*

*Alex was there when the families met for the first time, and his
patient, empathetic approach allowed him to depict the missing
men in the kind of detail that suggests a long period of observation.
That he never met either of them is almost impossible to believe.*

■　■　■

THEY FOUND what was left of him in the spring of 2014. Firefighters battling a huge blaze on Alaska's Kenai Peninsula first
spotted a boot in the dirt. Then they noticed some bones scattered across a wide grassy area. Fire crews in Alaska are used to

seeing the bones of moose, caribou, bears, and other large crea-
tures that live and die in these woods. So it wasn't until crew
members found a human skull that they stopped to consider that
the pieces might go together. The skull was resting on its side, the
face angled toward the ground. A few blackened molars clung to
the upper jaw. The lower jaw was missing.

The Alaska State Troopers arrived by helicopter and salvaged
what they could. "The bones were close to being ash," Lieutenant
Kat Shuey later recalled. "They weren't quite to the point where if
you touched them they would disintegrate, but close."

The remains were spread across an area about 60 yards in di-
ameter, presumably the work of scavenging animals. Also found
at the site were three hunting knives, two quarters, two metal
buttons, a zipper, and part of a Samsung mobile phone. All of
the items were charred to varying degrees, like most everything
else in the path of the Funny River Fire, which burned nearly
200,000 acres in the western lowlands of the Kenai Peninsula, a
remote corner of this remote part of the world, a place one local
described as "the *middle* of the middle of nowhere."

No one knew at the time that the Funny River bones would
set in motion a series of other discoveries, adding a surreal twist
to a long and disjointed tale of people lost and found and lost
again, and in the process reminding everyone involved of their
smallness in this vast land.

Troopers guessed that the bones were those of an adult male,
based on the size and style of the boot and the fact that in these
circumstances, the deceased is usually a man. But the condition
of the bones made determining the cause of death impossible.
The man may have gotten lost and frozen to death. He could
have tumbled down one of several steep embankments nearby
and broken his neck. He could have run into the wrong bear;
as many as 4,000 of them roam the peninsula, including some
of the largest brown bears on the planet. He might have eaten
poison berries, by accident or by design—the location was ideal
for someone who wanted to vanish, and Alaska is famous for at-
tracting dropouts, runaways, and end-of-the-roaders who wish to

conduct a life, and sometimes a death, in isolation. There were, to borrow one trooper's phrase, a great number of "equally plausible alternative inferences."

Within hours, news of the discovery spread from the firefighters' camps to the small communities along the Sterling Highway, the road that transects the peninsula. In the town of Soldotna, about 20 miles from where the bones were found, Dolly Hills got a call from one of her granddaughters. The granddaughter was upset. Why hadn't the police told them about the bones? Later, Dolly began to hear from people around town. They wondered the same thing that Lieutenant Shuey wondered aloud at headquarters, a question Dolly wasn't prepared to entertain quite yet. She listened and mostly kept silent. In private, though, she could think of nothing else: *Could it be Rick?*

When I first met Dolly, in January of 2005, her son Richard Thomas Hills had been missing for almost a year. I was working on a story about the phenomenon in Alaska of ordinary people disappearing while doing ordinary things. In Anchorage, the statewide coordinator of search-and-rescue at the time, Lieutenant Craig Macdonald, had told me about some recent cases, including that of Rick Hills. He described the case as tragic for the family but typical of what troopers dealt with almost every day. More than 3,000 people had been reported missing the previous year in Alaska, a state with a population smaller than San Francisco's.

Curious to know what Macdonald meant by "typical," I flew south to the Kenai, a peninsula shaped like the craggy profile of a T. rex's head, extending 150 miles southwest into the Gulf of Alaska. Glacier-topped mountains spread across the eastern and southern parts of the peninsula; marshy lowlands cover much of the rest. From the air, it was easy to see why Alaska attracts certain kinds of people—not just loners and misfits but explorers and adventurers as well, anyone drawn to wild, wide-open spaces.

Soldotna, a fishing town of about 4,000 people, sits along the Kenai River in the western lowlands. I was met there by Dolly

Hills and Heidi Metteer, Rick's longtime partner. Heidi and Rick had two children together, and he had also been raising her eldest, a daughter from a previous relationship, as his own.

Dolly was 53, petite and gregarious, with short black hair, glasses, and an angular face. She had a high, lilting voice that sounded cheerful even when she wasn't. Heidi was 33, tall and robust and dressed for the outdoors, but with a soft manner that seemed to belong inside. Heidi worked at a coffee shop; Dolly helped her husband, an electrician, run his business.

Dolly introduced Heidi as "my daughter," and I would come to know the two women as a unit. Dolly was the talker, the instigator who moved things along. Heidi was the thoughtful one, more apt to listen and absorb. Dolly seemed to rely on Heidi for steadiness, Heidi on Dolly for uplift.

"Praying 24/7," Dolly told me, was the only way she "didn't just lose it." She said she'd been reciting the Lord's Prayer silently, over and over, since getting up that morning. "I don't want to come across as super-religious," she added. "I swear now and then. And I like beer."

I spent two days with them, going over the investigation, discussing theories, and retracing Rick's last known movements. On February 24, 2004, he had been home from an oil-rig job for just a few days when he left Soldotna in his red Dodge truck to pick up a paycheck in Anchorage, about 150 miles away. The company confirmed that Rick had gotten his check that day, but his truck was found two days later, plowed into a snowbank in the town of Sterling, just 15 miles from home. The keys were in the ignition and his driver's license was on the front seat. In the center console was $292.

Rick's tracks in the snow—right foot dragging, as if he'd injured his leg—led into the woods. After about a quarter mile, he'd come upon a house and walked up to the back porch, perhaps hoping to find help. Then he'd wandered onto an abandoned airstrip, and there his footprints ended. Search dogs lost his scent, as if Rick had been plucked from the snow and lifted straight into the air. He was 35 years old.

Dolly and Heidi ruled out suicide: Rick had never shown any inclination, and they didn't believe he would abandon the children, who were 5, 9, and 13 at the time. He adored them; he had nicknames for each of them and took them fishing every chance he got. A couple of months before he disappeared, Rick made a secret trip to Anchorage to buy Christmas presents for the kids and then drove to a friend's house to wrap them, coming home with an armful of ribboned gift boxes. "It made him happy to see the kids so tickled," Dolly said.

On the day he left home for the last time, Rick had asked two of the kids whether they wanted to come with him. A man planning to kill himself wouldn't have done that. Heidi and Dolly also couldn't accept that he might have gotten lost and succumbed to the elements. "He spent a lot of time in these woods," Dolly said. "He knew them."

The two women feared that Rick might have been a victim of foul play. Devoted as he was to his kids, he had a wild streak. He liked to get high on cocaine or pills and then go out drinking all night, and he ran with a crowd of men and women who had been in and out of jail. For the sake of his family, Rick had tried many times to quit partying, only to be drawn back in. "But he would never not come home," Heidi said.

"Or call home, at least," Dolly added. "Even when he was impaired, he never failed to call."

After the police stopped searching, Dolly and Heidi kept the case alive. Dolly's husband, Tom, helped but mostly kept busy with work. The two women plastered the communities along the Sterling Highway with missing-person posters. They interviewed friends and acquaintances police had overlooked. Dolly recruited snowmobilers and pilots to go over the search area again and again. She even consulted psychics.

One, a British woman who lived in Anchorage, told Dolly that two men had been nearby as Rick was dying, that they had rifled through his coat for drugs and then left, and that Rick had frozen to death. The psychic seemed to intuit aspects of Rick's disappearance that matched what police had told Dolly and Heidi.

The two women came to believe she was closer to the truth about what had happened to Rick than anyone else, certainly closer than the Alaska State Troopers. She said it would be 10 years before they found Rick.

"Ten years?," Dolly replied. "We can't wait that long."

The first year was particularly hard on Dolly; she essentially stopped eating, and by the time I met her she'd dwindled to about 100 pounds. In the middle of telling me about one of their searches for Rick's body, she lost her train of thought and fell silent, then shook her head, as if trying to dispel some unpleasant notion. "If a truck came along and ran me over, I wouldn't care," she said under her breath.

I'd covered many stories of loss, but Dolly and Heidi's seemed especially cruel because it had no foreseeable end. They knew Rick was likely dead, but without his body, they couldn't rule out the possibility that he was somehow still alive, perhaps injured or in pain, or even held against his will. When they let their minds go there, the possibilities multiplied, became endless. They tried to block those thoughts, but they never went away completely.

By the end of my visit, I came to believe that whatever had happened to Rick couldn't have involved more prolonged suffering than what Dolly and Heidi were going through. Yet the two women would keep searching for the next 10 years. As I left to catch my flight home, they were bent over a map on the dining-room table at Dolly's house, discussing the logistics of dragging the Kenai River.

"It's just a couple guys in a boat," I heard Dolly say. "They drop a long pole with a big hook in the water, and the boat goes back and forth. The hook grabs onto whatever's on the bottom."

The e-mail appeared in my inbox in September 2014. In the years since my visit to Soldotna, I'd thought of Dolly and Heidi whenever I ran across stories of people who had disappeared. There was something about them that stayed with me, growing more vivid as the years passed and I suffered losses of my own. The image of two women studying a map, a single light overhead, spoke to me of an inner toughness rising to the occasion. A resilience equal to the worst thing that can happen.

Now they wanted me to call.

"You're not going to believe it," Dolly told me. "I hope you're sitting."

"We found him," Heidi said.

She and Dolly took turns filling me in. I'd never heard of the Funny River, much less the fire that had ravaged the Kenai. They told me a body had been found, and that its DNA had been tested.

"It wasn't Rick," Heidi said.

"It wasn't Rick," I repeated. "Who was it?"

For the next hour, Dolly and Heidi described a series of events that I could barely follow. They were still piecing the narrative together themselves. The three of us would wind up having regular phone conversations, trying to make sense of what had happened.

Four months later, in January of 2015, I flew back to the Kenai Peninsula. I arrived 10 years to the month after my first trip and found Soldotna exactly as I remembered it: a gritty little village trying to be a town, drab in its winter coat of month-old snow and ice. Dolly and Heidi had obtained a thick stack of official case files, many of them marked privileged. Among a hodgepodge of field reports, lab results, correspondence, handwritten notes, and transcribed witness accounts dating back to 2004 was a two-page letter from the director of the Alaska State Troopers, Colonel James Cockrell, dated August 28, 2014.

The letter had been hand-delivered by Captain Andy Greenstreet, the commander of the detachment that covers the Kenai. He'd knocked on the front door of the Hillses' tidy rambler on a Thursday, around 10:30 in the morning. Only Dolly was home. She called Tom and Heidi and told them to come to the house. When everyone was settled around the dining-room table, the captain started reading.

> Dear Mr. & Mrs. Hills:
>
>   I begin this letter knowing full well that mere words on a page cannot adequately express the magnitude of apology

which you and your family are due based upon errors made by the Alaska State Troopers. A failure on our part has created a circumstance which will undoubtedly bring you and your family a great deal of sorrow during the grieving process and leave you with more questions than answers.

Halfway through, Heidi interrupted him.

"Are you kidding me?" she said, glaring.

"Ten years," Dolly muttered.

"Are you *fucking kidding me?*," Heidi said.

Captain Greenstreet paused without looking up from the letter. He let Heidi's question hang in the air. "I felt for them," he told me later. He was relatively new to his post, and hadn't been involved in the investigation. He was just the messenger. By the time he finished, Dolly and Heidi were weeping.

"Ten years," Dolly repeated. It was just as the psychic had predicted.

That same morning, in Lake Havasu City, Arizona, Lieutenant Kat Shuey read an almost identical letter to a man named Leon Bennett. He was home alone that day; his wife, Bette, was sick and being cared for by relatives in Washington State. The Hillses and Bennetts hadn't known of each other's existence, but now their lives were inextricably linked, the peace of one family coming at the expense of the other's. Delivery of the letters had been coordinated so that they would get the news at roughly the same time.

"I didn't know what to do," Leon Bennett told me, recalling the days and weeks after Lieutenant Shuey showed up at his house. In early 2015, I traveled to Lake Havasu City to meet the other family that had gotten a knock on its door the previous August. Leon sat with his elbows propped on a small table, his hands clasped as if in prayer. He spoke slowly, his voice like gravel. "How could this happen?"

A retired contractor in his early 70s, Leon is a compact, sturdily built man, naturally reserved but with a lot on his mind. Bette

Bennett was in the last stages of a terminal lung disease. She was at home when I visited, only partially lucid, so I spent two days with Leon at the house of his sister, Jane Potter, who lives down the street. Jane and her husband, Leroy, are snowbirds, Alaskan residents who winter in the Southwest.

The Bennetts' only son went missing from his home on the Kenai Peninsula in 2005. His name was Richard too. He and Rick Hills must have crossed paths many times—at the Safeway and the hardware store, at gas stations and stoplights—given that they lived only a few miles apart along the same highway. But they traveled in different circles, and no evidence exists to suggest they knew each other.

Richard Bennett's family described him as a boy of few words who grew into a man of even fewer words. When he did interact with people, he was soft-spoken and kind, especially to his young nieces and nephews; at family get-togethers they would listen in rapt silence as he read children's books aloud—the only time many of them heard him speak at length. One of his neighbors in Alaska told me that Richard would occasionally come over for a beer, but wouldn't come in the house. He preferred to stay outside, on the front steps.

Richard was most comfortable in the wilderness. He'd fished and hunted since he was a child. One of Leon's favorite pictures is of Richard at age 5, wearing fishing boots given to him by his grandfather. The boots are too big; the tops reach all the way to his crotch. The boy is grinning from ear to ear. "For a long time, he never took them off," Leon told me. "He slept in those things."

In 2005, Richard was 39 and living alone in a trailer on the outskirts of Sterling, a short walk from the Kenai River and half a mile from the spot where Rick Hills's red Dodge truck had been found the previous year. I'd walked right past Richard Bennett's trailer when I retraced Rick's last steps, and Richard had probably been home. For several years, he'd struggled to find steady work. He did auto-body repair, but so did a lot of other people on the Kenai.

In August of that year, Jane and Leroy stopped by Richard's

trailer. They lived less than a mile away and hadn't heard from him for a while. They were startled to find the trailer completely cleaned out. Jane called Leon, who was living in Bremerton, Washington; he flew to the Kenai the next day. The three of them went to Richard's place and looked around in silence. Richard's belongings had been moved into a shed. Several large Rubbermaid bins were each labeled with the name of a friend or relative. A few were marked for Jane, with whom Richard had always been close. Inside she found household items: coils of rope, a few tools, frying pans, spatulas, mismatched bowls. "They were things he knew we could use," Jane told me. On a shelf were the titles to two old pickups, which Richard had signed over to her.

"If you would've told me 'suicide,' I would have said you were full of crap," Jane said. "Richard wouldn't *do that*. But seeing all his things packed up and labeled, the trucks signed over, it looked like he got his affairs in order."

Nothing was certain, however. Leon, Jane, and Leroy reported Richard missing to the Alaska State Troopers, noting that they hadn't found any of Richard's camping gear—his tent, sleeping bag, and mess kit—on the property, and that some of his guns were missing too. They learned that no one had seen Richard in several months and that just before Memorial Day weekend, he'd withdrawn his last $10 from an ATM in Soldotna.

Richard's closest neighbors, Frank and Nancy Kufel, retirees who lived down the road, appeared to be the last people who'd had contact with him. Nancy said that Richard had come over in March or April to use their fax machine to send out job applications, and that he had seemed despondent about his prospects. In mid-May, the Kufels noticed he was burning a lot of stuff in a large metal barrel. That's how people in these parts dispose of garbage, but this seemed far more than the usual amount. Then in June, the Kufels noticed what they described as "a tremendous amount of bird activity" in the woods across the street from Richard's trailer. Every seasoned Alaskan knows that a large number of ravens and eagles circling in one area means a carcass below, but

Frank and Nancy assumed it was a moose or a caribou or some other large animal.

The morning after they talked to the Kufels, Leon, Jane, and Leroy went into those woods, a dense forest of spruce, alder, and birch. They proceeded slowly, scanning their eyes over everything. After almost four hours, Jane entered a meadow and peered into a small, shaded clearing. Off to one side, next to a rotting log, something caught her eye. Jane felt her heart pound. "You guys better look at this," she said. The men rushed over, and the three stood in silence. It was a human skeleton, minus a head.

"It was just lying there on the ground, kind of turned on its side, legs stretched out," Jane later told me. "First thing I noticed, it had Levi's on. Richard always wore Levi's. Under the Levi's, blue sweats. Richard always wore blue sweats."

Leon can barely talk about the scene now, but at the time, he kept his emotions in check. He looked at the skeleton and thought it seemed about the right size. He felt the urge to touch it. He leaned down and gently turned the torso "to make sure it was what it looked like," he told me. "When my hand touched, I thought, *That's him.*"

The Alaska State Troopers came to the same conclusion. The skeleton was found about 300 yards from Richard's trailer. The accounts of Richard's state of mind, the approximate height of the skeleton, the jeans and sweatpants—they all added up.

Investigators sent a bone sample along with a swab of Bette Bennett's saliva to a Texas lab for DNA analysis, to confirm that the remains were indeed Richard's. But the lab warned that the test could take up to 18 months, and the Bennetts wanted to bury their son. They called the medical examiner's office several times, asking when the remains could be released. Both the medical examiner and the State Troopers were reluctant to declare the remains Richard Bennett's without DNA confirmation.

What finally tipped the scales for the investigators seems to have been the skeleton's right leg, which showed the markings of an old injury. Richard had fractured his shin and calf bones in a

1980 motorcycle accident. Investigators from the medical examiner's office tracked down the X-rays at Providence Alaska Medical Center in Anchorage and gave them to two forensic anthropologists. The anthropologists found them "consistent" with the markings on the skeleton. Robert Hunter, the lead investigator on the case, received the anthropologists' findings in March 2006 and discussed them with a superior. "We decided that with the information discovered during the investigation that it is reasonable to believe the human remains are that of Richard Bennett," he wrote in an official report on March 28.

The medical examiner's office released the remains, and the Bennetts had them cremated. On June 23, 2006, the family held a memorial in Anchorage. The next day, a small group hiked up a grassy hillside overlooking Lower Summit Lake, one of Richard's favorite places to hunt. Bette was still healthy enough to make the 20-minute hike from the highway to a picturesque clearing between two large birch trees. A high-school friend of Richard's, Harold "Hap" Pierce, dug a hole and buried the urn. Jane placed a wreath on the freshly turned soil. Under a blazing sun, Leon said a short prayer and bid farewell to his son.

For Leon, Bette, and Richard's two sisters, the ceremony marked the end of a nightmarish year. They could begin to move on. Jane felt relief too, but something nagged at her.

"There was closure in the sense that the family said goodbye and *maybe* he was laid to rest," she told me. "I still couldn't believe he would take his own life. I guess if he did it, he did it. But in the back of my mind, there were still questions."

"Like what?," I asked.

"Questions like 'Was that really him?'"

"Errors were made."

Lieutenant Kat Shuey says it with the practiced detachment of a 28-year police veteran. She isn't the one who made the errors. She's the one who uncovered them, and felt honor-bound to deliver the news face-to-face. Shuey spent 14 years as a trooper in the field. Now she's the deputy commander of the Alaska Bureau of

Investigation, a special unit within the Alaska State Troopers that handles, among other things, missing persons. Last year, 2,295 people were reported missing in the state. Many were runaways who eventually returned home, but some were people who will never be seen again.

"Families ask, 'How come you can't find our son? How come you can't find my husband?,'" Shuey told me. She understands why they ask. But, she said, "sometimes I think they forget how big Alaska is." Between the westernmost tip of the Aleutian Islands and the eastern edge of the Alaska Panhandle—a span roughly equal to the distance from California to Florida—a total of 1,332 law-enforcement officers keep the peace. About a third work in and around Anchorage, the only Alaskan community that can pass as a city. A few hundred more patrol towns and villages, mere flecks in the landscape. The rest of Alaska is policed by fewer than 400 troopers.

When someone goes missing in Alaska, search areas can be as large as entire states in the Lower 48, and considerably more treacherous. Alaska encompasses 39 mountain ranges, 12,000 rivers, 100,000 glaciers, and 3 million lakes. The mudflats can be like quicksand; ice and snow can erase a person's last traces. Landslides, avalanches, fissuring glaciers, overflowing rivers, and collapsing riverbanks all make travel unpredictable at best. Everyone I met there seemed to know of people still missing or "unfound." Dolly Hills herself lost a 13-year-old brother, William, in 1962. He was presumed drowned, but his body was never recovered.

In June 2014, soon after the discovery of the Funny River bones, Shuey asked for a list of people in the area who'd gone missing in recent years. At the top of the list were Rick Hills and Richard Bennett, whose last known locations were close together and only about three miles from the Funny River site. She wasn't involved in either case, and knew little about them.

While cross-checking records with the state medical examiner's office, Shuey learned that Richard Bennett's remains had been found and released to his family years earlier. This puzzled her—Bennett was still listed as missing in the police database. She went back to his file. Tucked among the documents was the notification letter that the Bennetts had been waiting for in the months after they'd found the skeleton. The letter, from the University of North Texas, concluded: "The individual represented by the unidentified remains F-3677.1 is excluded as a potential maternal relative of Bette P. Bennett." The DNA did not match. The body found in 2005 and released to the Bennett family in 2006 was *not* Richard Bennett.

Shuey was stunned.

The letter was dated November 5, 2007, some 16 months after the Bennett family had buried the remains of a man they'd believed was their son. Shuey said that the letter had been filed away by a clerk who no longer works for the Alaska State Troopers, and that the agency hadn't adopted electronic filing until 2012—facts that she acknowledges are no excuse and no consolation to the families.

"It was the Alaska State Troopers that failed," she told me.

Was it possible that the remains released to the Bennetts and now buried near Lower Summit Lake were those of Rick Hills, and the scattered bones found in the Funny River fire, Richard Bennett's? Troopers privately hoped so. That outcome would lessen the agony for the Bennetts, and the humiliation for the State Troopers. The medical examiner's office ordered a round of expedited DNA tests. The results came back in two parts. The first concluded that the bones found at the Funny River site were neither Rick Hills's nor Richard Bennett's. The second concluded that the original DNA sample taken from the remains released to the Bennett family in 2006 was in fact that of Rick Hills.

Three months after the Funny River bones were discovered, Shuey and another investigator found themselves speeding through the Arizona desert in the middle of the night to reach Lake Havasu City by morning. Both knew they were about to deliver upheaval to an unsuspecting family.

"The Bennetts had closure for eight years," Shuey told me.

"Now we have to go down there and take it away from them. We have to tell them, 'The remains you received in 2006 were not your son, and we don't know where your son is.'"

The letter Lieutenant Shuey read to Leon Bennett in Lake Havasu City ended exactly like the one Captain Greenstreet read aloud to Dolly and Tom Hills and Heidi Metteer in Soldotna: "I understand that there is nothing that I can say that can ever repair the devastation that your family is experiencing. For this, I am truly sorry. Sincerely, Colonel James Cockrell, Director, Alaska State Troopers."

Even in shock, Leon Bennett knew right away that he would never tell his wife about the troopers' visit. Bette had been so distraught when the skeleton was discovered in 2005, and so relieved—more than anyone else in the family—when they'd laid the remains to rest on the mountainside. Now she was on oxygen and struggling to breathe. She became confused easily. Sharing the news would have destroyed her. In Bette's final weeks, Leon muffled his sobs and strained to hide his devastation. There weren't many people with whom he could share the burden: Jane and Leroy and, it turned out, Dolly, Tom, and Heidi.

Dolly and Heidi contacted Leon shortly after getting the news. They felt bound to him by circumstance, and by their shared experience of a grief few others could understand. "If there's anything we can do, or if you just want to talk, call us," Dolly said. He offered the same.

Dolly and Tom spend winters in Phoenix, just 200 miles from Lake Havasu City, and the families decided to meet. They got together for the first time on a sunny Sunday morning in February 2015.

Everyone settled around the dining-room table at Jane's house, with Dolly and Tom at one end, and Leon, Jane, and Leroy at the other. On the table were photographs and police reports, dog-eared and riddled with Postit Notes. Atop one stack was Colonel Cockrell's letter to the Bennetts. Everyone glanced at it. "We have one," Dolly said. Nervous laughter.

The two families talked about "my Richard" and "your Richard" and human remains and bone fragments and detached skulls. Rick Hills's skull hasn't been found. Dolly and Heidi still suspect foul play, but they fear they may never know the truth about what happened to him.

The conversation turned to the uncanny similarities between Rick and Richard—two men close in age, roughly the same height, who disappeared in the same area about 15 months apart. They even wore the same kind of clothes, and both had old fractures in their right leg—Richard from his motorcycle accident, and Rick from playing hockey. Rick may have re-injured his leg when his Dodge plowed into the snowbank. That would explain why he had been dragging his foot.

"They told us there was no one else missing in the area," Leon said.

The case documents I read show that the State Troopers indeed did not consider that the bones found near Richard Bennett's trailer could have been anyone else's. In going through police reports, Dolly and Heidi counted 17 different troopers who'd had a hand in their son's case over the years. Of those, three were also involved in the Richard Bennett case. But the troopers didn't make the connection. "They said it was because they didn't put their reports in computers then," Dolly said.

She talked about how her family had searched and agonized for 10 years, only to find out that Rick's ashes were buried above a lake they drove past all the time on their way to Anchorage. After Captain Greenstreet delivered the news, Dolly said, it took another month to find the exact location of the urn. She, Heidi, and other family members hiked to the spot above Lower Summit Lake, held hands, and tearfully recited the Lord's Prayer before digging the urn out of the ground eight years after the Bennetts had put it in.

They wrapped the urn in a brown-paper grocery bag, and Heidi took it home. Late that night, she stared at the bag, beside her bed, and said, "I never thought you'd be in my bedroom again." Dolly laughed as she told the story.

The room went silent.

Dolly told Leon, Jane, and Leroy that they had chosen a beautiful spot at Lower Summit Lake. She thanked them.

"I want you to know he was well taken care of," Jane said.

"I want you to know that *we* know how you're feeling," Dolly said. "The hurting that never goes away, we know. We also know, the way this turned out. . . . It could have been the other way around."

This past July, I received an e-mail from Leon Bennett. There was no message, only a link to a story from the previous day's *Alaska Dispatch News*. The headline read, "Troopers Identify Human Remains Found During Last Year's Funny River Wildfire." The bones belonged to a Soldotna resident, James Allen Beaver, who'd been missing since 2011. He was 42 when he disappeared. Investigators had traced the Samsung phone to Beaver, but they'd decided to wait this time for DNA confirmation before releasing the bones to his family. Vast as the peninsula is, it can still seem like a small world. Rick Hills went to high school with James Beaver, and Heidi knows his brother Roy.

I called Leon.

His voice as gravelly as ever, he told me he was frustrated. He'd lost a son, thought he'd found him, and lost him again. He was frustrated that his grief felt so raw, as if Richard had disappeared just yesterday. And this time, he bore the grief without his wife. He had let Bette continue thinking that Richard had been laid to rest. "It was the right thing to do," he said. She died last April.

"I'm frustrated that the Alaska State Troopers aren't looking for Richard. They say they are, but I'm almost sure they're not," he said. "I'm frustrated that I'm not out there looking for him myself."

Leon was caring for one of his daughters, who was recovering from a quintuple bypass. He couldn't just drop everything and go off to the Kenai. All he could do from Arizona was check the news from Alaska every day for updates on the Funny River bones. He had quietly hoped the man would turn out to be his son, even though troopers had ruled out that possibility the previous summer. "I have zero confidence in them," he said. "So yes, it was in the back of my mind that it could be Richard."

With the bones now identified, a new thought has taken root in the back of Leon's mind: What if Richard is *alive*? It's less a hope than a torment, the reflex of a parent who has no evidence to the contrary, even if 10 years have passed and all signs point the other way.

Leon isn't the only one who's had that idea. Jane has always thought that Richard may have just wanted a clean start somewhere else. "We never found his firearms," she reminded me on several occasions. "And we never found his camping stuff." Richard's friend Hap Pierce told me he wouldn't be surprised if Richard one day knocked on his door. "I'd be pissed," he said, "but I wouldn't be surprised."

Alaska brims with stories of people who vanish and are given up for dead. Once in a while, the dead return. A woman named Lucy Ann Johnson made headlines a few years ago. Born in Skagway, on the Alaskan Panhandle, she eventually moved to British Columbia. Her husband reported her missing in 1965, and police learned that she hadn't been seen in almost four years. Police suspected he'd killed her, but they had no evidence, and he died in the late 1990s. Then, in 2013, the couple's only daughter, Linda Evans, went searching for answers and, to her shock and amazement, found her mother living with a different family in the Yukon Territory. The mother-daughter reunion is now Alaskan legend. Lucy Ann Johnson was 77 when her daughter found her. She had been missing for 52 years.

Leon Bennett believes his son may have wanted to leave his life. But what if he left it to find a *different* life? When he allows himself to follow this train of thought—that maybe Richard is roughing it in the wild, or hiding out in some tiny native village far off the beaten track—he feels a tinge of comfort. But then the not-knowing returns, and it keeps him awake at night.

"There's a possibility," Leon told me, speaking in a faint voice, as if not wanting to hear himself say it. "You don't want to dwell on it. He's probably gone. But you can't ignore that there's a possibility." The Alaskan bush would suit his son's temperament and skills. There are places out there with enough space for a man to remake himself without anyone bothering him. Places where people fish and hunt to eat. A single moose can feed a person for a year, Leon told me. "It'd be hard living. Not a lot of people could do it. But if there's anybody who could, it would be my son."

LAST BUT NOT LEAST: THE LONELY WHITE HOUSE BIDS OF TWO LONGSHOTS

Los Angeles Times, July 25, 2007

Introduced by **SAM HOWE VERHOVEK**, Tizon's colleague
at the *Los Angeles Times* and editor of this collection

Tizon really hated covering politics. I know this because it is one of many things that made us great colleagues at the Seattle Bureau of the Los Angeles Times. I'm a bit of a political junkie, so we never fought over who got to cover an election in the Pacific Northwest—or anywhere else. And while I generally find politicians interesting, it should come as no surprise to a reader of this collection, whose very theme is Alex's abiding interest in "invisible people," that my friend did not share this intrigue. At all. Politicians strive to be the very opposite of invisible. To him, it was all a charade.

All of this originally led me, in choosing stories for this collection, to skip over any of the campaign stories that editors coaxed—or pried—out of a recalcitrant Alex, which I picture him having written with all the enthusiasm of a hostage. But then one political story did pop out at me, because it is such a perfect Tizon take on a presidential race. Most reporters strive to cover the front-runners; Alex was interested in the losers at the back of the pack. Of course!

Of course, he would want to cover them. If Alex Tizon covered horse racing, he'd want to know about the long shots, the has-beens, and the never-weres; if he covered Wall Street, probably with a gun to his head because I can't imagine him ever doing such a thing willingly, he'd be much more interested in the people who lost their shirts than the star stock pickers beating the market. Likewise with politics: Of course, he'd want to know what makes men or women keep running a race when they are so far behind—in the polls, in raising money, and in the very attention paid to them—that they have become . . . invisible.

Here, he lets the candidates, and their true-believer support-
ers, answer the question. He does it respectfully; there's a lot more
empathy in this piece than there is mockery, even if this is a story
about guys who have no chance of winning. And he takes each man
seriously, which is perhaps the most powerful element in this story.
Even as the self-proclaimed cognoscenti on cable news were ignor-
ing Mike Gravel and Ron Paul, a fate akin to death in politics,
Alex was listening to them. He wasn't so much skeptical about their
prospects or their strategies or their fund-raising as he was interested
in a simple question: Why do you think you should be president of
the United States?

· · ·

ONE IS A DEMOCRAT, the other a Republican. They've never
met but share much in common: Both wear dark suits and sneakers, for one. Neither has a lot of money. Both are running for
president.

Mike Gravel and Ron Paul. Mike and Ron. Their names, sharing space at the bottom of the polls, seem increasingly linked.
Each came out swinging in the debates and scored points for candor and quirkiness and, in Gravel's case, crankiness.

The oldest of the declared candidates, Gravel, 77, and Paul,
71, have become the campaign's upstarts. They've helped draw an
audience that might otherwise not have tuned in to the earliest-
starting primary season in U.S. history.

After the first debate, Gravel generated more Internet traffic
than any other Democratic contender except Sen. Barack Obama
of Illinois. Through much of June and early July, "Ron Paul" was
among the top three most frequently searched terms on the Web.
Paul's YouTube videos were viewed 2.3 million times.

So who are these guys? Can two old men in rubber shoes win
their parties' nomination to be leader of the free world?

MIKE GRAVEL, former senator from Alaska, has just flown in to
Portland on a red-eye from Indianapolis.

He rode economy in a middle seat in row 25, landed in the

City of Roses after 2 A.M., grabbed some sleep and strolled into the hotel restaurant just past 11 A.M.—the cutoff time for breakfast.

"Would there be any chance you could manage one more breakfast?" Gravel asks the gum-chewing hostess. "I'm sorry . . . ," she begins. Then someone from behind whispers to her that this man is running for president. He's important.

The hostess looks the candidate over.

Gravel smiles at her like a man to a favorite grandchild. Was this the same person whom commentators, after the first debate, called cantankerous?

He wears the obligatory uniform of male presidential hopefuls, dark suit and tie, and looks top to bottom like a decent enough fellow, with his thinning white hair and rimless spectacles. The hostess glances at his shoes: black strap-on Velcro walkers.

She sighs. "This way," she says.

He orders eggs, hash browns and toast with honey. He talks about his flight. "My feet were hurting so bad I couldn't sleep," he says. His voice, coincidentally, sounds gravelly. Gravel (pronounced gruh-VELL, as in his old campaign slogan, "Give Hell, Gravel!") suffers from neuropathy and chronic back pain, so traveling can be agony. Meditation helps him. In-flight movies too.

At one point during the meal, a supporter, Deborah Petri, 38, who has driven down from Tacoma, Wash., to meet him, approaches to shake his hand. "You're my hero," Petri tells the candidate. "I love you."

She, like many other supporters, loves him despite his deficits—or perhaps because of them. His numbers in most national polls remain below 1%. Broke, jobless and politically marginalized, Gravel can't help but relate to the struggling masses. He's one of them.

His story in sum: former Army counter-intelligence officer; married to second wife, education consultant Whitney Stewart Gravel; father of two grown children; twice bankrupt; U.S. senator from Alaska starting in 1969; gained a national reputation as a maverick lawmaker willing to go against his own party; best-known for his theatrical opposition to the Vietnam War.

In 1971, Gravel read aloud passages of the Pentagon Papers, a secret government report describing U.S. military decision-making in Vietnam, entering 4,000 pages of the 7,000-page report into the Congressional Record. The report fueled the movement that eventually forced the end of the war.

But after a dozen years in the Senate, Gravel lost his seat in 1981 and disappeared from public life—until April 2006, when he became the first Democrat to declare his run at the presidency.

Gravel had become angry over the government's inaction on the Iraq war, which he considers immoral. He also wanted to bring attention to a project he had worked on privately for more than a decade: the concept of governing by "national referenda." His idea, which he calls "the National Initiative," is to turn the American people into one giant legislative body.

The people, once and for all, would decide on the most pressing issues, from illegal immigration and healthcare to the war in Iraq and the war on drugs; he considers both wars disastrous.

At his age, it was now or never "to accomplish something, more than what I've already done, before I die," he says between bites of toast. "Our chances of winning are remote. But you never know. Lightning could strike."

Jimmy Carter, Michael S. Dukakis and Bill Clinton were relative unknowns when they entered the races for the 1976, 1988 and 1992 Democratic nominations. Carter and Clinton went all the way, of course.

During the first Democratic debate this spring in South Carolina, Gravel scored laughs and stole the show with his old-coot routine. He said the front-runners "frighten" him with their unwillingness to rule out the use of nuclear weapons. "Tell me, Barack," Gravel said in the most quoted line of the debate, "who do you want to nuke?"

His performance started what supporters call "Gravelmania."

"I couldn't believe he just turned to the other candidates and asked them a serious question," says Nick Urban, 24, a campaign volunteer from Olympia, Wash., who had driven to Portland with Petri. "It was just so surprising. He made it a real debate."

Gravel lobbed another grenade during Monday's debate, when he accused fellow Democrats of selling out the party.

"Look at where all the money is being raised right now," he thundered. "It's the hedge funds. It's Wall Street bankers. It's the people who brought you what you have today. Please wake up."

Gravel, who claims to have "zero net worth," began his campaign in debt and continues to struggle financially. The latest figures show his campaign has raised $175,000 but has spent $197,000.

No chartered planes or suited chauffeurs await him. In fact, with breakfast done, he needs a ride.

Gravel is in town on a sunny Saturday to speak at a Unitarian Universalist event exploring the relevance of the Pentagon Papers. He must be at the Oregon Convention Center in 30 minutes and has not arranged transportation.

Urban volunteers to drive. He hadn't expected to be put to work but appears glad to help his man out.

"I get shotgun," Gravel says.

The candidate and his press secretary, Alex Colvin, pile into Urban's old green Saab along with Petri, and the car speeds off.

At the convention center, the candidate meets up with an old political ally, Daniel Ellsberg, the former military analyst who leaked the Pentagon Papers to the New York Times. The two white-haired men share a private moment before Ellsberg introduces the candidate to a crowd of several thousand.

Ellsberg's words seem to capture the abiding essence of Gravel, and Ron Paul too, and for that matter all underdogs who face impossible odds.

"The fear of looking foolish is what keeps people in line all their lives," Ellsberg tells the rapt audience. He glances at Gravel at the speaker's table. "Here is a senator who is not afraid to look foolish."

In cyberspace, Gravel continues to generate buzz, but no one knows whether it will translate into votes. On his official website, one recent discussion topic began with this intriguing title: "Mike Gravel and Ron Paul as third-party Pres/Vice Pres Ticket!"

"Hey Gravel," says one post. "Give Ron Paul a call!"

IN THE LOBBY of the Hyatt Regency in downtown Kansas City, Mo., the sea of people does not part for Paul, who is here to speak at a National Right to Life Committee convention. The sea hardly stirs, in fact, as he makes his way to the hotel coffee shop one floor down.

Paul descends the escalator like he moves across the country: unrecognized except by a passionately loyal few. Like the 50-something woman wrapped in scarves who approaches the table where Paul and his campaign manager, Kent Snyder, have just seated themselves.

"I want you to know I think you're so real," she gushes at Paul. "I wish I could give more." Scavenging the bottom of her purse, the woman digs out a crumpled $10 bill. She hands it to him and rushes off, scarves fluttering.

"Usually they put it in an envelope," Paul says.

Snyder snatches up the bill, because every dollar helps. It's been predicted that serious contenders for the nominations will have to raise tens of millions by the end of the year to compete. Paul, as of mid-July, has raised $3 million. Plus, now, $10.

Ron Paul stands 6 feet slightly hunched, with graying hair and brows over crinkly eyes that turn into slits when he laughs. His suit hangs loose over a slender frame. A onetime high school track star in his native Pennsylvania, he once ran the 100-yard dash in 9.7 seconds. Paul now sports a bad knee; thus the sneakers.

His demeanor could be described as the opposite of commanding. Avuncular comes to mind. Kindly. Almost ministerial, which fits with the family story that Paul once considered becoming a Lutheran minister like two of his brothers.

His resume in brief: Air Force veteran, gynecologist and obstetrician who has delivered 4,000 babies, married with five children and 17 grandchildren, 1988 Libertarian candidate for president and 10-term Texas congressman from the Gulf Coast. He calls himself a champion of the Constitution. His nickname, "Dr. No," comes from his consistent opposition to big (or even midsized) government, taxes and war.

Paul says he'd prefer to spell his nickname "Dr. Know."

"I'd like to think I study the issues," he says.

In the second GOP debate, he offered an almost scholarly explanation for growing anti-American sentiment abroad. America's policy of intervening in foreign affairs, especially in the Middle East, he said, partly explains Islamic anger.

"We've been bombing Iraq for 10 years," he said.

It was at that moment that Kansas City resident Richard De-Young, 28, a software engineer, decided Paul was his man.

"I was absolutely floored by his candor," DeYoung says. "He's not about trying to pander to the American people. He's about giving his take on the truth."

When supporters asked him to join the race two years ago, Paul resisted. But the supporters—many from the Libertarian pocket of the Republican base—persisted, and Paul relented, partly egged on by his frustration over the current crop of candidates. None of them, he believes, would end American involvement in Iraq immediately. Paul says he would.

"Things were getting worse. More men were dying in the war, and Ron felt responsible for what was going on," says Carol Paul, the candidate's wife of 50 years. The couple talks on the phone two to three times a day. She makes him chocolate chip cookies to take on the road.

"I worry for him," she says. "He gets very tired."

Paul is the last of four Republican candidates to speak in front of the conventioneers on a hot Thursday afternoon. Afterward, half the room applauds, and the other half looks him over, seemingly unmoved.

Later the same day, about 500 supporters gather in an antiquated downtown theater for a rally. It is a crowd of believers. They roar and chant and hold banners announcing "the Ron Paul Revolution" and cheer wildly when the candidate, looking slight on the grand stage, takes the podium.

He shields his eyes from the lights. He shoves a hand in his suit pocket. He thanks the crowd and says how great it is to be in Kansas, which raises eyebrows because he is in Missouri.

"People ask, 'How come you're doing so well on the Internet?'" Paul says. His speech is countryside-slow. "It might just be that freedom is a popular idea." Big applause.

In 20 minutes of oration, Paul tells not a single joke. True to form, he mentions the Constitution frequently. "Almost every problem we have is because we didn't follow the advice of the founding fathers and the Constitution." Bigger applause. "What we want is noninterference by the government in our personal lives." Standing ovation.

On the stage, he displays no tendency to grandstand, no attempt to be winsome or even likable, although his sincerity seems to compensate. Paul's charisma seems to be that he has none. Charm, in this circle, equates to phoniness.

"The media say about me, 'He did all right but, boy, he's not very charismatic,'" Paul says. "Maybe I should take classes."

Outside the theater, under a scorching summer sun, a handful of supporters wave Ron Paul placards to endless passing cars.

The latest CNN poll shows Paul at about 2% nationally among registered Republicans.

"Go, John Paul!" someone screams from a pickup.

"It's Ron!" a sidewalk supporter screams back.

The revolution has a ways to go.

PART V

VILLAINS

JOHN MUHAMMAD'S MELTDOWN

Seattle Times, November 10, 2002

Introduced by **JAMES NEFF**, former investigations editor of the *Seattle Times* and current deputy managing editor of the *Philadelphia Inquirer*

*everal weeks into the harrowing Beltway Sniper story, the un-
folding drama took a turn that snapped the* Seattle Times
*newsroom to attention: Assassin John Muhammad and his young
sidekick recently had been living in our area. And as we would learn,
Muhammad had actually started his twisted national crime spree
with a fatal revenge shooting in nearby Tacoma.*

*Six reporters from the investigations and metro teams roared
into action, breaking exclusives that led our industry in exposing
the troubled lives of the two suspects and the twists and break-
throughs in a frantic police investigation that spanned the nation.
Despite the award-winning effort, the relentless daily scoops and
disconnected, unused fragments in the reporters' notebooks called
out for something more: quickly putting these hard, bright pieces of
reporting into a mosaic that illuminated the greater story—a task
that fell to Alex Tizon, who had yet to join the story.*

*It needed to be a swift turn, for our readers and for Alex—a
week and half, to my memory. He immersed himself in the stack of
stories, underlying documents, and interview notes while beginning
his own reporting.*

*But how to tell the tale? Alex starts the story in Seattle and ends
it fourteen months later with the capture of Muhammad and the
young Lee Boyd Malvo. Layered on top of that time line, in an
order that blends into the chronology, is another motif: Muhammad's life in themes—family man, military man, angry man, and
so on—that hide beneath Alex's driving story and give it rewarding
logic. Working from home to focus on his task, Alex wrote and
rewrote. Pulling a final all-nighter, he nailed it, delivering "John*

Muhammad's Meltdown," an astonishingly insightful and compel-
ling account of "a pained, pathological grifter whose only genius
was his personal predilection to commit violence from a distance."

· · ·

THE SMILE WAS ABSENT that day. The million-dollar smile
he flashed whenever it served him, the gleam of winsome pearl
that charmed women and men from Baton Rouge to Bellingham.

On that day 14 months ago, inside a small courtroom in Tacoma, John Allen Muhammad could barely gather his thoughts.
He was dumbfounded. He was losing his children.

"Your honor, could I say something?" Muhammad said, his
voice unexpectedly soft but unhesitating.

"Just a moment, sir," said Judge Mark Gelman. The judge was
all business. He explained that the sole reason for the hearing was
to enforce a court order giving full custody of Muhammad's three
children to their mother, Mildred.

"Your honor," a flustered Muhammad interjected. "Can you
please tell me what's going on?"

The judge explained further.

Muhammad responded: "Are you telling me the reason I won't
be able to keep my children is because I don't have the proper
paperwork?"

Before the hearing was over, he asked the judge two more
times: "So I can't see my children?"

In the odyssey of the man accused as one of the two Beltway
snipers—his apparent descent into a calculating kind of madness—this 18-minute hearing, tape-recorded on Sept. 4, 2001, in
Room 260 of the Pierce County Courthouse, may have been the
tipping point.

His life had already plunged into disarray and bitterness. But
the final loss of his children, according to those who knew him
best, was "the snap," the veering onto the road of no return.

Muhammad, 41, took a 17-year-old boy, Lee Boyd Malvo, with
him. Their odyssey would apparently span the continent, leaving

at least 14 people dead, five wounded and a nation shuddering once again at its vulnerabilities.

Muhammad's friends and family wonder whether they ever really knew the man who last month smiled so handsomely on the front pages of every newspaper.

"I thought he was a man of high integrity," says longtime Tacoma neighbor Leo Dudley, emphasizing the word "thought."

Some media profiles have depicted Muhammad as a mastermind, a Svengali, a cunning strategist who had crafted his car into what *Newsweek* described as a "Rube Goldberg killing machine."

Yet more evidence provides a contrasting impression: Muhammad as a pained, pathological grifter whose only genius was his personal predilection to commit violence from a distance.

Though he captured the nation's spotlight for almost a month—which may speak mostly to the rarity of serial sniping—it's clear that Muhammad was no master, except to Malvo. And for quite some time, he was of questionable mind.

He may have been more bully than Svengali. His so-called killing machine was a $250 junker with a fold-down seat and a hole in the trunk.

If anything was Rube Goldbergesque, it would be the persona of Muhammad himself, a tangle of fictions held together by separate strands of disaffection.

He was a man of multiple identities, exemplified literally by his use of as many as 22 aliases. More than that, he was radically different, even contradictory, things to different people: Devout worshiper and chronic adulterer. Righteous father and habitual liar. Gentle neighbor and gun nut. Finally, decorated veteran and self-styled enemy of the state.

Who was he at the core?

More will emerge over time, but the 12 months before the first Beltway sniper attack—the countdown to his own demise, much of which took place in the narrow corridor between Bellingham and Tacoma—reveal that he was fueled by a number of compulsions.

He was bitter against the United States, just as he was against the forces that separated him from his children. He was an angry ex-husband, and an angry member of the Nation of Islam, a Black Muslim who considered the U.S. a terrorist state.

He defended the 9/11 attacks, which happened seven days after the fateful custody hearing.

The degree to which his personal bitterness merged with militant ideology, or whether one exacerbated the other, may never be known. Muhammad himself may not know.

Why did Muhammad and Malvo focus their attack on the Washington, D.C., area? Was it to paralyze the control center of the nation Muhammad had fought for and had come to despise? Was it to extort the $10 million he and Malvo demanded in one of their taunting missives to police?

Or was it, as his ex-wife Mildred and her family believe, a perversely circuitous plot to kill her? She lived in hiding with their children in Clinton, Md., and Muhammad had located them.

In the end, if he is convicted, the conclusion may be that Muhammad's motivation was as multifaceted as the man himself. Maybe he was an angry father, an angry Black Muslim and an extortionist.

Or maybe he was simply angry.

At least one man in his past is not surprised that Muhammad now sits in solitary confinement in a Virginia jail, that he awaits trial for murder and that he almost certainly faces the death penalty.

Retired Sgt. Kip Berentson, more than a decade ago, intuited that Muhammad might someday turn to murder. Berentson served over him in Saudi Arabia during the Gulf War. Neither one liked the other.

One incident in particular caused Berentson to conclude that Muhammad was a bomb ticking. Since the incident, involving a grenade, Berentson has kept a piece of paper with Muhammad's name and dog-tag number in his wallet.

"In the back of my mind," he said, "I knew our paths would cross. Like, 'Until we meet again.'"

When news broke of Muhammad's arrest Oct. 24 at a Maryland rest stop, a part of Berentson recoiled in terror; another simmered in guilt. He knew.

"That face has been in my mind for 11 years."

THE COUNTDOWN BEGINS—At the time of the custody hearing in Tacoma, Muhammad was living on and off in a homeless shelter 122 miles to the north, at the Lighthouse Mission in Bellingham. It's in the waterfront district, a gritty, industrial section of town. The mission sits like a three-story box across the street from the factory where Georgia-Pacific makes toilet paper.

Malvo, the Jamaican whom Muhammad had molded into a surrogate son since they connected in the Caribbean the year before, lived with him at the shelter until June of this year. The two became familiar figures in the area's nooks and watering holes. They stood out, first, because they were black in a very white town and, second, because they cut such striking figures.

Malvo's smile was even more winsome than Muhammad's. Both were handsome, well-mannered, clean and not merely fit but muscular. Standing 6 inches taller at a sinewy 6-foot-1, Muhammad was the obvious leader. He walked with chest out and back straight, with a countenance that beamed a soldierly self-assurance.

"Sturdy" is how one friend describes him. He had the ready smile, but rarely laughed or broke out of a certain seriousness. "Intense" is how others describe him. Like someone with a calling.

When the shelter shooed away the overnighters at 7 each morning, Muhammad would wander into a nearby tavern and sip $2 Budweisers. "He'd start right in," says Millie Ulmer, morning bartender at the Waterfront Tavern. "He did three or four sometimes, then he went up the street" to another tavern.

He would sit three stools from the cigarette machine. Regulars remember him as polite, friendly, a bit aloof. When he wasn't watching one of the many TVs, he would appear to be thinking. He seemed to have a lot on his mind.

In the afternoons, Muhammad and Malvo would walk to Stuart's Coffee Shop, a few blocks away, and play chess. They would work out at the YMCA, spending two to three hours lifting weights. Muhammad reportedly bench-pressed 350 pounds, nearly twice his weight.

For four months after the custody hearing that took away his three children, ages 8, 10 and 12, Muhammad went through the motions of trying to win them back legally. He journeyed from Bellingham to Tacoma once a week to consult with an attorney who'd agreed to take his case pro bono.

But he knew it was probably futile. Mildred had left the state with the kids and had gone into hiding. Legal maneuvering would do no good if they couldn't be found.

Muhammad knew this from first-hand knowledge.

In March 2000, in the midst of the acrimonious divorce, Muhammad had abducted the children and gone into his own hiding, first in Antigua, then in Bellingham. He had the kids for 17 months, until a Whatcom County sheriff's deputy tracked them down at the elementary school where they were enrolled under fictitious names.

Then, the custody hearing, and now it was Mildred's turn to disappear. Months passed, and Muhammad's trips to his lawyer became less frequent. In February of this year, he stopped going altogether.

"He dropped off the radar screen," says the lawyer, John Mills.

Muhammad was devastated; Mills knew that. He, along with friends and family on both sides of the country, attests to Muhammad's fondness for children, his own most of all.

Muhammad fathered at least five children with three different women in his life, but it was the last three, the ones he had with Mildred, with whom he felt most bonded. They were his soft spot. They were his one pure love.

After it became clear that he would not get them back through the courts, that he might never get them back, or even find them, something inside him melted down.

"A nervous breakdown" is how one of his closest friends, Robert Holmes of Tacoma, describes it: "I know John lost it because he lost his kids."

But even Holmes had no idea to what depth Muhammad's anger had plunged, nor to what lengths he would go for revenge. Police believe Muhammad and Malvo may have committed their first killing during the period of this meltdown.

In starting a pattern of criminal sloppiness, the pair apparently killed the wrong person.

Sometime during the day of Feb. 16, police allege, Muhammad or Malvo or both knocked on the door of the Tacoma home of Isa Nichols. Nichols had kept the books for Muhammad when he ran a mechanic's service, and had sided with Mildred in the custody dispute. She had helped police try to track down Muhammad and the kids.

But Nichols was out on an errand when the knock came. Her niece, 21-year-old Keenya Cook, paused from changing her baby's diaper to answer the door.

Cook was shot in the face and died in a heap.

It was purely a revenge-murder, police say. As pure as it could be in the increasingly murky world of John Allen Muhammad. Ideology or hatred for America played no role. That particular hate was a whole other cauldron coming to a boil.

A DETONATION—A few days after the attacks on the World Trade Center and the Pentagon, Muhammad, still living intermittently at the mission, wandered into the Horseshoe Restaurant, which boasts of being the oldest place in Bellingham for "great food, fine tobacco and a place to meet with friends over a good beer."

He picked a stool at the bar in the Ranch Room. A few stools away, on the other side of the L-shaped counter, a small group of locals sipped their own morning beers and vented their outrage at Osama bin Laden. One said the United States should bomb the hell out of al-Qaida.

Muhammad took exception. In a calm, even tone, he told the men that the CIA had sponsored a lot of terrorism in the world, and that the U.S. was itself a terrorist state. The group glared at the stranger who interjected himself into a private conversation.

One man came unglued.

He was a local fisherman and crabber named Drew Sandilands. He is 47, with weathered hands and a wiry, slender-strong build. If anyone in the group could have physically challenged Muhammad, it was Sandilands. And if anyone had reason to, it was he: His cousin was the airline pilot of one of the jets that was hijacked and slammed into the Trade Center.

Sandilands told Muhammad to get out or he would "get his ass whupped."

Another man in the group, Tracy Ridpath, held Sandilands back.

As calmly as he had walked in, Muhammad walked out into daylight and out of trouble. Sandilands followed him outside, but Muhammad was already gone. The fisherman later told his buddies that he had a feeling Muhammad was a terrorist.

Others in Bellingham, post 9/11, had the same feeling. Three people, on three separate occasions, reported their suspicions to the FBI.

Their calls went unheeded. The bureau says they weren't compelling enough to investigate.

One of the calls came from the Rev. Al Archer just a month after the terrorist attacks. Archer, director of the Lighthouse Mission, observed Muhammad for two months before contacting the feds.

It was Muhammad's polite demeanor, excessive to the point of phoniness; it was his smoothness and businesslike air; it was the big duffel bag that he carried with him everywhere; it was his soldierly control over the young Malvo; most of all, it was the trips he took to the East Coast, Louisiana, the Caribbean.

Not many men at the shelter got phone calls from travel agents. It was as if Muhammad was using the shelter as a base of operation.

Indeed, it seems, Muhammad was a man on a mission. Independent of any known terrorist group, it appears, Muhammad began his own sort of jihad.

His surname had not always been Muhammad. He was born

John Allen Williams and raised by relatives in a strict Baptist home in Louisiana.

While stationed in the Persian Gulf, he read "The Autobiography of Malcolm X," the tale of a street-tough ex-con who became a leading minister in the Nation of Islam. The Nation was an American creation, an amalgam of black nationalism, Jehovah's Witnesses doctrine and certain Islamic teachings, launched in the 1930s.

It is, many mainstream Muslims say, a heretical offshoot of their faith. The Nation of Islam teaches that the black man is the God of the Universe, the father of civilization, and the white man is the Devil. An impending Armageddon, the sect teaches, will end with the destruction of, specifically, the United States, the bastion of the Devil.

By 1992, while stationed at Fort Ord, Calif., Williams was drawn to the sect led by Louis Farrakhan and became a follower.

In 1997, while living in Tacoma, he officially converted to the faith, slipping out of his mechanic's overalls and dressing in a suit and tie to attend weekly meetings of a Nation of Islam study group in Seattle. Like many in the Nation, he started calling himself Muhammad and legally changed his name last year.

The Nation's focus on sobriety and family values was for a while a powerful influence on Muhammad, friends say. He reached out to two sons from other women, whom he had neglected. He doted over the three children he'd had with Mildred. For a time, until he apparently reverted to philandering, his marriage seemed strong.

Ultimately, though, there are signs that the Nation—and, in particular, its strong anti-American message—had a darker influence on a troubled mind.

Though the controversial Farrakhan has condemned the snipers' shooting spree—one of the victims was an African-American man with his own ties to the Nation of Islam—the sect's language echoes through one of the notes left for police by the alleged Beltway Snipers.

"Call me God," the note reads. Muhammad's Black Muslim

brothers at the Seattle study group routinely greeted each other as "God," a former member says.

The sniper note ends with, "Word is bond," a quote contained in the Nation of Islam's main text, the Supreme Wisdom.

When The System took Muhammad's children away in the spring of 2001, it may have accelerated his hunger to destroy it. The Armageddon was approaching.

THE PERFECT SILENCER—In the months after the custody hearing, Muhammad and Malvo were hatching plots. They revealed aspects to numerous people, but not always consistently or truthfully.

They told at least one friend in Tacoma about plans to build a silencer for a rifle, and they expounded with contained glee on the lethal possibilities. The pair even practiced target-shooting, neighbors say, in a backyard of a densely populated section of Tacoma.

Back in Bellingham, Muhammad spoke to a gunsmith, Glen Chapman, about altering a rifle. Chapman recalls Muhammad's story about shortening the firearm for mailing purposes as "the phoniest thing I ever heard."

Muhammad divulged graphic details of his plans to a man he met at the YMCA—so graphic that the man got scared, cut off communication and eventually reported Muhammad and Malvo to the FBI and police.

The man, Harjeet Singh, 35, is a New Delhi–born Sikh who has lived in Bellingham since 1989. He got to know Muhammad and Malvo in the weight room. With time, Muhammad greeted Singh like a Muslim brother:

"As-salamu 'alaikum." Peace be with you, in Arabic.

Singh replied, "Wa 'alaikum salam." Peace be with you, too.

Singh says Muhammad praised the 9/11 hijackers for causing more damage to the United States than an army could have done. Singh himself did not condone the terrorist attacks—"250 people from India died in the World Trade Center," he says—but he shared Muhammad's outrage over decades of U.S.-sponsored violence overseas.

It wasn't until an afternoon in May that Singh realized Muhammad's anger was altogether a different animal from his own. As the three of them sipped tea in a cafeteria near the YMCA, Muhammad and Malvo scanned the room cautiously. Muhammad then pulled some items from a duffel bag.

Among the items, Singh says, were a shiny 8-inch pistol silencer, a blueprint for a rifle silencer and a 20-inch axle rod that Muhammad said could be bored and converted into a rifle silencer.

Muhammad asked Singh if he knew anyone in the Sikh community in Canada who could do the job. Singh said he didn't, and besides, why did Muhammad need a silencer? Singh says Muhammad replied that he wanted to shoot a tanker truck on the highway and make it explode, or shoot a police officer and then, as officers gathered for the memorial service, set off a bomb, killing as many officers as possible.

"They were serious," Singh says. "I got scared."

From that point, he took pains to avoid the pair, even instructing his wife to tell them he no longer lived with her. He says he hasn't seen the two since that day in the cafeteria, but he recalls another conversation that has become more haunting in retrospect.

Sometime last spring, in late March or April, Muhammad went out of town and Malvo spent the night with Singh and his family in their north Bellingham apartment. Without his father figure around, Malvo turned loquacious. Singh says Malvo told him that he and Muhammad had already shot and killed two golfers in Arizona.

Singh thought Malvo was bluffing, and didn't give the comment much thought. But last week, Arizona investigators revealed that they are investigating a mysterious murder last spring for a possible tie to the Beltway Snipers. A golfer had been shot from a distance by a high-powered rifle, on a Tucson golf course on March 16.

At that time, Muhammad and Malvo were in Tucson visiting Muhammad's sister, who lived just a few blocks from the course.

If the duo were responsible for that slaying, it means that by the time they showed off their duffel bag of goodies to Singh in

May, they may have already killed at least two people—Keenya Cook in Tacoma, and the golfer, Jerry Taylor, in Tucson—and possibly more.

Meanwhile, between their various trips, the pair continued to work out at the Bellingham Y daily, sometimes twice a day. They would eat lunch at the Community Food Co-op. One week in April, they bunked down at an apartment with some students from Western Washington University they had met at a coffee shop.

Some afternoons, Malvo would go to the library to do research on guns. Singh recalls that, too: Malvo was obsessed with guns.

FATHERLESS BOYS—It may yet turn out that Malvo played more of a role in the shootings than a mere minion following orders. He allegedly wrote the sniper notes and made key phone calls to police. Only his fingerprints were found on the rifle used in the Beltway shootings.

Police now believe Malvo pulled the trigger in at least some of the shootings, if not most or all of them. How much he did under pressure and how much was self-driven remains unclear.

Muhammad was the clear authority, but "it's not going to turn out that [Malvo] is some robot," said one federal investigator.

In fact, those who know them say the two have much in common—including difficult, fatherless childhoods.

In Muhammad's case, his mother died of cancer when he was 5 and his father abandoned him and his four siblings. They were raised in Baton Rouge, La., by an aunt and by his grandfather, a former prison officer who beat the children when they crossed him.

Malvo was raised by an itinerant mother, Una James. Although she seems to have been dedicated to him, her days were spent trying to feed, house and clothe them both, first in their native Jamaica, and then on the Caribbean island of Antigua.

It was there that Muhammad and Malvo connected.

In the middle of his divorce, Muhammad had taken his three children and fled to a house on the island made available to him by a friend. Among his activities there, authorities say, was trafficking in false passports and immigration visas.

Una James, who was consumed by a desire to live in the United States, was one of his customers. She paid Muhammad for false ID and headed to Florida, planning to retrieve her son once she got settled.

Malvo, left to fend for himself, gravitated to Muhammad. They fit hand-in-glove, moving naturally into a father-son relationship. Neighbors eventually heard Malvo call Muhammad "Dad."

Muhammad had a soft side for fatherless boys. But his way of being a father would strike some as being a drill sergeant. His years in the Army apparently had given him a paradigm through which he would relate to the rest of the world.

Even his own kids were treated like his troops, and Malvo, the new recruit, moved in with them in the tiny house the family occupied on Antigua.

At times, Malvo showed flashes of violence, neighbors say. One, Malvia McKen, recounts that when her 5-year-old son touched Malvo's basketball, the teen struck him in the stomach with a piece of pipe.

After about a year and a half on the island, Muhammad returned to Washington state with his natural children and Malvo, with the false identity of his natural son. That identity stayed with him. In Bellingham and from that point forward, Muhammad introduced his companion as his son.

The Immigration and Naturalization Service later discovered that Malvo had entered the U.S. illegally, and he was to face an INS hearing this month. Some speculate that the young man's probable deportation might have also played a role in the timing of the pair's long and final road trip.

In the end, it might have seemed to them, they had only each other.

"HE COULD GET ANYTHING"—How they funded their various cross-country trips—indeed, how Muhammad made a living—is a puzzle still being pieced together.

Based on Muhammad's bragging to various friends and relatives over the years, he was a mechanic, teacher, franchise owner, real-estate baron, music producer and Special Forces sniper.

Some were outright lies; others contained a kernel of truth. He was indeed an auto mechanic. During the most stable part of his marriage to Mildred in Tacoma during the 1990s, Muhammad ran an auto-repair business that thrived for a while, then fell apart. Close friends say that as the couple's marriage disintegrated, primarily because of Muhammad's chronic womanizing, so did the business.

Mildred's brother, Charles Green, who lived with the family for stretches at a time, has said Muhammad made a habit of taking sex from female customers as pay for his auto services. Family friends in Tacoma corroborate the story.

During the time Muhammad ran the business, Express Car/Truck Mechanic Services Inc., he was also known in Tacoma as a man who sold black-market car parts, stolen goods and counterfeit documents.

Some of that continued on Antigua. As former Antiguan police officer Augustin Shepherd said about Muhammad: "Anything he wants, he can get it."

As in Tacoma, whatever scams Muhammad ran on Antigua remained small-time, limited to a small circle of clients. Neither his legitimate businesses nor his cons lived up to Muhammad's bragging. In court documents, he said he left the island because it was too backward and he had no means of supporting his children.

Back stateside, Muhammad, along with Malvo, apparently soon found another means of obtaining cash: hitting the road, killing and robbing.

Muhammad took to calling his charge by a new nickname: "Sniper." Malvo was seen in Bellingham in April wearing a T-shirt with the insignia "BCRA Sniper '97." The initials stand for British Columbia Rifle Association. No one at the association knows how Malvo got the T-shirt.

THE FINAL TRIP—The people at the Lighthouse Mission would see Muhammad and Malvo for the last time in June, about a month after the meeting in the cafeteria with Singh. Whatever plot the two had developed by then, it was about to shift into a higher gear.

From that point, more than ever, the pair lived like vagabonds, staying with various friends and acquaintances for brief periods, then moving. They appeared to spend most of the early summer in Tacoma, painting houses and sometimes staying in a duplex owned by Robert Holmes, one of Muhammad's closest friends.

Holmes and Muhammad had met as soldiers when both were stationed at Fort Lewis. Holmes, also a mechanic, was a big man, a former Golden Gloves boxer and someone who could deal with Muhammad as an equal.

One day in June, Muhammad showed Holmes a Bushmaster .223-caliber rifle, a civilian form of the M-16 military assault rifle. Holmes said Muhammad told him he was going to take it to a firing range for "zeroing," which means aligning the scope to shoot accurately.

"Can you imagine the damage you could do if you could shoot with a silencer?" Muhammad told Holmes.

Two weeks ago, it was revealed that the gun used in the Beltway shootings had "disappeared"—likely stolen—from a Tacoma gun store called Bull's Eye Shooter Supply last summer. It was a Bushmaster .223.

Muhammad took a rifle, perhaps that one, when he and Malvo rode a Greyhound to Baton Rouge in July. Family members recall the two appeared tired and haggard. Once rested, Muhammad brimmed with stories that, in hindsight, sound almost delusional.

He showed the rifle he kept in a case inside his duffel bag. He claimed to be a member of an elite Special Forces team on a secret mission. Malvo, he said, was part of the team. He asked where in Baton Rouge he could buy ammunition for his weapon.

The Special Forces didn't supply ammunition? one relative wondered.

During the visit, "I'm freaking out a little," says Edward Holiday, a cousin who once idolized Muhammad. "He's not in a hotel, needs a haircut, he's not clean and he has no car. I thought, John is running from something."

During that visit to his hometown, Muhammad seemed to go out of his way to talk to and visit with people he hadn't seen in years—old classmates, distant relatives, acquaintances. In some cases, he spoke and behaved as if he were acting out a final farewell.

And as he did so, he wrote his own eulogy, built largely on lies: He and Mildred were still together, living in the Virgin Islands. He had bought her a Jaguar. He had other houses in Canada and in Washington state.

Muhammad and Malvo left Baton Rouge sometime in August. They told everybody their final destinations were Washington, D.C., and eventually Jamaica. (The accused Beltway Snipers would later demand $10 million from the federal government to be placed in a bank account in Jamaica.)

But before heading East, the pair briefly went back West, where Muhammad eyed a 1965 Lincoln Continental at a Tacoma garage. His interest focused on the size of the car's trunk. But at $3,500, the Lincoln was out of his range.

In the first days of September, police say, Muhammad and Malvo made their way to Trenton, N.J. On Sept. 10, Muhammad, with the help of a friend now in custody, bought the now-infamous blue 1990 Chevrolet Caprice for $250 from a place called, portentously, Sure Shot Auto Sales.

Muhammad and Malvo put in a lot of miles in the month of September. They looped south to Alabama and Louisiana, then to the D.C. area. Police say they left a bloody trail along the way. Authorities have linked the duo to at least five shootings that month—three in Maryland, one in Alabama and one in Louisiana. Another September murder, in Atlanta, is suspected to be their work as well.

Some appear to have been committed at close range, the others from a distance.

The motive for these shootings appears on the surface to be robbery, but some investigators say there were the beginnings of a "sport aspect" in these assaults. Muhammad and Malvo, it seemed, had developed a taste for shooting human beings.

LEARNING TO KILL—"Sniping plays into the notion of the killing act as a 'game,'" says Dr. Jeffrey Smalldon, a forensic psychologist in Ohio who has consulted in about 180 death-penalty cases.

In 1993, Smalldon performed one of the most comprehensive psychological evaluations ever done on a homicidal sniper. The subject was Thomas Lee Dillon, known as the "Outdoorsman Sniper." Dillon killed five outdoorsmen in the rural counties of southern Ohio in the late 1980s and early 1990s.

Smalldon says there seem to be striking parallels in the personalities of Dillon and Muhammad: Both were profoundly disaffected, were preoccupied with control and dominance but bridled against authority. Both felt unappreciated by society and appeared to have passive-aggressive personalities, a tendency to express anger indirectly or in a nonconfrontational way.

The crime of sniping, which can be described as a passive-aggressive act, "has a certain kind of appeal to a certain kind of person," Smalldon says. A criminal sniper purposefully avoids contact and objectifies the victim so that killing is, in Dillon's words, "no more involving [physically and emotionally] than picking off a bottle at a dump."

Both Dillon and Muhammad were passionately interested in guns, and both were engrossed, even defined, by the world of the military. The two men share these last two traits with nearly all of the high-profile sniper-killers of the past half-century: Charles Whitman, U.S. Marines, 14 dead and 31 wounded on the campus of the University of Texas in 1966. Mark Essex, U.S. Navy, nine dead and 19 wounded in and around New Orleans in 1972. Lee Harvey Oswald, U.S. Marines, one dead—the president of the United States—in 1963.

"The ability to watch a human being's head explode and to do it again and again," writes David Grossman, a former military psychologist who once helped develop programs to turn soldiers into more efficient killers, "that has to be learned."

Once learned, some find it impossible to unlearn. In a recent essay, Vietnam veteran and Pulitzer-Prize-winning novelist Tim O'Brien says:

"If you get a guy who's unbalanced, I don't know if you're able to re-teach that kind of person [civility and nonviolence] once something in him has been awakened by the whole environment that encouraged death."

Snipers form a tiny subset in the world of serial killers, but they still conform to the general rule: Serial murderers do not stop until they are forced to stop or killed.

It is the ultimate dark addiction, a true road of no return.

By the end of September, Muhammad and Malvo, now outfitted with a jerry-rigged shooting perch in the trunk of their Caprice, were well on their way down that road. Their body count may have already been as high as nine. Police had not yet connected the dots.

CRITICAL MASS—Retired Sgt. Berentson, the man who has kept Muhammad's name and dog-tag number in his wallet for the past 11 years, says the road should have dead-ended for Muhammad years ago.

Why Muhammad didn't end up behind bars in 1991, neither Berentson nor anyone else in the U.S. Army's 84th Engineering Company can explain. In the first months of that year, the unit was in the Middle East preparing for the ground-attack phase of the Gulf War.

The story, according to Berentson and at least two other former members of the 84th, was that Muhammad threw a thermite grenade into a tent housing 16 of his fellow soldiers.

Thermite grenades—made of finely granulated aluminum mixed with a metal oxide, and blasting heat up to 1,200 degrees—are used to destroy equipment during battle. The attack could easily have killed or maimed, but all 16 in the tent, some coughing and choking, escaped unharmed.

Berentson was in the tent. He says the grenade went off near him and near a staff sergeant with whom Muhammad had fought earlier that day. The Army's Criminal Investigation Division, Berentson says, concluded Muhammad (then named Williams) was the lead suspect.

Muhammad was led away in handcuffs and eventually transferred to another company pending charges. He had been court-martialed twice before for lesser incidents while serving in the Louisiana National Guard. But an indictment over the grenade incident never materialized, and Muhammad's Army file has no record of it.

Muhammad's side of the story, as told to his then-wife Mildred, was that after he was accused of the attack, he was hogtied and humiliated by his fellow soldiers in a way that he would never forgive or forget. The experience, Mildred told a Washington Post reporter, would change him permanently.

Whatever the truth, there are former members of the 84th who are not only unsurprised by the horrific accusations now facing Muhammad, but who have been expecting something like this for years.

"He had a warped mind capable of doing it," Berentson says. "I should have done more. Maybe it would have prevented the killings."

In early October, Muhammad was seen in Clinton, Md., in the very neighborhood where Mildred and their children lived in hiding. Clinton is a suburban enclave about 15 miles southeast of the District of Columbia.

At that point, at least three of the sniper shootings had occurred. Mildred on Friday went public with her belief that she was not only intended to be killed, but that she was the whole reason for the murder spree.

"This was an elaborate plan to make this look like I was a victim so he could come in as the grieving father and take the children," she told The Washington Post. "They all died because of me."

Mildred knew Muhammad perhaps better than anyone else. She knew what he was capable of doing. She was in the same courtroom with him on Sept. 4, 2001, as Muhammad expressed his incredulity at the judge's ruling. It was the last time she saw her ex-husband before fleeing. Maybe it was something in his voice that day, as he asked the judge over and over:

"So I can't see my children?"

Long before Muhammad and Malvo's first alleged killing, Mildred was already watchful. He had threatened to kill her before and, in some things, she knew he was fully capable of following through.

Early in the evening of Oct. 2, a 55-year-old man was shot and killed in the parking lot of a grocery store in nearby Wheaton, Md.

The next day, five people would be shot and killed as they went about the ordinary movements of their lives—one mowing a lawn, one mailing a package, one crossing a street, two filling their cars with gas—all of them cut down by a distant evil, shattering entire webs of families and communities in an instant.

The spree reached critical mass, and America would for the first time wake up to a horror whose boundaries have not yet found an end.

THE STORY OF A DRIVE-BY MURDER AT BALLARD HIGH

Seattle Times, March 8, 1998

Introduced by **JIM SIMON**, reporting colleague of Tizon's
at the *Seattle Times*, former managing editor of the newspaper,
and current managing editor of *Honolulu Civil Beat*

I once joked with Alex that he could turn nearly any assignment into a quest to answer the Big Question. He never was much interested in settling for black-and-white answers—and never stopped trying to understand the world through the lens of those he wrote about.

To me, that's what gives "The Story of a Drive-by Murder" its power.

Alex frames his jailhouse portrait of Brian Ronquillo as an attempt to understand the un-understandable—how a popular teenage girl wound up murdered outside her Seattle high school by a short, middle-class kid who fired eight bullets into a crowd of students.

Alex, who covered gang culture for years, traces with spare but vivid detail how Ronquillo first attached himself to the 23rd Street Diablos as if he were joining a social club. With a few of Ronquillo's mannerisms—the tapping of his skull to indicate "hard head," the repeating of the phrase "I really don't think much"—he conjures an image of the shooter coping with an endless future behind bars.

Finally, with a simple statement from the mother of the dead teenager—"the heart can break so many times"—Alex eloquently captures the grief that destroyed two families.

Alex once told an interviewer that the stories he worked on inevitably became personal. Rereading this piece now, some twenty years later, I'm struck by the very personal investment Alex made as a reporter in trying to piece together elusive truths.

■   ■   ■

WALLA WALLA—The boy who killed Melissa Fernandes has grown into a man. A small young man with a bald head. Brian Ronquillo is 20 years old, no longer the blank-faced adolescent without a clue. He knows stuff now. At the very least, he knows that lives can be undone in a single moment.

The knowledge shows on his face, the look of someone sober after a long drunk spell. The eyes suggest a kind of regret. The mouth forms a straight, penitent line. Right now, though, he's drawing attention to his shaved skull.

"Hard head," he says, raising a finger to a spot above his temple. He says he got caught up in a bad way, didn't listen to admonitions, and this—tap-tap-tap—is why he ended up here, serving 52 years in the Washington State Penitentiary.

As an explanation, it doesn't say much about why he did what he did outside Ballard High School in Seattle four years ago this month.

But what theory could explain how a bright, talented 16-year-old student with a clean record and wide-open future, who came from a loving, stable, middle-class family that provided every material thing he needed—how could someone like this wrap a bandanna around his face, point a gun at a crowd of students and pull the trigger, not once, but eight times?

Most agreed Ronquillo was immature, eager to impress and loyal to the wrong crowd. His attorney, Anthony Savage, said as much during his trial, but Savage also ascribed a tragic quality to his client: Here was a basically decent kid who made a single, disastrous mistake.

Ronquillo and his family say his 52-year sentence was too harsh for his first and only criminal offense. They say he did not get a fair trial. The state Court of Appeals, however, said he did, and denied Ronquillo's appeal last week. Now he and his family are preparing to petition the state Supreme Court to review the case.

As the trigger man in what was arguably the most notorious Seattle killing of 1994—the only murder ever of a student on

Seattle School District property—Ronquillo embodied the worst fears of a gang culture out of control. Seattle police recorded an all-time-high number of drive-by shootings that year.

Fernandes' mother, Tammy Fernandes, 39, spoke for many when she said Ronquillo got what he deserved and should be given no options, "just as 'Missy' was given no choice."

At the end of Ronquillo's trial, Tammy Fernandes spoke of closure and of healing. She's experienced neither. She says she relives those last moments with Melissa every day. The memory of her daughter's face in the hospital "sits right here at the top of my brain. It doesn't go away. I can't tell you how much it hurts.

"I wonder if he hurts, too."

Ronquillo didn't testify at his trial and said nothing publicly except at the end, just before he was sentenced. He apologized to the Fernandes family and to his own family for causing so much pain. It was a short, mechanical statement. Tammy Fernandes doesn't even remember it. In her mind, and in the public's mind, Ronquillo has been mute since the shooting.

Ronquillo has told friends he's grown up in prison. He claims to be six inches taller and four years smarter. He squirms when asked, face to face, if he has also grown in perspective, grown enough to understand the gravity of what he did on March 23, 1994.

BRIAN RONQUILLO walked into the interview room wearing white Converse sneakers, blue jeans and a sweat shirt. He had a slow, loose-limbed way of walking, which in some circles translates into "cool." He seemed at home in the room, a tiny cinderblock chamber with a guard station outside the door.

He slumped in a chair and constantly ran a hand over his head, as if the questions were too hard. He bounced his knee as he did throughout his trial. The bald head made him look meaner than he was. He still had a boy's voice.

As he spoke, it became apparent he was not someone given to deep reflection, although a clear intelligence came through. When talking about subjects he liked—cars, girls, movies—he smiled and laughed.

But with questions about Melissa Fernandes or "the incident," as he called it, he grew uncomfortable and acted as if his head hurt. His constant refrain was, "I really don't think much."

"Do I understand the gravity of my crime? Yeah, I won't lie, it was a pretty bad crime, you know. But, I don't know. I guess when I got locked up, I just—pssshhhht—shut out everything. I really don't think much. I block out everything emotionally, you know, so I don't feel much. If you think too much in here, it'll wear you down and break you mentally.

"I don't want to be some ding going crazy up on the third floor [psychiatric ward]. In juvenile, people were like, 'Man, they just gave you 52 years, if I was you, I'd commit suicide.' I said, 'But I'm not you. I'm a lot stronger.'"

Survival is something he was proud of—barely out of his teens, not quite 5 1/2 feet tall, living in a concentration of the meanest men in the state and holding his own.

He hasn't been raped, bullied, nor even been in a fight. He spends his days listening to music on the radio or on cassettes sent by his sister. He watches TV and reads entertainment magazines. "I'm not too swell on books," he said. At night he sleeps with headphones, filling his head with music, as if to block out thought.

HOME IS A 10-BY-12-FOOT CELL in a high-security wing of the prison. He has two cell mates with whom, he said, he's become close. His part of the cell, which consists mostly of the top-left bunk, displays signs of his professed changed life: two Catholic rosaries, three Bibles, four pictures of his family taped to his headboard.

Some things he couldn't change, like the blue dots tattooed between the knuckles of his fist—two dots here, three dots there—signifying the number 23. That was the name of his gang, the 23rd Street Diablos, more commonly known on the streets as simply The 23rd, named after a street on Seattle's Beacon Hill.

This was not a subject Ronquillo wanted to talk about. He could hardly even say the word "gang," so damaging has the word been to him. He referred to it only as "the life," as in: "I don't know what happened. Somewhere along the line, I got caught up in the life."

Survival was not an issue for Ronquillo growing up. The picture that emerged from court records and interviews was of a stable, industrious family that had earned its place in the ranks of the comfortable middle class.

His parents, Bonifacio and Myrna Ronquillo, worked long hours, she as a toxicologist, he as a technician for the U.S. Postal Inspection Service. They lived in a spacious home in Shoreline.

Bonifacio, a retired Navy man, also received a good pension. Deeply religious, he didn't drink or smoke, and required a military efficiency from his family: up at 6 A.M., showered and dressed and bed made by 6:45, breakfast together by 7 or 7:30.

Ronquillo and his sister, Maryann, seemed to thrive under the strict guidance. At St. Luke's, a Catholic K-8 school a few blocks from home, both kids were popular and got good grades. Ronquillo made a name for himself as a rap artist, winning the school's talent show in his last year before attending Blanchet High School in North Seattle, where he became an honor student his freshman year.

He was a little guy, not even 5 feet tall at the time, with a round face and a full, bushy head of hair. Friends described him as a clown, full of energy and willing to play the fool for laughs. "He was always the one to say, 'Let's do this, let's do that,'" a former classmate said.

He was heavily influenced by rap music. He began to take on the walk and talk of his favorite rap artists, saying "Whassup cuz?" and "Whassup blood?" as a way of greeting friends and rivals.

In his sophomore year at Blanchet, classmates said, he started taking on "a gang look" at a time when it was just becoming fashionable—the baggy clothes, tilted baseball caps and oversized coats. But Ronquillo also seemed to acquire the attitude: the nonchalant cool and the respect-me-or-else pose of a street fighter.

That year, Ronquillo was implicated in three separate graffiti incidents and was asked to withdraw from Blanchet—the only blemish on his record.

He transferred to Shorewood High School and seemed to fully embrace "the life." He skipped classes and let his grades drop. By that time, Ronquillo and his father butted heads frequently. His father's strict ways no longer suited him and his new friends.

Ronquillo managed to keep his life with The 23rd a secret from his family and church. They attributed the boy's change to adolescent rebellion. And a lot of it was exactly that. But Ronquillo's friends had a nasty habit of carrying guns and firing them.

If it weren't for the guns, The 23rd would be just a cluster of mischievous boys who happened to dislike other clusters of mischievous boys. The gang was not into dealing drugs (although some smoked marijuana) and didn't have a clearly marked turf.

"They were basically a social group," said Tom Nakao, a gang-intervention counselor who had close ties to the gang. "At least that's how they started. They talked tough, they acted tough, but most of these kids were not hard core."

The 23rd was a loose-knit, casual group of friends with numerous overlapping circles of classmates, cousins and acquaintances. Most were of Filipino descent, although there were whites and other Southeast Asians among them.

The gang roughly broke down into a North End group, made up of younger kids like Ronquillo, and a South End group made up of slightly older kids living on Beacon Hill and in the Rainier Valley.

Members of the two groups went to dances together and played pool or hung out at friends' houses listening to music. A few got into trouble with the law for car prowls and theft. Some had been kicked out of school for fighting.

But individually, outside the context of the gang, they often impressed people with their politeness and deference. It wasn't an act. If anything was an act, it was the gangster pose. This duality in behavior was broached several times during court hearings. Kathy Powers, Ronquillo's juvenile probation officer, testified that Ronquillo "essentially led two lives."

What held the boys of The 23rd together was a common infatuation with that other life, one immersed in the "gang culture," made up of certain strains of music and dress and codes of conduct. The boys liked to think they lived according to the "code of the streets" even though many lived on spacious tree-lined avenues in the suburbs.

They got into the life because they wanted to. It gave them camaraderie, excitement, status—a low status in the eyes of adults, but in the upside-down world of adolescent rebellion, low was good; low was cool.

The gang also gave them power. The more power, the better. And what more glorified tool of power was there for the common man, or boy, than the handgun. Only a few members had them. It became frightfully clear that most knew little about how to use them, and knew less about their deadly force.

THE 23RD STREET DIABLOS will be remembered most for this:

The victims in the gang's three most destructive acts were all innocent girls. None of them were intended victims. In each case, the shooter seemed astonished his bullets caused harm. Twice, the bullets killed.

The first shooting happened July 3, 1992, when a car full of 23rd members dueled with another car on Interstate 5. In the other car was a member of a rival gang called the Bad Side Posse. Both groups were from South Seattle, and had had a run-in earlier in the day at Boom City, a strip of fireworks stands on the Tulalip reservation north of Everett.

On the way back to Seattle, someone in the BSP car threw a metal pipe at the Diablo car, and the BSP car sped ahead. The driver of the Diablo car, Huy Vu Nguyen Dang, shot three times at the BSP car. One bullet struck 17-year-old Carrie Tran in the back of the head. She died the same day. Tran, a recent graduate of Seattle's Ingraham High School, was not a BSP member.

Dang, 19, on the other hand was a known member of The 23rd and had the tattoos to prove it. He was sentenced to 33 years in prison. Because the shooting happened near Everett, Dang's trial took place in Snohomish County and was not widely reported in Seattle.

A police report stated that Dang "was shocked that he killed someone" and wanted "to express to the victim's parents how he did not mean it."

The second shooting took place in a parked car in North Seattle on Feb. 22, 1994. Jerome Reyes, then 17 and a member of The 23rd, was showing off a .38-caliber revolver to two teenage girls seated next to him.

While playing with the safety latch, he accidentally fired the gun, shooting Erica Segalbaum, a ninth-grader from Edmonds. The girl was hit in the left arm and chest and suffered a punctured lung but survived.

Reyes was charged with third-degree assault. His father, a minister, pleaded to the judge that the shooting was accidental and that his son was "truly and sincerely remorseful." The judge released Reyes under the restrictions that he observe a curfew, handle no firearms and stay away from further trouble.

A month later, Reyes was one of 11 people arrested after the murder of Melissa Fernandes. Reyes was blamed by everyone as the instigator. It began when three members of the Bad Side Posse, The 23rd's old rivals, called Reyes a punk and chased him off the Ballard High School campus.

Two days later, on March 23, 1994, Reyes returned with two carloads of 23rd friends to the exact location where he was run off—near the corner of Northwest 68th Street and 14th Avenue Northwest—on the north side of the school, a BSP hangout.

One of the people in the lead car was Brian Ronquillo.

The 23rd and BSP had a running rivalry since before the I-5 shooting. The BSP were mostly Laotian. If traced back far enough, one would probably find the conflict began with a Filipino kid getting into a fight with a Laotian kid.

In the process of calling in allies, a gang conflict was born. The hostility escalated even as the origin was forgotten. That's how it often happened. The animosity became a given. As Reyes later said during the trial: "We don't like them, and they don't like us."

The 23rd members arrived at Ballard High around lunch

hour, got out of their cars and confronted a group of BSPs, but the 23rd members fled when someone said a police car was in the area. The BSPs laughed at them.

A little more than an hour later, about 1:30 P.M., two carloads of 23rd members returned to the school. In the interim, Ronquillo had borrowed a gun from a friend and put it in his backpack. It was a Mac-12 semiautomatic handgun, a weapon originally developed for the military.

It's doubtful Ronquillo had ever fired a gun like this. Former members of the gang say they don't think he'd ever fired a gun, period. When asked the question in person, Ronquillo said, "I can't talk about that."

The crowd outside the school had changed. Now there were only two BSP members standing around with other students. Melissa Fernandes was next to them. It was just after fifth period, and she was waiting for her mother to pick her up.

Fernandes was well-liked, pretty and sociable, and tough in her own way. She was known as a peacemaker and lover of animals, and told anyone who'd listen that she wanted to be a marine biologist. She wanted to see the world, and had friends who wanted to see it, too. She mingled in many circles, and knew the young men in the two approaching cars.

She was regarded as a friend of The 23rd, and had no reason to fear them. Witnesses said that, as the cars approached, Fernandes actually walked toward them. Some said she was going to try to calm the situation; others said she was just going to say "Hi." She never had a chance.

As the lead car, a red Nissan Sentra, got within 10 to 12 feet, Ronquillo, in the front passenger seat and wearing a blue bandanna over the bottom half of his face, pulled the Mac-12 from his backpack and began firing. Investigators later said that, based on witnesses' reports and ballistics, Ronquillo continued firing even after the car had passed the crowd.

Most of the people standing around, including the two BSP members, hit the ground. Fernandes stayed standing, and one witness said she had a look of incredulity on her face. She was turning away when she was hit with a bullet just above and be-hind her left ear.

The bullet broke into four lead fragments as it hit her head. The fragments tore through different sections of her brain. Ex-aminers later said brain activity probably stopped immediately. She fell to her knees, clutching the back of her head, and fell face forward. Someone turned her over.

"The last memory of her will scar my life forever," said Va-nessa Reeder, a classmate at Ballard. "I ran outside. . . . There was my best friend lying on the ground in a pool of blood. She had an inanimate expression on her face, with two tears stream-ing down."

Fernandes was taken to Harborview Medical Center where she underwent surgery. Before the surgery, "I held her toes, I held her feet, I held her arms and fingers, I laid on her chest," her mother, Tammy Fernandes, said. "She just looked at me. I'll never forget that image, her looking at me."

Tammy Fernandes said Melissa was unrecognizable after sur-gery. "She was different. It wasn't my daughter anymore." Melissa Fernandes was taken off life support and died 22 hours after she had been shot.

A police officer who later questioned the suspects said: "The fact that they hit her has really stunned them. Most of them didn't think anyone was to be killed or that Melissa Fernandes would be the victim."

The shooting took place on a Wednesday afternoon. By the following Saturday night, Seattle police had arrested 11 people. All 11 were convicted of various charges in connection with Fer-nandes' death.

Ronquillo and Cesar Sarausad, the driver of the red Nissan, were tried together as adults.

Ronquillo was convicted of first-degree murder and sentenced to 52 years. Sarausad got second-degree murder and 27 years. Sarausad also appealed his conviction and is awaiting a decision. Reyes plead-ed guilty to manslaughter and was sentenced to eight years.

The other eight defendants pleaded guilty to rendering crimi-nal assistance and were back on the streets by Christmas. One of those boys, Lucas Gosho, 20, was convicted of a nonfatal drive-by shooting last year at the Alderwood Mall in Lynnwood. He was sent back to prison for six years.

Ronquillo's appeal was based partly on the argument that he did not intend to kill anyone, least of all Fernandes. This essen-tially was his defense during the trial: He'd meant only to scare his rivals and apparently was a bad shot.

His appeals lawyer, Eric Nielsen, argued that, to be convicted of first-degree murder, which requires proof of premeditation, the court had to show that Ronquillo was specifically trying to kill Fernandes, and neither the police nor prosecutors presented any evidence of that.

A conviction of second-degree murder or manslaughter, Nielsen said, would have been more fitting, and the penalty more appropriate—20 to 30 years less than Ronquillo's current sentence. Nielsen has until April 1 to petition the state Supreme Court to review the case.

The Ronquillo family added the disappointment of last week's appellate-court ruling to a list of emotional setbacks. Trauma-tized by the loss of a son and the instant notoriety of their name, the family moved from Shoreline to a house north of Lynnwood. Twice a month, they drive 10 hours round trip to Walla Walla for a two-hour visit with Brian.

"I just want my son home," said a somber Myrna Ronquillo, 46. This is her constant refrain. It seems to answer every question. Myrna Ronquillo has tried to stay busy, working two full-time jobs, to keep from dwelling on her pain. "We have to stay strong. We have two kids, and we have to take care of them."

Her husband, Bonifacio Ronquillo, 48, when not working at the Postal Inspection Service, can often be found in the sixth-floor law library of the King County Courthouse. There, he pores through law books, looking for anything that might help in his son's appeal.

"Who would have thought this could happen to my family? We tried to do everything good for my son," Bonifacio Ronquillo said. "Now we will do everything we can for his appeal. Even if we have to go all the way to the Supreme Court. Even if we lose everything we own."

Brian Ronquillo once again knocked on his head. "Matigas ng ulo," he said, which in his Philippine dialect meant "hard head."

If he'd listened to his father about staying home, or to the dream he'd had two weeks before the shooting, in which a black angel warned him something terrible was going to happen—maybe he'd be playing hoops at the playground instead of sitting in a guarded room being asked whether he was sorry for his crime.

He said he prays for Fernandes and her family every night, and asks for forgiveness from God. He even recited the prayers verbatim in the interview room. Yet something about his remorse wasn't quite persuasive.

Ronquillo never saw Melissa Fernandes fall to the ground, her head punctured, never saw her being loaded onto an ambulance and driven away. Those images can't haunt him because he didn't see them. He was long gone.

The drive-by shooting may be one of the most cowardly of violent acts precisely because it's committed simultaneously with fleeing. There's distance between the act and the result. The shooter often doesn't see the damage inflicted, and doesn't have to acknowledge it, except in the abstract, like in a video game.

To many young people enamored with "the life," gangs are partly a game to begin with. And for the uninitiated, a drive-by can be part of the game—a detached, bloodless activity with no immediate risks.

AFTER THE SHOOTING AT BALLARD, seen by dozens of witnesses, the two carloads of 23rd members went to Seattle's Northgate Mall to play video games. One wonders whether any thought at all was given to possible consequences.

A welcome one was that the 23rd Street Diablos died.

Tom Nakao, the gang intervention counselor, said the shooting depleted their ranks and shook up the members so much, the group stopped gathering and never resumed. "I've never seen a group so vilified by the press as hard core disappear so quickly," he said.

"They realized all of it happened over nothing really. Nothing. Now they're a whisper of the past."

Seattle police say gang activity is down on all fronts. The number of drive-by shootings last year, 36, was the lowest in this decade. The year of the Ballard shooting, 1994, there were 77.

Sgt. Steve Martin of the SPD gang unit said the explanation for the decrease is simple: Many of the hard core gangsters—the leaders, the trigger men, the big-time drug dealers—are in prison. They won't be there forever. A few are beginning to trickle out now, and Martin said his unit is anticipating "an upswing" in activity in the next year or two.

Ronquillo, in a fleeting moment of reflection, offered up a morsel of wisdom for those caught up in the life.

"All I've got to say is look at me," he said. "I was 16 when I got locked up. I've done four years. I've got 48 to go."

He raised both hands, like two sides of the scales of justice. "Over here, you're 16 and free and having fun. Over here, you're 16 and sitting in the penitentiary for the rest of your life. Just weigh that."

To be sure, Ronquillo has weighed his actions at Ballard High School over and over again. He understands the enormous waste, as only a young man facing a half-century in prison can.

As for the pain he's caused others, Tammy Fernandes doubts Ronquillo can know its depth. She tells how, four years after the murder, her 14-year-old, Nicki, "still aches for Missy," sometimes going for days without speaking or leaving her room. And how her 5-year-old, Kelly, points to every church on the road and says, "There's Missy's house."

The heart can break so many times, Tammy Fernandes says. Each time, she holds it together by force of will because she has to. Sometimes, she crumbles into a grief so private, she can't share it with anyone.

In those moments, she says she knows Brian Ronquillo will never comprehend what his one blind act has done. It is her refrain. He'll never know how far the one bullet traveled. In her mind, it hasn't stopped.

PART VI

ECCENTRICS

ONWARD CHRISTIAN SURFERS:
SPREADING THE GOSPEL ON WAIKIKI

Los Angeles Times, May 31, 2006

IN AN OLD NUCLEAR BUNKER, THIS GUY
HAS THE LOWDOWN ON UFOS

Los Angeles Times, March 28, 2008

Introduced by **SAM HOWE VERHOVEK**,
who appreciated that Tizon took him seriously

"*Surfers for Jesus*": *In the hands of most reporters, this is a joke,
a punch line, a chance for a soft feature with a few jokes
about folks with the nutty idea that the Son of Man came not to
serve but to surf. Or maybe it's not really a story at all: Who cares
whether a bunch of surf bums have religion or not?*

*Likewise, a guy in a nuclear bunker out in the sticks, tracking
UFOs. More giggles and gags.*

*But Tizon saw stories, and he didn't jump for any of the predict-
able punch lines. For the surfers, he got what they were all about,
or at least how they understood themselves:*

> *Jesus preferred the company of those on society's lowest
> rung: prostitutes, tax collectors and fishermen. In some
> realms today, that rung would include surfers, often viewed
> as loafers and deadbeats or pleasure-seeking Bohemians
> who forsake everything for the perfect wave.*

*When it came to the UFO connoisseur, again, let the man have
his say: "The work of studying UFOs," he explained to Tizon, "is of
immense consequence to every living thing on this planet."*

Tizon took these people seriously, treated them respectfully, and

*listened to them intently—that much is obvious in reading these
stories. That was so often his approach, and, as a fellow journalist, it's one of the things I admired most about his reporting. More
important, this was his approach to life.*

. . .

ONWARD CHRISTIAN SURFERS:
SPREADING THE GOSPEL ON WAIKIKI

HONOLULU—If Jesus were alive today, he would be a surfer. He
would mingle with fishermen and beach bums and lay his mat
on the sand among the scantily clad. Instead of walking on water,
he would ride waves on a carved piece of fiberglass, keeping an
eye out for anyone who needed saving.

This is what Dean Sabate and his friends believe.

They are surfers for Jesus. Today they are on Waikiki Beach
doing what they believe Jesus would be doing. While others
might see a frolicking crowd, Sabate and his group see sprinkled
among the masses a few lost souls who need tending.

"This is our ministry, being out here, being in the ocean,
making friends," says Sabate, 42. He is a former pro surfer, muscular and bronzed.

"We don't go thumping people on the head with a Bible. We
come out here, enjoy the water and talk to people," he says. "We
just allow God to work."

LOST SOULS INCLUDE THE LONELY, the poor, the hopeless
and the worn out. These are plentiful in paradise, though they're
not always easy to spot. In Sabate's experience, those who seem
together may be the least together people on the beach. You can
hide sadness behind a pair of shades.

He knows. Just seven months ago, Sabate, once considered a
surfer prodigy, was aimless and living in a park on the other side
of Oahu. A pastor found him, befriended him and introduced
him to a group of Christian surfers. Now Sabate leads a group of
"surfer missionaries" doing their thing. There are about a dozen

of them here on this postcard-perfect afternoon. The sun blazes down through blue skies. The surfers spread out like a platoon on patrol.

Waikiki is a haven for tourists but also draws its share of the homeless and wayward. Everyone is a potential convert.

One of the surfers, Dave Strigl, 38, takes me out on the water. We paddle on boards around Mamala Bay. His ultimate goal, as with most missionaries, is to bring people into a relationship with Jesus.

But the surfers don't rush it. They're willing to wait months, even years, for a conversion, a sort of incremental nudging into faith. On these outreach trips, they're mostly interested in developing friendships. The surfers' approach in one line: "Make friends first, God will do the rest."

On the water, there's no talk of Jesus, but death comes up.

"See that sea turtle?" Strigl says, gesturing toward an approaching shell.

"I didn't know sea turtles came this close to shore," I say.

"It could mean sharks," Strigl says, smiling. It is a nudge. Sharks could cause death and death leads to the afterlife. The afterlife is a natural segue into God. That talk would come later.

The surfer missionaries do beach things: sunbathe, stroll, swim, surf, staying alert to any likely encounter with a stranger. Inside the surfers' van, in case anyone shows interest, is a box of Christian tracts. On some occasions, the surfers gather at the beach and pray, then hand out the tracts to people who approach.

On a grassy spot above the beach, Sabate chats with a surfer named Scott, who has stopped by. He is a friend from Sabate's days on the pro circuit. Sabate was born and raised in Hawaii and seems to bump into friends at every beach. Scott is separated from his wife and doesn't know what to do.

"Only God can heal a broken relationship," Sabate tells him.

On-the-spot conversions generally don't happen. A good day is when a single conversation leads to a single invitation to a Bible study. The main thing, according to the group's philosophy, is to hang out with the needy like Jesus did. Jesus preferred the company of those on society's lowest rung: prostitutes, tax collectors and fishermen. In some realms today, that rung would include surfers, often viewed as loafers and deadbeats or pleasure-seeking Bohemians who forsake everything for the perfect wave.

After three hours on the beach, the surfer missionaries re-group, pile into their van and head for the hills above Honolulu. The van chugs up a winding road into the heart of Kalihi Valley, a lush ravine of low-income houses and apartments.

An upright surfboard by the side of the road marks the spot where the van turns onto a long dirt driveway. The driveway leads into a three-acre compound of ramshackle buildings with tin roofs. This is home base.

IT USED TO BE a kimchi factory. Since 1997, longtime mis-sionaries Tom and Cindy Bauer have used the property as head-quarters for their ministry called Surfing the Nations. Sabate and Strigl are leaders in the group.

The ministry is part relief agency, missionary training camp and surfers' crash pad. The group surfs in the early mornings, serves for most of the day, then surfs again in the late afternoons.

Service can include outreach, cleaning house for the disabled and holding surf workshops for young teens. In between the surf-ing and service, surfers study the Bible, attend missionary classes and maintain the compound. They spend two hours a day pray-ing and meditating.

About 25 people stay on the property in separate bunkhouses for men and women.

It is a revolving population. They range in age from teenagers to mid-lifers and come from all over the world and all Christian denominations. They stay for a few days or a few years, depending on their financial arrangement. Surfers raise their own support—frequently from home churches—to pay for travel and personal expenses such as cellphones and clothing.

Living is cheap. The property is owned by Grace Bible Church, where the Bauers have attended for years. Room and board are provided, and surfboards supplied. Surfboards lean against and cover entire walls and hang from the rafters.

The room where workers once washed cabbage for the kimchi is now a community center with a ceiling made of surfboards. The walk-in freezer is a makeshift sound studio (for aspiring surfer musicians). The garage is an office, and above that is where the Bauers live—a modest, well-tended apartment furnished with donated and salvaged furniture.

Cindy Bauer manages the office and makes sure the place runs on a schedule. She is in her 50s, energetic and cheery. Tom Bauer, 56, is the head surfer dude, the spiritual leader of the community. They have four grown daughters, two still living at the compound.

The concept of a surfer's ministry came from Tom. A native Californian and surfer since childhood, Tom owns 70 surfboards.

"I didn't choose to be a surfer. I was called to be a surfer," says Tom, a silver-haired man who feels no compunction saying things like "Stoked!"

Unfortunately for him, he tried to merge his two loves—surfing and Jesus—in the early 1970s when some in the church establishment (he belonged to several churches in California) frowned on beach culture. He was told he'd have to choose one or the other, and for years he kept those two aspects of his life separate.

Some traditionalists viewed the beach—associated with flesh and drugs and beatnik rebellion—as "not a place where good Christian folk assemble," says David Morgan, a humanities professor at Valparaiso University in Indiana. He says there will always be some traditionalists who disapprove of "any subculture that freely intermingles pleasure with religious practice."

The irony is that the Sea of Galilee, where Jesus supposedly walked on water, was likely a place with a rich beach culture, Morgan says. "If you're an itinerant preacher like Jesus of Nazareth, you're going to go where the people are, and one of those places is the beach."

The idea that Jesus today would keep company with surfers, Morgan says, "has some sociological support to it."

The Bauers moved from California to Hawaii in 1979 as missionaries. They started the surfers ministry 18 years later. For them and the other surfers at the compound, surfing is a spiritual experience. Part of it is just being immersed in God's creation, Sabate says. "And there are times when the waves are really big and you think you could die, and there's no one to turn to but God."

About six times a year, the Bauers and their sun-tanned corps conduct missionary trips abroad—to places like Indonesia, Sri Lanka and Papua New Guinea—to open surf clubs, run surfing contests and share their faith.

Niklas Ericksson, 34, has spent much of his life since 1999 at Surfing the Nations. He is from Sweden, where he works part of the year for a diaper company. The rest of the year he lives here.

Sometimes, he says, he can't believe how good life can be as a surfer missionary. Yes, you are poor but you experience a deep inner peace. You serve God, and sometimes "you're out there in the water with friends, you're in this beautiful place, you're doing what you love, and you think:

"This is awesome."

THURSDAY IS FEEDING THE HUNGRY DAY at the compound. Just as the sun rises above the hills, the surfers begin setting up tents and tables just off the gravel parking lot. In the community center, others pack boxes of food donated from a food bank. The boxes are passed along a human chain until they reach the tables.

The food line is scheduled to begin at 10 A.M., but a few people start arriving about 9 A.M., hobbling up the long gravel driveway. Others come in borrowed cars and trucks. About 12% of Hawaii's population suffers from food shortages, according to state agencies. Many of the needy live right here in Kalihi Valley, but people come from all over Oahu. They've heard about the food program by word of mouth at the beaches.

After they line up, sign in and collect their food boxes, the people sit around the compound and visit with the surfers.

"These people are my friends," says Jane Chu, 58, who has

driven 45 minutes from Pearl City. "It's not just 'Come and get your box and go.' They want to get to know you."

Chu's husband, disabled from a construction injury—"He fell 25 feet onto concrete and broke his back"—receives $2,400 a month in worker's comp. Rent is $1,900. The boxes of canned food and fruit collected here will help feed an extended family.

In the parking lot, a young man with a black bandanna around his head and slightly menacing eyes directs the cars coming in and out. His name is Jeddy Basques, 19. He has 15 brothers and three sisters. His parents are in prison for drug-dealing. Basques is one of the many orphaned souls profoundly touched by the surfers. He comes to the compound several times a week for Bible study and prayer.

"Sometimes Tom [Bauer] takes me to the beach with my brothers," he says.

The flow of cars continues until well past 3 P.M. By the end of the day a few hundred people will have come and gone. Basques helps the surfers put everything away, working side by side with Sabate. With the day's work done, the surfers go their separate ways. Some take naps, some write letters home, some go to the mall.

Sabate makes a quick round of the premises to see if anyone wants to go to the beach. Strigl does.

A few others say they'll meet them at the regular spot on Waikiki. Sabate and Strigl throw surfboards in a van and hop in.

Strigl starts the engine.

"Wait," says Sabate.

Strigl glances at Sabate quizzically, and then remembers.

They both close their eyes and bow their heads.

"Lord, we thank you for this day," Sabate says. "We pray that you may protect us out there in the water. We pray that whatever we do, we give you the glory. We pray that you may use our gifts and talents to serve you. Please use us. In the name of Jesus, we pray. Amen."

. . .

IN AN OLD NUCLEAR BUNKER, THIS GUY
HAS THE LOWDOWN ON UFOS

HARRINGTON, WASH.—"That door," he says with dramatic pause. "That door weighs 4,000 pounds. It's been reinforced to withstand a nuclear blast."

Peter Davenport has a radio voice, the kind of exaggerated baritone that cuts through walls and most doors, but not this one. This is solid steel and a foot thick.

It is Davenport's door, which opens into a tunnel leading below ground to what was once a nuclear missile complex here in the desert of eastern Washington.

The Air Force decommissioned the site in the mid-1960s and it sat empty for most of the time since.

Davenport, longtime director of the National UFO Reporting Center, a nonprofit clearinghouse and 24-hour hotline for UFO sightings, bought it for $100,000 two years ago to turn into his new headquarters.

Why does a man buy an old windowless missile complex deep underground, only to spend his days tracking unidentified objects flying through the sky?

Davenport doesn't have an answer. Furthermore, he doesn't need one. As a full-time UFO investigator and possessor of one of the world's most comprehensive, though unofficial, UFO databases, his life already runs counter to convention.

The center, in continuous operation since 1970, is known worldwide among those interested in UFOs: scientists as well as people surfing the Web. The hotline is posted on various UFO websites, and calls—as many as 20,000 in a year—come from people who believe they've seen or experienced something beyond the ordinary, potentially involving extraterrestrials.

If the case seems compelling and is a short flight away, Davenport will investigate in person. He takes written reports, records testimony and consults experts in specialty areas.

Davenport, 60, is a passionate, cerebral man with a haughty disdain for the media.

"I do not countenance fools," he had said earlier that day, almost as a warning. "The work of studying UFOs is of immense consequence to every living thing on this planet. If I sense you are wasting my time, I will be blunt."

His life revolves around a question, namely: "Are we alone in the universe or are we not?" He believes there are clues behind the monstrous door that he now faces.

He picks up a shovel. He has not been to his missile site in weeks, and 3 feet of snow blocks the doorway. He breaks up chunks and shovels them to the side.

It is 34 degrees on a late March afternoon, the sun just beginning to set over this patch of land 50 miles west of Spokane. Not a single house can be seen—only snow and mounds of barren terrain and the occasional frozen tumbleweed like rolled-up cobwebs in the distance.

A wrenching sound breaks the silence. Davenport has pried open the door. He tilts his head, then squeezes through sideways before disappearing into darkness.

"HE'S NOT THE NORMAL GUY on the street, but crazy? No. He's not crazy," Robert B. Frost says of Davenport, whom he's known for most of the last two decades. The former chief engineer for Boeing's portion of the B-2 bomber project, Frost met Davenport, a fellow techie, in Seattle.

"The guy's brilliant," Frost says. "Personally, I think he's going to prevail on this thing."

By that, Frost means time will prove Davenport correct on his hunch that UFOs represent a real phenomenon.

Although mainstream science tends to dismiss the subject, along with Bigfoot and the Loch Ness monster, a number of prominent scientists and much of the public—as many as 60%, according to polls—believe UFOs exist and should be studied. As a corollary, a large number of astronomers believe life in other parts of the universe is not only possible but likely.

Among the famous, former President Carter, anthropologist Margaret Mead, psychiatrist Carl Jung and astronaut Gordon Cooper reported seeing a UFO or proclaimed a belief in UFOs as representing visitations from extraterrestrials.

Last fall, Rep. Dennis J. Kucinich, at the time running for the Democratic presidential nomination, made headlines by admitting he had seen, in the 1980s, a strange "triangular craft" hovering above a rural area of Washington state.

In a way, Davenport's destiny was sealed, by his own reckoning, at age 6. In 1954, while sitting in a car with his mother and brother at a drive-in theater in St. Louis, he looked out the window and, there in the sky, a bright red disc hovered then— whoosh—disappeared into the horizon.

"If there was a seminal moment," Davenport had said earlier. "That would be it."

He read and eventually wrote widely on the subject as a sideline to his education, which included earning degrees in biology and Russian at Stanford University and graduate degrees in genetics and the biochemistry of fish at the University of Washington. He became founding president of a Seattle-area biotechnology company, BioSyn Inc., and nine years later, in 1994, sold his stock and made a small fortune.

That same year, he got a phone call from Robert Gribble, a retired firefighter in Seattle, who for two decades had acted as a one-man clearinghouse for UFO information and operator of a 24/7 national UFO hotline (206-722-3000).

Gribble wanted to pass the torch. Davenport accepted and has been director of the National UFO Reporting Center since, keeping the same hotline and funding the operation out of his own pocket. Costs can range from $500 to $5,000 a month, depending on travel.

Davenport has few other expenses. He never married, never had kids. He drove old cars. For a dozen years he ran the center out of a rented home near Seattle's University District. Then he got the notion that he wanted his own missile site.

"There was an allure to the idea," he says he told friends. Davenport, who had long been interested in aircraft and rocketry, had heard of missile silos for sale in eastern Washington.

One in particular was going for a bargain price: Atlas Missile Site No. 6, in which the previous owner had killed and dismembered a visitor. Long-haul truck driver Ralph Benson was convicted of murder in 2004 and was suspected in at least one other murder when he died in prison two years later. Davenport bought the site from Benson's sons.

"I DON'T KNOW about the kind of people who buy these things," Davenport says, his voice trailing off in the darkness. He leaves the steel door propped open, and fumbles for lights.

A series of clicks, and the room turns pale yellow. He stands in an entryway, all concrete and steel, and dank like a cave. On each side is a tunnel.

He takes the tunnel to the right, clomps down a metal tube about 50 yards long. It is large enough for him to walk through without bending. The tube leads to a cave about the size of a basketball court. Piles of debris can be seen in the semi-darkness.

"Launch control room," he says with his radio voice.

Davenport offers up specs (corroborated by military documents): The ceilings are 16 feet high, the walls 18 inches thick. The complex, made of 3 million tons of concrete, can withstand a blast 50 times the power of the Hiroshima bomb at a distance of 1.6 miles.

He returns to the vestibule and enters the other tunnel, similarly constructed, which opens into another cavernous space: the missile room.

The complex was known as a "coffin launcher." This is where the Atlas missile rested flat. Above, the ceiling was a sliding metal door, which opened as hydraulics raised the rocket for launching.

Toward the back of the missile room, shrouded in darkness, sits Davenport's life work: a collection of tens of thousands of reports on UFO sightings from all over the world. He has files from long before the television show "The X-Files" brought the paranormal to prime time.

The information is meticulously labeled and filed in a long row of mismatched metal file cabinets. They form the shape of a miniature city skyline.

The plan was to live and work in here. But the site needed more work than expected. The place leaks. The ventilation isn't good, and there's a little bat problem.

For now, the center's phone and answering machine will stay at Davenport's Harrington apartment, a few miles away, until Missile Site No. 6 is fixed up. Davenport is doing most of the fixing up himself.

Shadows flicker as he shines his flashlight around. He walks to the nearest cabinet, opens a drawer and randomly pulls out a thick sheaf of files. Call logs. A file for every month. A sampling of entries:

Jan 6, 1995. 0:15. Warm Beach, WA. Two women observe a strange "rope of light," with a bright sphere attached.

Jan 6, 1995. 17:30. Glendo, WY. Mother and son witness large glowing craft maneuver into cloud. Pursued by mil. aircraft.

Jan. 7, 1995. 5:00. Makapuu Point, HI. Man and wife observe bizarre hump-backed triangular object over sea. Opaque windows.

Davenport says that of the vast majority of UFO sightings, up to 90% are explainable: weather balloons, military aircraft, satellites and the like. Many more prove to be hoaxes.

But then there's the tiny percentage, maybe only a handful each year, where something was definitely seen—often by multiple reliable sources—and that defy explanation.

He believes that clues lie buried in these hill-sized mounds of paper that he has meticulously cataloged, if only the government or a university would do the research.

"I'm willing to share data," he says. "I'm willing to throw all of it to anyone who wants to know."

There have been few takers.

Someday, he says, a UFO event could take place that would prove irrefutable, and then people would be forced to make a leap in consciousness as big as stone-agers into cyberspace. If that happens, the files in this underground castle could take on new significance. Or not.

Either scenario comes with a burden. Arthur C. Clarke, author of the classic novel "2001: A Space Odyssey," who died this month in Sri Lanka, once said: "Either we are alone in the universe or we are not. Both are equally terrifying."

Davenport slams the drawer shut. He sighs.

Outside, the sun has set and the evening sky has darkened enough for celestial bodies to become visible. The constellation Orion appears in the southern sky, and Mars twinkles too.

"Not many people would waste their lives pursuing such an elusive subject," Davenport says on the drive home. His car is an 18-year-old gray Crown Victoria with a quarter-million miles. The windshield is cracked. "Sometimes I don't know why I do it."

Then he remembers Elger Berg of Seattle.

Berg was a carpenter and mechanic. He had waited 64 years to tell the story of something he had seen outside a small village in Alaska when he was a young man: a cigar-shaped craft with blue-green lights that flew over his head and disappeared into the mountains.

After hearing Davenport on the radio, Berg sought him out to tell him about the UFO. Four months later, in early 2001, Berg died at age 84.

His story, which Davenport captured on cassette, is the only record of the incident. If someone, anyone, ever wants to look into it for whatever reason, the tape and accompanying notes await in a safe place, in a city of file cabinets, under the desert.

MRS. LEU, TEAR DOWN THAT WALL!
A U.S.-CANADA BORDER FLAP IN HER YARD

Los Angeles Times, May 26, 2007

Introduced by **MILLIE QUAN**, senior editor
for projects at the *Los Angeles Times*,
who was Tizon's editor at the newspaper for five years

*T*his is a rather ordinary kind of newspaper feature story—a small story about ordinary people caught in a ridiculous circumstance. It's of little broad import, and Tizon doesn't pretend otherwise. Yet he somehow manages to elevate the story into a sort of parable about the fate of modern men and women caught up in the dumb, bumbling machines of government.

How does he manage that?

Start with the reporting. Always start with the reporting. A lot of reporters will come back from a reporting trip with notebooks or tape recorders full of conversation—and nothing else. Tizon didn't just take notes. He took prisoners. He listened to people. He watched them.

The story is packed with information, with what might seem like minutia. Shirley-Ann Leu, faced with an incomprehensible situation, responds with incomprehension: "She raises her hands above her head and mimes pulling her hair out."

He pays attention to the small detail that will fix an image in the reader's mind: "Shirley-Ann pads around the wall to the edge of her property and places a foot in the ditch, her fuzzy black house slipper set daintily against the dirt."

Yeah, we should all remember fuzzy slippers.

Stories like this have a tendency to portray the people as caricatures and, especially if they are older, as cute. There is none of that here. There is no sentimentality. Instead, there is respect, a deep empathy for the glory of ordinary folks. He captures the dynamics of the couple's relationship.

"We were supposed to retire and spend our days in peace,"
[Shirley-Ann] says.

Herbert, an exceedingly genial man with gray at the tem-
ples, sits nearby, smiling, letting his wife do the talking
and occasionally chiming in with a "Yes, yes. That's right."

The writing is conversational, at times slyly funny. It never
plods, even in the little history lesson contained within. Tizon
points out the ludicrousness of the situation but doesn't take sides
in any obvious way. He describes the situation and lets its inherent contradictions speak for themselves. How can you not love a
bureaucrat who describes his own agency as so small and unimpor-
tant that it is mere "budget dust"?

.   .   .

BLAINE, WASH.—The invisible line that divides Canada and the
United States runs along a shallow ditch just beyond Shirley-Ann
Leu's backyard, so close she could cross the border in a single
hop.

At 72, Shirley-Ann, a retired hairdresser, shows no such inclination. But some in her care—namely 11 Pomeranians, two toy
poodles and a young neighbor girl whom she baby-sits—appear to
her all too eager to jump the ditch and roam wild across Canada.

To prevent this, Shirley-Ann and her husband, Herbert, 69, a
retired electrician, built a 4-foot-high concrete wall. They saw it
as a perfect solution. The wall would enclose their wards and also
keep their sloped backyard from crumbling into the ditch.

Little did they know it would instigate a bona fide border conflict.

The Leus now find themselves in a legal fight against the U.S.
government, which has the support of the Canadian government.
The outcome will determine whether the wall stays, which party
will pay if it has to be removed, and to what extent border authorities can control development on private property.

Because the Leus' wall is part of a larger project that includes a driveway, walking paths and patios—the entire outdoor part of their quarter-acre lot—the couple have stopped all construction until the case is resolved. The work involves heavy machinery, and the Leus don't want to pay the extra cost of doing the project piecemeal.

In her backyard, Shirley-Ann stands amid mounds of lumber and rebar, looking as if she is about to cry.

"We were supposed to retire and spend our days in peace," she says. "Instead. . . ." She raises her hands above her head and mimes pulling her hair out. Her pink wire-rimmed glasses scrunch up against her face.

Life for the couple has been complicated—and tense—since they moved from Hawaii a year and a half ago to this rural border town 110 miles north of Seattle. The wall dispute, involving an obscure agency and a little-known treaty, is only the most aggravating part of the strange reality of living next to an international boundary.

How could she explain it?

Shirley-Ann pads around the wall to the edge of her property and places a foot in the ditch, her fuzzy black house slipper set daintily against the dirt.

"That's Canada," she says, her words weighted with the notion that her foot is now subject to the rules of a different nation.

Running parallel to the ditch is a two-lane road, Zero Avenue, part of the Canadian municipality of Surrey. A handful of homes dots a rolling landscape of fields and pastures. Cars zip past at highway speed although the signed limit is 50 kilometers an hour (31 mph).

Every few hours on Zero Avenue, a Royal Canadian Mounted Police vehicle drives past. At the front of the Leus' house, on the American side, the U.S. Border Patrol makes regular passes along West 99th Street. The Leus say it took a while to get used to the patrol cars passing day and night on both sides of their house.

Underground sensors hidden on the edges of Zero Avenue detect all kinds of movement. One neighbor on the American side, Bob Boulet, says every time he mowed his backyard last year, he set off a sensor and a Border Patrol helicopter came whizzing by within minutes. Boulet says he asked the Border Patrol to mow the lawn for him so he wouldn't bother them anymore. The agency didn't find the request amusing.

Between Boulet's house and Shirley-Ann's, a surveillance camera swivels atop a 40-foot tower, watching and recording the goings-on in a 360-degree panorama.

All of this, for Shirley-Ann, translates to one thing: "Don't even think about crossing the road," she says, moving her foot back to the United States. "Try it. They'll come after you."

Which is why, in her mind, it would be disastrous if one of her dogs or the little neighbor girl were ever to jump the ditch and cross over. First, they could be run over by a car. But if they made it, how would she get them back?

The quickest legal way to retrieve them would be to drive west two miles into town, get in line at the truck crossing at Highway 543, show her documents, and drive back east onto Zero Avenue. It could take 10 minutes to get there and as long as three hours to get back, depending on traffic.

Or she could take her chances and run across the street. If she were caught, she could face a range of penalties. Crossing the border without passing through an official point of entry breaks the law on both sides.

On the U.S. side, according to Border Patrol Agent Joseph Giuliano, deputy chief in the Blaine office, a border-jumper could face a $150 citation or up to a $5,000 fine and six months in jail.

Walking back to her house, Shirley-Ann says: "People come visit and see where we live, and they flip out."

THE U.S.-CANADA BORDER runs along the 49th parallel and stretches 5,525 miles over mountains, forests and prairies; through lakes, rivers and bays; from the tundra of the Arctic Ocean to the shores of the North Atlantic—the world's longest undefended boundary.

Both countries have announced plans to create a coast-to-coast "virtual fence" with high-tech monitoring equipment, but vast stretches of the border remain largely unguarded. In many remote areas, mostly in the West, the only clue a boundary exists at all is the presence of a boundary monument: a 5-foot-tall concrete obelisk.

There are supposed to be about 8,600 such markers along the border, spaced so that at each marker, the next one can be seen. Some obelisks have toppled or been vandalized; others have been worn down by time and neglect.

Behind the Leus' house, bramble bushes shroud the markers along Zero Avenue, and much of the street corridor is overgrown with cottonwood and cedar trees.

A former fishing and logging town, Blaine, population about 4,000, is best-known as the northern terminus of Interstate 5 and the third-busiest checkpoint on the U.S.-Canada border, screening about 7 million passenger cars a year.

East of the border station, on the outskirts of town, a little neighborhood surrounded by woods sits in relative isolation. It is a motley collection of old and new houses, old and young residents, and vacant lots still to be developed.

Besides the rural feel, the neighborhood's biggest appeal is hinted at by the name of one of its main streets: Canada View Drive. On this road, which becomes West 99th Street, the houses along the ditch look out at British Columbia's lush Fraser River Valley and beyond to the Coast Mountains.

It was this view that first hooked Shirley-Ann and Herbert. Their stucco ranch-style house had been built with large picture windows facing Canada.

"Look at that," says Shirley-Ann, sitting in a bay window of her living room.

Herbert, an exceedingly genial man with gray at the temples, sits nearby, smiling, letting his wife do the talking and occasionally chiming in with a "Yes, yes. That's right."

Their story in sum: lived in Hawaii 48 years, married 42 years, no children, recently retired. The couple found their fixed income didn't go very far in Honolulu. "Some days we were living on pork and beans and toast," Shirley-Ann says. Herbert smiles in affirmation.

In 2005, the couple sold their home in Hawaii and moved here, where land was cheap and they could be closer to Shirley-Ann's relatives in Canada. And where the pooches, now kept in a chicken-wire cage at the side of the house, could roam in a big yard.

They hired a contractor to build the wall. Workers cleared the ground in August and poured the concrete in November. The wall stretched 85 feet and cost $15,000. In January came the knock at the front door.

THE MAN IDENTIFIED HIMSELF as a field engineer for the International Boundary Commission. Shirley-Ann vividly recalls the conversation:

"He says to me, 'Your wall violates the treaty.'"

"I have no idea what you're talking about," she responded.

"The Treaty of 1925," the man said, handing her a brochure. "Someone will be contacting you." Before the man left, Shirley-Ann asked a question she has asked numerous times since. "Who are you again?"

She and Herbert had never heard of the International Boundary Commission. Neither had the city of Blaine, which had approved the wall and issued the permits. "I was surprised too," says Blaine City Manager Gary Tomsic, referring to the IBC. The treaty was news to him.

The official name is the Treaty Between Canada and the United States of America to Define More Accurately and to Complete the International Boundary Between the Two Countries.

The document, signed by then–U.S. Secretary of State Charles Evans Hughes and Canadian Minister of Justice Ernest Lapointe, established the IBC as a binational agency with one commissioner in each country, and charged the agency with maintaining an "effective" boundary. This meant, in part, maintaining a clear 20-foot-wide "boundary vista," or swath—10 feet on each side— along the entire border.

In a hand-delivered letter to the Leus in February, the IBC told the couple that the wall, although inside their property line,

encroached 30 inches into the boundary vista and would have to
be torn down or moved.

"If the wall is not removed and/or relocated . . . then the commission may itself cause the wall to be removed and the expenses
for the removal will be invoiced by you," wrote the U.S. commissioner for the IBC, Dennis Schornack.

In April, the Leus filed the first lawsuit ever brought against
the agency.

The Leus' lawyer, Brian Hodges, says the IBC has no authority
to condemn property or regulate development on private lots without providing adequate notice to owners and local governments.
The fact that Blaine officials knew nothing about the boundary-
vista setback, Hodges argues, indicates the agency had not done a
satisfactory job of notifying the public.

In a phone interview from his Washington, D.C., office,
Schornack said he could not comment on the Leus' case except
to say property owners close to the border had "a common-sense
obligation" to inquire about federal restrictions. He added that
property owners in past conflicts willingly obeyed IBC requests.

Schornack's half of the agency (the other half is in Ottawa)
has an annual budget of $1.4 million. "Budget dust," Schornack
says.

The amount is barely enough to accomplish the agency's primary mission, which is to maintain a clearly visible boundary.
This means hiring work crews to go into remote areas with chain
saws and machetes. Some sections in Alaska, Washington, Idaho
and Montana have not been cleared in decades.

In a sense, the IBC is a victim of the historically good relations
between Canada and the U.S., said Deputy Commissioner Kyle
Hipsley.

Because "we've always been friends with Canada," Hipsley
says, the work of the agency isn't seen as an urgent funding priority in Congress.

Schornack and Hipsley say they hope Congress will realize
the importance of their work: The agency has asked to double its
budget for 2008.

In Seattle, the U.S. attorney's office is preparing a response on behalf of the IBC. The deadline is in June. The Leus continue to stare out at the construction site that would be their backyard.

Shirley-Ann, unable to set her dogs loose or plant flowers in the garden, pores over documents related to the case. Stacks of paper litter the floor beneath her chair in the bay window.

Occasionally she glances out at the view, as if trying to remember something. Every once in a while she issues a statement directed at the world.

"Retire in peace. Ha," she says.

"Yes," says Herbert, still smiling. "That's right."

THIS LAW AIN'T NO FRIEND OF HIS: ELVIS THE CABBIE FIGHTS FOR KINGLY ATTIRE

Los Angeles Times, August 24, 2003

Introduced by **BRIAN LINDSTROM**, documentary filmmaker
in Portland, Oregon, who wrote salmon gut–speckled *rengas*
with Tizon between shifts at the Cordova canneries

F *or me, there is one line that stands out in Alex Tizon's Cab Elvis piece, a revealing and heartbreaking quote from David Vernon Groh: "The former waiter and ice-cream vendor said he'd like to have a family someday but is 'too poor to have a wife and kids.'" Suddenly, Mr. Groh—and his goals and dreams—come into sharper focus, and there is a lot more at stake than just a seemingly capricious dress code.*

I wish I knew how Alex elicited that response from Mr. Groh. But even if I knew the exact question he asked, I'm not sure I'd share it, because to do so would risk reducing to a formula Alex's singular ability to empathize, as if the question could be separated from the keen mind and massive heart that produced it. I bet Mr. Groh felt seen, heard, and even understood by Alex in a way that we all need and deserve.

One day in 1991, an envelope from Alex, postmarked from the Philippines, arrived in my mail. I was always excited to receive his letters. Often, they included rengas, *collaborative poems where you alternate lines with your collaborator(s). Alex, firefighter-in-training Tim Davis, and I kept ourselves marginally connected to our respective muses writing* rengas *while working grueling summers in our youthful days in salmon canneries in Cordova, Alaska. The* rengas *would be speckled with fish guts by the time they circulated among the three of us before finding a home in one of our journals.*

But this envelope contained only a photo. On a boulder near a river, Alex sat beaming, surrounded by eight members of his extended Philippines-based family, all lit from within with that spe-

cifically Tizonian joy of simply being together. On the back, in that distinctive, delicate yet sturdy handwriting that I have come to miss dearly, Alex wrote, "I'm the short one with dark hair."

Another envelope, this one from 1997. No renga, no photo, just a copy of the investigative articles Alex wrote for the Seattle Times exposing corruption in federal housing for Native Americans. In the margins of the article announcing his Pulitzer Prize for the series, Alex wrote, "I want you to be proud of me, Brian."

And a last envelope, not addressed to me but containing the name of the winner of the 2015 Oregon Book Award for General Nonfiction. I was in the front row, sitting next to Alex. His tie undone, Alex sat there with no apparent sense of expectation or apprehension. If his image had been a photo, the caption would've read, "Here is a man with nothing at stake." When his name was called, he waited a beat and then laughed. As if to puncture any possibility of pomposity, Alex bounded to the stage, laughing the entire way and delivered an admirably incoherent speech about the importance of laughter and wine.

Being with Alex was a first line of a renga, an invitation, a beckoning to both go deeper and laugh at yourself. Around 2012, we reunited after being out of touch for several years. Seemingly out of nowhere, after a long night with many friends, he told me about having done and experienced about all that he needed to. He said he was tired and if the end was near, he could handle that. He didn't mention and may not have known he'd go on to write his memoir or his brilliant, searing masterpiece about his beloved Lola, "My Family's Slave," for The Atlantic. I tried to comprehend what he was telling me. He watched as my face contorted, and then he laughed.

. . .

SEATTLE—It used to be when David Vernon Groh walked down the aisles of Pike Place Market, he was greeted simply with "Hi, Elvis!" Which is what you expect when you're an Elvis impersonator.

But these days, the regulars at the downtown market greet him with rallying cries: "We're with you, Elvis!" and "Don't give up!" and "Go get 'em!" A bumper sticker circulating around town reads: "Free Elvis."

Besides being an Elvis impersonator, Groh, 37, is a cab driver. One day, about two years ago, he fused his two identities and became "Cab Elvis," the only taxi driver in town with jet-black sideburns, a bright red jumpsuit (with matching cape) and a song repertoire that included "Hound Dog" and "Love Me Tender."

Customers loved it; the tips multiplied. City inspectors were not as enthusiastic.

Mostly it was the red jumpsuit they objected to. The city fined him for violating the taxi driver dress code. One thing led to another, and Groh is in the middle of a legal battle grandly referred to by his fans as "Elvis vs. the City of Seattle" or "the King vs. the Emerald City."

At issue, according to Gary Keese, the assistant city attorney handling the case, is whether there is a constitutional right to dress like Elvis.

"They say yes. We say no," Keese said.

On a recent day, Groh appeared glum. He was sitting in a small booth at the Athenian restaurant in Pike Place Market, sipping black coffee and telling his story. Groh lives in an apartment above the market and spends much of his free time among its patrons.

At 6 feet 2, he's three inches taller than the real Elvis but not quite as chiseled in features. He's got the hair, the contemptuously curled lip and the paunch. He can switch to Elvis-talk in a snap—"Thankyou vurrah much"—but at the moment doesn't appear to be in the mood.

Litigation will do that to a king of rock 'n' roll, and perhaps more so to a regular guy like Groh. The former waiter and ice-cream vendor said he'd like to have a family someday but is "too poor to have a wife and kids."

He started the Cab Elvis thing to make a little extra money and to cheer people up, including himself. "It brings so much joy to so many people, and it brings joy to me," Groh said. "What could be wrong with that?"

His fame started small and has remained relatively modest, if you don't count the Japanese press. A slick Japanese monthly did a two-page spread on him, and a Japanese-language travel guide featured Groh in his full Elvis regalia as one of the highlights of visiting Seattle.

Much of Seattle didn't pay much attention to Groh until his tangles with city officials became public. Now he's a full-blown hero to some.

Locals couldn't resist the notion of Elvis going up against City Hall.

"There are so many bad things going on in the world," said waitress Catherine Strange, "and they [city bureaucrats] are worried about Elvis. Jeeesus."

In fairness to city bureaucrats, they have nothing against Elvis personally. In fact, the rules governing taxi cabs in the city were drawn up six years ago in response to public complaints. Apparently, some cab drivers didn't dress well, smelled bad and failed to maintain a hygienic atmosphere in their cars.

So the regulations included a dress code.

For Groh's employer, Red Top Taxi, that meant black pants and a blue dress shirt for all cabbies. In May, a city inspector issued Groh a $60 citation for wearing the red jumpsuit. Groh appealed and lost. The city warned him that fines would double if he was caught violating the code again.

Late last month, with the help of a local attorney who took on Groh's case pro bono, Cab Elvis sued the city, asserting that it had violated his freedom of expression. The suit contends the dress code is unconstitutional and silly. A hearing in King County Superior Court is tentatively scheduled for December.

Meanwhile, Seattle City Councilman Richard Conlin said he would introduce legislation, possibly next month, that would provide for exceptions to the taxi driver dress code.

Conlin said that colorful characters who present no harm to the city should be encouraged because it helps create "a lively street scene."

At the Athenian, Groh sipped his coffee and kept his head low so as not to attract attention. It didn't work. The hair does it every time. A dishwasher from the back spotted him and yelled: "How's the lawsuit of the century going?"

A woman at a nearby counter saw him and said, "I can't believe what they're doing to you. Hang in there."

Groh smiled that curled-lip smile and said, "Thankyou vurrah much."

PART VII

ORACLES

"OLD LADIES DO WHAT WE CAN": DISPATCHES FROM A NEW NATION

Seattle Times, September 18, 2001

Introduced by **JACQUI BANASZYNSKI**,
Tizon's assigning editor at the *Seattle Times*
for two years

*T*he 9/11 assignment that became "Crossing America" was vague: Look for America. Alex Tizon would have appreciated my reference to a favorite Simon and Garfunkel song and then countered with something darker, probably from Leonard Cohen. He always pushed beyond the easy surface to the murkier depths beneath. And yet his writing could be deceptively direct and simple.

Consider this, the third of his thirteen stories from the road that September. He found himself in Missoula, Montana, still searching for a focus to an ill-defined patchwork that, we hoped, would form an American quilt. He spotted two older women "having a picnic at a park," sat with them over iced tea, and found a story many reporters would have driven past. He was working fast, by remote, and under the emotional pall of the time.

When he filed this story, I challenged his opening reference to "little old ladies" as sexist and demeaning. But he earned it through his reporting and writing: "They called themselves that," he told me, and then he wrote about them with a combination of humor and respect.

When I sent the story to the news desk, editors challenged its placement on Page One: There was no real "nut graf," that line that sums up the "why" of the story. And any thin tether to relevance didn't come until nine gentle paragraphs in. Tizon bristled at the convention of the nut graf. But in this piece, as in much of his work, it can be found in quiet, elegant moments (quoted below with my emphasis). He is not stitching a quilt but weaving a tapestry.

In paragraph 1 he references 9/11 without hitting readers be-
tween the eyes:

> *While driving through the eastern foothills of the Bitterroot*
> *Mountains one late afternoon, as* the nation neared a new
> and terrible one-week mark. . . .

In paragraph 8 he draws a description of America from a song
many think should be the national anthem:

> *They went 50 mph over the Bitterroot range, soaking up*
> the purple mountains' majesty. . . .

And in paragraph 9, the so-called nut graf, he ties these two "old
ladies" to the collective struggle to find a response to the terrorist
attacks:

> *Today's mission, so far thwarted, is to* find an American
> flag *for their Midas.*

. . .

MISSOULA, MONT.—What do little old ladies do in times of
war? While driving through the eastern foothills of the Bitterroot
Mountains one late afternoon, as the nation neared a new and
terrible one-week mark, I met two and asked them.

They were having a picnic at a park. The table was covered
with white linen, and over it sat a white take-out box of Chester
Fried Chicken and a couple of jug-sized cups of Lipton Ice Tea.

Mary Boles is 70 with bleached-blonde hair and blue mascara
under bifocals that cover a third of her face. Vera Moulton is 65
going on 85, if you count mileage rather than years. She's led a
hard life and doesn't mind showing the wear and tear. She carries
a Buck knife, which she was using at the moment to cut into a
drumstick. The women wear identical outfits: red shorts, sleeve-
less plaid shirts and white sun hats.

They're the senior Thelma and Louise of the Northern Rockies, which is to say, two women on the open road, guided by fate and moxie, and the whim of the moment, but without the guns and boyfriends—"We're past those silly things." Besides, they have husbands waiting for them back home.

"They're both on oxygen," Mary says.

"Emphysema," Vera says.

The women drive a 1977 Midas motor home. They travel year-round together, two bingo-playing bandits on a lark. When not traveling, they're home taking care of their husbands.

Last week, they left their hometown of Newport in northeastern Washington and, like us, crossed the Idaho Panhandle into Big Sky country. They went 50 mph over the Bitterroot range, soaking up the purple mountains' majesty before descending into the lush, bustling valley town of Missoula.

Tomorrow or "whenever we feel like it—ha!" they'll head south to visit one of Vera's sisters. But today's mission, so far thwarted, is to find an American flag for their Midas.

The picnic was a break from their exhaustive search at Wal-Mart, a few miles down the road from the park.

"We walked down every aisle for an hour," Mary says.

"A whole hour," Vera says. "Every aisle."

Eventually, a Wal-Mart clerk informed them the store was all out but was expecting a shipment any day. This was the case all along our route so far.

Stores that sell flags sold out in a flurry, so frantic has been the demand. The Stars and Stripes have appeared everywhere—windows and billboards and porches, along city streets and country roads—and in venues not customarily known for patriotic displays: over a urinal at a truck stop, the entrance of an adult book store. Where it might have typically said "wash me" in the back of a dusty semi, someone had finger-drawn a flag and the words "Go USA."

Mary and Vera, like a lot of us, are looking for some way to help. What Mary really wants to do, she says, is drive to New York City and tell the person in charge there—"I guess that would be the mayor"—to put her to work.

But like a lot of us, she can't venture too far from home. Her sick husband could need her ASAP. So instead she and Vera decided to contribute in other ways.

Whenever they could, they shopped at stores that donated part of the proceeds to the cause. They gave money, like at Wal-Mart, where a Red Cross volunteer had set up a table. They wore ribbons to remember the dead.

The volunteer at Wal-Mart gave them each red ribbons with white stars, which they pinned over their hearts.

They attended church services and candlelight vigils. They prayed. A minister friend says we should never underestimate the power of a praying grandmother because their words have seniority in that realm.

Little old ladies have always pitched in during war—sewing military garments, working the less-strenuous jobs in munitions factories, raising money, baking cakes and keeping spirits up, not to mention giving up husbands and sons and grandsons to the battlefield. Vera's father fought in the first World War; her husband, in the second.

They can't carry bazookas, but "old ladies do what we can," Mary said.

"Yep, whatever we can," Vera said.

CROSSING AMERICA:
"WE NEED TO PRAY DEEP"

Seattle Times, October 2, 2001

Introduced by **ALAN BERNER**, who drove across the United States with
Tizon twice—taking the photos while Tizon wrote the words

*A*lex and I were headed east and hoping to meet up with Wendell
Berry, the poet and novelist, the Kentucky-born activist.

We weren't able to arrange it, so we drove to Louisville to find
the gym where Muhammad Ali had trained.

Turned out it was now a gym with only two baskets and nobody
in it.

That evening, a chance meeting with a person leaving a restaurant—he wanted to know who we were, what we were doing, and
what kind of cameras we were holding—led to his suggestion that
we speak with a pastor who had marched with Dr. Martin Luther
King Jr. and had baptized Colonel Sanders.

In the morning, we followed him to a West End church.

As we drove by a modest century-old home, we spotted Ollie
May Walls and her mother, Birdella, sitting on the well-worn porch.
A giant Stars and Stripes hung on the broadside of the clapboard.

We looked at each other and knew: They were going to be this
stop's story.

We spent time with the Reverend Charles Elliott and then immediately headed over to see Ollie May and Birdella.

It was practically a church service—call-and-response.

Ollie May did most of the talking, and Birdella would say,
"Amen" or "Praise be to Jesus."

At one point, Ollie May called the terrorists Kamikazmi-nauts.

"Is that a word?" Alex asked. "Can I use that?"

He said, "If it isn't a word, it should be."

We spent most of the day with them, brought back dinner, and
then continued our journey east.

· · ·

LOUISVILLE—The Expedition raced through the last of the High
Plains, cut through the Great Lakes states of Illinois and Indiana,
and as the sun set on our 16th day on the road, our truck rolled like
a tired old buggy into this elegant Southern city on the Ohio River.

Here we met a mother and daughter named Birdella and Ollie
May Walls. They had God on their minds. And they'd noticed
that much of America seemed to be thinking of God right now,
or at least dropping his name.

"An airplane goin' into a building will do that," said Ollie
May. "Praise be to Jesus," said Birdella.

Their chairs rocked on a creaky porch. Birdella is 74; Ollie
May, 49. They live on public assistance in a century-old clapboard house on the West End. Mother and daughter spend a lot
of days rocking on the porch and talking to neighbors passing by.

The "West End" is what people say when referring to the
black section of town. It's a wide area that varies from tidy little
flats to desolate brick sprawls—the South's version of "projects."
The young Muḥammad Ali, born Cassius Clay, came from here.
A main boulevard is named after Ali, one of the best-known Muslims in the world.

The West End butts up against downtown, a striking contrast,
with its wide streets and pillared European-style government
buildings. A statue of King Louis XVI of France stands across
from City Hall with its grand architecture.

Louisville is one of the oldest river ports in the country, and
also the northernmost Southern city of any size. In twang and
style, it's closer to Memphis than Chicago.

Birdella and Ollie May came to the big city from the hills of
Tennessee. "Country folk" is how they describe themselves. They
were raised up on grits and church hymns, and God was as much
a part of life as the Great Smoky Mountains that rose up and shel-
tered them.

Ollie May used to be a nurse's assistant, but she found it harder
to compete with younger, more educated workers. Maybe she wasn't
cut out for city living. A part of her never left the Tennessee hills.

The day we visited, she wore overalls, a flannel shirt and a straw hat over pigtails. She did most of the talking. Her face was as stretchy as a rubber band, her voice, happy as a banjo. She referred to the terrorists as "Kamikazmi-nauts," which if it isn't a word, should be.

Birdella, a wizened old matriarch with cataract eyes, rocked and mostly kept quiet. When you thought she was asleep, she'd blurt out "amen" to correct you.

The two sometimes spoke in duet, as in church liturgy, with Ollie May extemporizing and Birdella affirming.

Ollie May: "We're foot-wash Baptists."

Birdella: "That's right, but don't look at our feet."

On Sept. 11, Birdella and Ollie May recited the Lord's Prayer out loud several times, alternating lines. They went to church, where the pews were packed, as they've been in churches all across the country.

Ollie May: "Faith and trust in God. It's all coming out now and bringing us together."

Birdella: "Amen. God is good."

Not everybody in the neighborhood took such a generous view of the sudden outpouring to God. Next door stood King Solomon Baptist Church, an imposing building with a red-brick facade, where two ministers expounded on the divine reasons for the attacks.

The Rev. Charles Elliott Jr., a dapper, gray-templed man whose claims to fame include marching with Martin Luther King Jr. and baptizing Colonel Sanders, worked himself to a froth, pounding a table and reaching a crescendo of indignation.

"God won't destroy America, but he'll give America a whuppin'! That's how I see this. I see it as America getting a whuppin', and we're getting a whippun' because we have strayed so far from righteousness!"

Elliott knew that evangelicals Jerry Falwell and Pat Robertson were criticized for making similar statements on TV. But, unlike those two, he won't apologize and won't take back the words. When he was done sermonizing—the second he finished—Elliott changed back to the soft-spoken gentleman we met at the door.

Others in the black religious community spoke about the disingenuousness of praying to God only in times of crisis and ignoring him all other times.

"I hear people saying, 'God Bless America,'" said the Rev. Franklin Hill III, a radio personality known in town as The Spiritual Doctor. "Be real. God has been blessing America. He's blessed America abundantly, and America has taken him for granted."

Elliott and Hill agreed whatever the reason, people turning to God could be a real opportunity for spiritual renewal—if it's done humbly and with a seeking attitude.

But being spiritual during war, they cautioned, wasn't the same thing as recruiting God to your side, which they see as foolish. What army doesn't think God is on its side?

Seek the truth, they said. That's all.

Across a vacant lot, back on the porch, Birdella and Ollie May rocked on their creaky chairs. They didn't want to clutter up their thinking with all this theologizing.

Ollie May: "I don't know nothin' about religion. I just know the Lord. And I know the Lord wants us to come together, all of us—black, white, brown, rich, poor, whatever—even the Kamikazmi-nauts. We need to pray deep. We need to get together and pray all the time.

"It's the only way."

Birdella: "Have mercy, Jesus."

Their porch was built 105 years ago, and gave the impression that a strong wind could blow it down.

It was now a rickety ledge on which two women perched. The porch was part of a house of broken windows. The windows looked into a home with no telephone. The home was on the edge of a neighborhood forgotten by the rest of the city.

Mother and daughter had each other, and little else, except the God they brought with them from the hills of Tennessee. They were a trio. And tall buildings crashing only made them sit a little closer to one another.

ACKNOWLEDGMENTS

This book was both a joy and a sadness to produce. The sadness, I will try to consign to this paragraph only. Alex left all those whom he loved far too soon, and his readers are bereft, too, since he had many more years' worth of unique stories to tell. For me personally, it was a privilege to work with him and to be his friend—and while it's an honor to edit this collection, it's tragic to be doing so at this early date.

Now, the joy. Tizon's widow, Melissa, and his two daughters, Dylan and Maya, are wonderful people and such enthusiastic supporters of this project. I join them in hoping that this collection may inspire some in the rising generation of writers and reporters. If Alex's legacy is reflected in their work, and if it leads them to see the invisible and to tell their untold stories, this book will be a success.

I am also grateful to several of Alex's siblings and other members of his extended family, and to his many friends; they all provided me with insights that helped shape the important choices about what to include in the book.

This collection includes more than Alex's work—it is enriched immensely by the introductions to each story, which focus on the various skills, insights, and other special touches he employed in putting them together. I am deeply grateful to each and every one of the contributors, who were all editors or reporting colleagues of Alex's and who, I'm certain, share the hope that this book will be put to good educational use.

A few special shout-outs, first to David Boardman, Alex's long-time chief editor at the *Seattle Times* and now the dean of the Klein College of Media and Communication at Temple University. Dave was an early and enthusiastic proponent of this book and, indeed, of Alex's career.

Lynn Marshall, who along with Dave is one of the "introducers" in the book, was so much more than a researcher in the Seattle Bureau of the *Los Angeles Times* when Alex and I worked there. She was a friend, confidante, muse, and teller of jokes. There were hard days and there were fun days, which I guess is pretty much true of newspapers everywhere—Lynn made every one of those days better, for Alex and for me. Even on deadline. *Especially* on deadline.

Jose Antonio Vargas appreciated Alex and his work for all the right reasons, and I am very grateful to him for writing the Foreword to this collection, as I am to Cheryl Strayed, of *Wild* fame, for her endorsement.

At Temple University Press, a collection of marvelously talented people brought this book home and made it real. I am grateful to Aaron Javsicas, Sara Jo Cohen, Joan Vidal, Kate Nichols, Ann-Marie Anderson, Gary Kramer, Heather Wilcox, Ashley Petrucci, and Marinanicole Dohrman Miller. Each of you made the book better, and I thank you.

I owe a final word of loving gratitude to my wife, Lisa, who was at Alex's funeral with me and thus was there at the moment the idea for this book rose on the horizon; she urged me, as she always does, to seize the day.

ALEX TIZON (1959–2017) was a Pulitzer Prize–winning journalist whose writings include numerous articles for such publications as the *Seattle Times*, the *Los Angeles Times*, and *The Atlantic*, as well as the memoir *Big Little Man: In Search of My Asian Self*.

SAM HOWE VERHOVEK is a former reporter for the *New York Times* and the *Los Angeles Times* and the author of *Jet Age: The Comet, the 707, and the Race to Shrink the World*. He is also a contributing writer for *National Geographic* and an adjunct faculty member at Seattle University and the University of Washington.